A CHANCE TO HARMONIZE

ALSO BY SHERYL KASKOWITZ

God Bless America: The Surprising History of an Iconic Song

A CHANCE TO HARMONIZE

HOW FDR'S HIDDEN MUSIC UNIT SOUGHT TO SAVE AMERICA FROM THE GREAT DEPRESSION—ONE SONG AT A TIME

SHERYL KASKOWITZ

PEGASUS BOOKS
NEW YORK LONDON

A CHANCE TO HARMONIZE

Pegasus Books, Ltd.
148 West 37th Street, 13th Floor
New York, NY 10018

Library of Congress Cataloging-in-Publication Data is available.

ISBN: 978-1-63936-571-5

10 9 8 7 6 5 4 3 2 1

Printed in the United States of America
Distributed by Simon & Schuster
www.pegasusbooks.com

For Ben, Ezra, and Elliott

CONTENTS

Author's Note   xi

Prologue: The Key West Experiment   xiii

1   Music as a Social Function   1

2   In the Slough of Despond   17

3   Musical Engineering   33

4   Cooperation Is Our Aim   48

5   New Wine in Old Bottles   59

6   Delight in What It Is to Be American   74

7   What Are People Singing Now?   84

8   Look Down That Lonesome Road   99

9   Government Song Woman   114

10   We Ain't Down Yet   131

11   Wayfaring Stranger   146

12   Let the People Themselves Make the Music They Need   158

13   New Ground   170

     Epilogue   189

     Acknowledgments   199

     Notes   203

     Index   231

We in the United States are amazingly rich in the elements from which to weave a culture. We have the best of man's past on which to draw, brought to us by our native folk and folk from all parts of the world. In binding these elements into a national fabric of beauty and strength, let us keep the original fibers so intact that the fineness of each will show in the completed handiwork.

—President Franklin D. Roosevelt on the
occasion of the first National Folk Festival, 1934

AUTHOR'S NOTE

If you'd like to listen to some of the recordings mentioned in the book as you're reading, you can find a selection of music tracks organized by chapter on my website (sherylkaskowitz.com).

THE KEY WEST EXPERIMENT

What happened in Key West during the Great Depression could be the plot of a Hollywood musical. It would begin with a young Judy Garland wearing a modest but threadbare sundress, pulling a small wagon down trash-lined streets. She would pass the abandoned navy yard, crumbling factory buildings, and boarded-up storefronts. She would walk by the bustling corner saloon, waving and calling "Hiya, Joe!" to the bartender. Nearing the town's only hotel, she would park her wagon under a palm tree and say hello to the street vendors nearby: the couple with two adorable tykes selling coconuts, the old fisherman selling his day's catch from a bucket. She would pull aside the burlap covering her wagon to retrieve her handwritten sign, "LIMES FOR SALE," and a small crate to sit on. Maybe she would sing dreamily about what Key West used to be like, when the streets were filled with soldiers and sailors and factory workers and tourists and fishermen and divers, when she could enjoy the beauty of the island without worrying about having enough to eat. The song over, the camera would zoom out to show no buyers in sight for any of the vendors, who all looked weary and forlorn, a stark contrast to the beautiful beachside scenery. But soon an earnest young man would approach—played by Mickey Rooney—striding confidently, wearing shorts and holding a clipboard. "Hey everybody!" he would call. "Let's put on a show!"

⌘

Key West had fallen mightily from its perch as the wealthiest town in the United States back in the 1880s. Beginning in the mid-1920s, the island lost its pineapple-canning and cigar-making factories, all its military posts (Navy, Army, and Coast Guard), its fishing and sponge-diving industries, its status as a port-of-call for passenger ships, and its rail line. The Key West economy was already shaky before the Wall Street Crash of 1929, and by 1934 it was by some measures the US town hit hardest by the Depression, with its city government in debt estimated at five million dollars. Storefronts stood empty in dilapidated buildings; trash accumulated on the streets as regular garbage collection ceased. As people left the island to look for work elsewhere, its population dropped from nearly twenty thousand in 1920 to about twelve thousand in 1934, with more than three-quarters of those who stayed now unemployed and on the federal relief rolls. After visiting Key West in the spring of 1934, *Harper's* magazine reporter Elmer Davis wrote that those not on relief "seemed to be living mostly by selling rum to one another." Key West was more than just broke—it "had lapsed into a state of mass melancholia." On July 1, 1934, the city council took the extraordinary step of declaring bankruptcy and handing over its governing power to the State of Florida. Governor David Sholtz, in turn, declared a state of emergency and asked the Federal Emergency Relief Administration (FERA) to take over the island, hoping the ambitious New Deal program could save it from ruin.

That's where the "let's put on a show" protagonist enters, in the form of FERA southeastern regional director Julius F. Stone Jr. Appointed to lead the agency's Florida efforts after serving in its New York office, Stone was just thirty-two years old but appeared older, with a receding hairline and trim moustache giving him the look of a good-hearted yet stern middle school teacher. As a former stockbroker with a PhD in chemistry from

Harvard, Stone may have fit the stereotype of a meddling Yankee intellectual, but his enthusiasm for rehabilitating the island proved infectious. Arriving on the island shortly after the FERA takeover in July 1934, Stone began by inviting residents to city hall assemblies, where he outlined his plans and tried to recruit volunteers. "Your city is bankrupt," he told one crowded assembly. "Your streets are littered and filthy; your homes are run-down and your industry gone. We will begin by cleaning up. Then we will rebuild." Within a few days, more than one thousand unemployed people had signed up to help. Forming a line three blocks long, they moved across the city together picking up trash. The group, which Stone dubbed the Key West Volunteer Corps, soon swelled to more than four thousand residents, partly paid a small amount from the relief rolls but essentially volunteering their time to clean up their city. At the same time, FERA's social service department provided direct relief to needy families, distributing food, setting up a health clinic, and bringing in public health educators to avoid a feared typhoid fever outbreak among the island's underfed residents.

Stone's vision was to give the island a complete makeover to become a tourist destination to rival the Bahamas—and to do it in five months, before the winter vacation season began in December. He and his team of eleven FERA staffers moved into vacant houses on the abandoned naval base and got to work. Along with the volunteers, they built beach huts, playgrounds, a park, and a swimming pool. They renovated abandoned homes into guest houses, remodeled the once-elegant Casa Marina Hotel, planted coconut palms around the island, and installed landscaping along major roads. They tore down the most dilapidated buildings and spruced up restaurants, bars, and nightclubs. Indeed, it seemed that the only one of Stone's initiatives that didn't come to fruition was his strong recommendation, following Bermuda's famous example, that everyone involved in FERA activities wear shorts. The idea never took off except among a handful of staffers. Shorts had never been part of Key West culture, and the idea gave Stone away as an out-of-towner and represented a step too far for many residents.

But beyond the cleanup and the building and the choice of attire, it was Stone's decision to involve artists in the project that puts Key West at the root of this story. Stone turned to Edward Bruce, director of the Public Works of Art Project within the Department of the Treasury. Bruce had been putting artists from around the country to work on murals in government buildings, and Stone asked him to send twelve out-of-work artists to Key West. Every week, each of these artists was expected to create three watercolor landscapes depicting the beauty of the island, which were then used in brochures, postcards, and wall art. Painters also created murals for restaurants and bars until, as the art program's director Adrian Dornbush remembered, "pretty soon there wasn't even a little dirty spoon restaurant that didn't have huge murals on the walls."

The use of art in this Key West project went beyond painting. Artists taught residents how to make handicrafts from local materials to sell to tourists: ash trays and buttons carved from coconut shells, hats and purses made from palm fibers, other trinkets made from shells and fish scales. A furniture designer from New York set up a woodworking studio on the island to create furniture for houses rented to VIP visitors. Realizing that tourists would expect entertainment and festivals, Stone incorporated performing arts into his scheme, with residents, artists, and FERA staffers forming a marimba band (hoping to reflect Key West's Cuban heritage), a choir, a folk dancing troupe, and a theater group called the Key West Players.

In October 1934, Stone had his literal "let's put on a show" moment, announcing that his FERA program would stage a festival in February—featuring an open air presentation of Gilbert and Sullivan's *The Pirates of Penzance*. Stone likely saw the operetta as the obvious choice, given Key West's reputation as a nineteenth-century pirate city. In the first of many made-for-Hollywood plot twists in the Key West story, the professional director Stone had hired was injured in a car accident, so Dornbush needed to fill in. He soon found hidden talents on the island. The FERA artists had already set to work on the sets for the outdoor theater, but one of the painters also had a knack for designing costumes, and another took on the lighting design. Avery Johnson, a painter from Chicago, turned out to have a lovely baritone and was cast as the Pirate King. They found music and dance directors among the island's winter residents, recruited local musicians for the orchestra and the chorus, and discovered a talented singer to play the lead soprano. When they couldn't find a tenor who could hit the high notes, they brought a singer over from Miami, where they also recruited musicians to fill out the orchestra. They rehearsed and constructed their outdoor stage that fall, alongside all the other renovations on the island, with everyone wondering whether anyone would show up to see all their hard work.

Finally, when winter came at the end of 1934, so did the tourists. Between December 1934 and April 1935, Key West had more than thirty thousand visitors, providing the influx of money and jobs everyone had hoped for. The *New York Times* proclaimed that Key West had become "a clean and shining tourist haven." In his *Harper's* article Davis swooned at the art colony atmosphere that Stone had inadvertently created by bringing artists together, describing the new Key West as "Greenwich Village, Montparnasse, Provincetown—on a little tropical island."

Of course, not everyone was so smitten with FERA's experiment. At Pena's Bar, regulars broke into applause when owner Antonio Pena Morales refused to accept a truckload of murals sent by FERA, deeming them too large to adorn the famous bar's walls. Famous Key West denizen Ernest Hemingway, who the *New Yorker* called "an outsider who deeply resented the presence here of other outsiders," was a vociferous critic of the New Deal in general and of its encroachment on his beloved island in particular. He railed against New Dealers as "starry eyed bastards spending money that somebody will have to pay," and his Key West novel *To Have and Have Not* seethes with contempt for Stone and his program. For many conservatives off the island, Key West encapsulated the worst of the New Deal's overreach and overspending, and critics blasted Stone as a dictator, a "terrible tyrant" who was wasting government funds, meddling in private enterprise, and even "encouraging wine, women, and song" with the program's loans to nightclubs and bars. But such criticism was far outweighed by glowing press coverage, fueled by a Key West PR team that continuously provided cheerful, illustrated stories about the island's beauty and its miraculous transformation.

On February 19, 1935, as the orchestra played the first notes of the *Pirates of Penzance* overture in the outdoor theater overlooking the water, the full moon appeared on the horizon, right on cue. The night was unusually cold and windy, but the audience of more than three thousand residents and visitors stayed until the final curtain, when they gave a loud standing ovation that continued until Dornbush came out from backstage to take a bow alongside the cast. If that moment of triumph wasn't enough of a Hollywood ending, it turned out that the tenor from Miami had fallen in love with the local soprano who played the female lead, and the two decided to get married and settle in—where else?—Key West.

That triumphant performance followed by wedding bells may be where the Hollywood musical version would have ended, but for this story, Key West was just the beginning.

❦

In addition to its success as a tourist spot, the Key West experiment appeared to achieve one of the New Deal's unquantifiable goals: to improve morale and provide a sense of hope to people suffering from the impact of the Great Depression. Even though Stone had focused his efforts on catering to potential tourists, the program also had intangible benefits for those living in Key West—the community action to fix up the town, the new skills acquired in craft-making, and the joy of creating music and theater all helped to boost islanders' sense of hope and pride in their community. One regional FERA official who visited the island that spring detected a dramatic shift in outlook among its residents, as he reported to FERA director Harry Hopkins: "This program has completely changed the attitude of the population of Key West from one of apathy to one of energetic hope." This sense of hope also took root among Key West's new colony of artists, many of whom had been struggling and out of work before coming to the island. Reflecting on his time at Key West, Dornbush later said, "Somehow you felt actually as if you had, for the time being, escaped the Depression somewhat."

In the spring of 1935, Key West became a laboratory of sorts, a popular field trip site for other New Dealers to see what the government could do if given the chance. Proclaiming it "the New Deal in miniature," Davis wrote in *Harper's*, "If the experiment being conducted there works out, it may be repeated with variations elsewhere." Newspapers dubbed Key West "New Deal Town" and "Brain Trust Island" (named after FDR's inner circle of advisers) because it had become such a favored destination for government administrators.

Among New Dealers visiting the island that winter was Undersecretary of Agriculture Rexford G. Tugwell. As one of the most progressive members of the administration, he was often denounced by conservative critics as "Rex the Red," plotting to upset the social order, but the press couldn't help but mention that he was also "young, curly-headed, and handsome," with some dubbing him "the handsomest of the Brain Trusters" and the "best dressed man in the administration." At Tugwell's confirmation hearing, conservative senator Ellison D. ("Cotton Ed") Smith even framed those Hollywood good looks as a strike against the nominee, complaining that Tugwell was "a very handsome gentleman who would starve to death" as a farmer, and thus had no place in the Department of Agriculture.

When he visited Key West, Tugwell had something new on his mind. The winter of 1935 marked a turning point for the New Deal—a pivot from the focus on emergency relief during its first two years toward more expansive initiatives aimed at reform and long-range planning. As part of this shift, Tugwell would soon become the director of the Resettlement Administration, a sprawling new agency that, among many other responsibilities, would oversee a group of government-built homesteads in rural areas across the country. These planned communities would house people hit as hard by the Great Depression as those in Key West—"stranded communities" made up of farmers whose land had failed, miners whose mines had shut down, and unemployed urban workers willing to try rural life. Key West's tourism angle might not work on homesteads situated in remote unincorporated areas, but Tugwell saw in Key West a model for what the federal government could accomplish.

Tugwell first came to Key West on February 4, 1935 (during the last few weeks of *Pirates* rehearsals), writing in his diary that he stayed with Stone for a few days, toured the town, and met a number of FERA artists. He noted that he visited again during the last week of March but provided no details about his activities. During one of these visits, Stone had invited Dornbush to join them for dinner, and the next evening, Tugwell asked Dornbush to come see him alone. As Dornbush remembered it later, Tugwell "was intensely interested in everything that we were doing" and wanted something similar for the new Resettlement Administration, admitting that he didn't know exactly what it would look like.

When, a few weeks later, Tugwell invited him to come to Washington and work for his new agency, Dornbush asked for time to think it over. On the one hand, he had always considered himself to be a painter first, one who happened to have a knack for administration, and this new role would mean putting aside his own art completely. Dornbush, who was openly gay, may have also worried about the buttoned-down culture of Washington after having spent the past two years in progressive art colony settings. Before coming to Key West, he had served as director of the Stone City Art Colony in Cedar Rapids, Iowa. Founded in 1932 by Grant Wood—a painter more famous and less open about his sexuality than Dornbush—Stone City served as a haven from both the Great Depression and traditional societal expectations. A newspaper profile of Dornbush noted that the tall, debonair painter "must have found paradise" among the other young artists and the idyll they had created. In Key West, he shared a spacious house on the naval yard with three or four FERA artists, later remembering it as "a very, very congenial and delightful atmosphere." But now, Dornbush saw that Stone didn't really need him anymore. With Key West's art program running smoothly, he knew one of the other painters could easily take over as director. He was intrigued by the idea of expanding on what they had accomplished in Key West. He decided to accept Tugwell's offer and began to make arrangements to leave the island for Washington.

Dornbush signed his official appointment documents and oath of office on May 1, 1935—the day after President Roosevelt wrote the Resettlement Administration (RA) into existence with Executive Order No. 7027. The massive new agency, allotted a budget of more than $375 million, would absorb forty-six disparate programs for the rural poor that had been managed by other New Deal agencies at the local, state, and federal levels—what Tugwell ruefully described as "everybody else's headaches." For Tugwell, bringing all these programs under one agency would allow a more unified approach to tackling what he saw as interconnected problems at the heart of the Depression. His solution would involve conserving land by turning submarginal farmland into federal forests and parks, resettling those farmers into new communities on better land, and providing financial loans and grants to small farmers who were living on good land but needed help getting through tough economic times.

In its first few months, the RA's Washington offices were distinctly *un*settled. Without a dedicated headquarters to house its rapidly growing staff, its workers were scattered throughout a handful of office buildings across the city. When no other offices could be found to accommodate its seemingly endless need for space, the RA arranged to convert the fifty-four-room Walsh mansion on Massachusetts Avenue into a makeshift office for some of its staff. The DC press loved to recount how government workers installed electrical outlets, desks, and telephones within the opulent ballrooms where Mrs. Evalyn Walsh McLean had once worn the Hope Diamond and entertained royalty.

In the spring of 1935, Dornbush reported to a more modest government office building to begin his new post in the Planning Division, composed of a group of advisers Tugwell had assembled to answer the rather daunting question, "What influence do we want the Resettlement Administration to have on the current and coming course of events in America?" Dornbush's new job title of "senior social economist" seemed to indicate a role that would require a different set of credentials than his two years of college, art studies in Europe, and work experience teaching art and directing art colonies. In fact, the job that Tugwell had in mind for Dornbush was so new that it didn't fit any existing titles within the federal government's bureaucracy, so his staff had found a job description that seemed the closest fit, to help avoid red tape in getting Dornbush's appointment approved quickly. In the description of his expected duties, the only indication of something unusual was hidden in the fourth item: a focus on "matters pertaining to the field of arts and crafts and their relation to community life."

Arts activities on the RA homesteads were meant to foster a cooperative spirit that would go beyond simply boosting morale during tough times, as they had done in Key West. The hope was that they would help to inspire a larger ideological shift from rugged individualism to a new sense of collective purpose, laying the groundwork for a collectivized, cooperative society that Tugwell and other progressive New Dealers saw as the only way out of the Great Depression. For Tugwell, voluntary democratic cooperatives were the logical solution to the world's economic problems—sound alternatives to both the individualistic chaos of capitalism and the involuntary collectivism enforced by fascist and communist regimes. He declared cooperation to be the "easiest, most natural thing in the world." Historian Paul Conkin describes the RA's efforts as "one of the most open breaks with the individualistic tradition in American history," explaining that "these communities were to be examples of a new, organic society, with new values and institutions." The RA's communities embodied a vision that FDR articulated in his first inaugural address in 1933, declaring, "We now realize as we have never realized before our interdependence on each other; that we cannot merely take but we must give as well; that if we are to go forward, we must move as a trained and loyal army willing to sacrifice for the good of a common discipline."

In his first months as an unlikely senior social economist, Dornbush took field trips to the RA's homesteads and continued to ask Tugwell what he wanted the agency's new arts program to look like. As one newspaper column described their conversation, "Was he expected to make the farmers paint, organize barn dances, or start classes in pottery-making, or what? Faced with the question, Tugwell paused. Then he smiled and said, 'Yes.'" Tugwell had said he wanted to infuse the RA homesteads with "community art," and he would leave the details up to Dornbush. He wanted whatever they had done in Key West to be adapted to the RA, but instead of a focus on tourists, it would be largely for the benefit of the struggling homesteaders themselves. He wanted furniture for their new homes. He wanted artists to teach them handicrafts, painting, weaving, woodworking, and music. He wanted operettas, choirs, and folk dancing—not to entertain tourists, but to raise morale, build community, and create hope. It was all part of Tugwell's larger, transformative vision for the agency—and for American culture overall. But in the summer of 1935, no one knew what it would look like, or what it could become.

CHAPTER 1

MUSIC AS A SOCIAL FUNCTION

When Margaret Valiant left Memphis at age eighteen, she promised herself that she would only return to the South if she had a round-trip ticket. Her recent move to Washington, DC, was the closest she had come since then, but the notarized document she had just signed, with a layer of color-coded carbon copies attached to its thick off-white stationery, would soon propel her even farther south. By signing, she took the official oath of office for her new government job: field instructor in music for the Resettlement Administration, effective as of yesterday—January 7, 1936. When she learned that the offered salary of $1,440 per year was the lowest for her pay grade, she said, "Well, our country is in trouble. I'll take the minimum." In addition to the signed oath, a one-page memorandum listing the assignments for the six field instructors determined her southward direction: Under her name were the words, "Cherry Lake Farms, Cherry Lake, Florida."

Margaret likely knew very little about what awaited her in Florida. On a map, she could have seen that Cherry Lake was an unincorporated area in Madison County, just a few miles south of the Georgia border. She would have understood that Cherry Lake Farms was one of many homesteads run by the Resettlement Administration (or "RA" in the New Deal lexicon). She was told she would be returning to Washington at least twice a month for meetings, so she knew she would be keeping the round-trip-ticket promise she had made to herself long ago. But it was now certain that this new government music job would bring her back to her roots in the Deep South after an absence of nearly twenty years.

⌘

Margaret Valiant Brahan was born on February 22, 1901, in Como, Mississippi. After her mother died giving birth to Margaret's younger sister when Margaret was two, she was shuttled between increasingly distant relatives, first with her father's well-off sister in San Antonio, Texas. At age eight, she was sent to live with her older half cousin, whom she always called "Aunt Annie," in Plum Point, Mississippi. It was a small rural community close to the Tennessee border: "farming country," she described it later, "where we grew everything we ate—except, we got coffee by the sack, green, and we roasted it in the old kitchen oven. And we got sugar by the barrel. And we got flour by the barrel. Other than that, everything we ate, we grew on the ground around us, and we grew it ourselves." Through middle school, she walked a mile and a half to a one-room schoolhouse, where she remembered learning a "smattering of this and that," taking especially to Latin, language, and spelling. As the only girl, she filled in playing first base on the boys' baseball team since they were always short of players and she "could run like a rabbit." When Aunt Annie somehow found the money to buy a piano, Margaret jumped up and started playing it while it was still on the wagon, waiting to be unloaded.

In 1914, after Aunt Annie's husband died, the two moved to Memphis, where Margaret attended a public high school and soon began formal piano lessons. After a few years, her piano teacher sensed a larger musical talent and arranged for her to receive a six-week scholarship at the Cincinnati Conservatory of Music after high school. Arriving in Cincinnati in the fall of 1919, Margaret discovered a new universe—going to her first symphony, ballet, and opera—and knew she couldn't go back to her old life. When the six-week scholarship ended, she stayed in Cincinnati and continued her studies at the conservatory, paying her own way by picking up accompanying jobs at the conservatory and playing pipe organ at movie matinees.

Margaret had a magnetic presence. She was striking and tall, with dark hair and brown eyes, a quick wit, and an easy laugh. She later said, "I never thought of myself as pretty, if I ever was. But I must have had some sort of *bearing*." Her time in Cincinnati brought her into contact with a group of powerful and wealthy friends who welcomed her into their social circle, allowing her to reinvent herself completely. This survival strategy of what she called "acquiring friends rather than money" would become a repeating pattern and one of her life's guiding principles.

Margaret's reinvention began at the end of the school year in 1921, when Bertha Baur, the head of the Cincinnati Conservatory, invited her to spend the summer at her house in Lake Champlain, New York. There, Margaret served as a sort of "court musician" at Ms. Baur's elegant parties, accompanying dancing on the piano and entertaining guests with singing performances. During that summer in the Adirondacks, Margaret encountered a group of wealthy women who would become her friends, patrons, and protectors. First, she met Matilda Steuart, the daughter of a prominent New York lawyer with whom she hit it off immediately. Matilda introduced Margaret to the new (and much younger) wife of her father's client Noah Slee: Margaret Sanger, the birth-control activist with a complicated legacy.

The first thing her new patrons did was host a benefit concert among their wealthy friends to raise money for Margaret to buy a new wardrobe. She collected $90 (as she later said, "I don't think I'd ever had $90 in my whole life") and went with her friends on a shopping spree in New York City, trading in her handsewn pink and blue organdy dresses for something more sophisticated: a navy-blue dress, tan shoes, elegant gloves, a red velvet hat with a pheasant feather the same color as a small mink coat. Her new friends helped pay for Margaret's last year at the conservatory, where she switched her focus from piano to voice and finished her degree in 1922. After she had spent a few years in Cincinnati teaching piano and working as a school accompanist, Steuart, who was studying art in Paris, invited Margaret to join her. Once in Paris, Margaret was able to secure a scholarship to study voice at the Paris Conservatory, launching her into a promising performing career and a new cosmopolitan life of travel between Europe and New York City.

After two years of study at conservatories in both Paris and Milan, Margaret had her Paris debut in a vocal recital on April 13, 1926, at the Salle des Agriculteurs in Paris, a prominent concert venue at the time (with an eerily prescient name, given the work she would do in the RA's rural communities). She was already performing as Margaret Valiant, having dropped "Brahan" after so many Europeans seemed to have trouble pronouncing it. The program began with three operatic arias, followed by a set of traditional Spanish songs and African American spirituals. A review in the *New York Herald* noted that she appeared nervous at the beginning of the program and her voice "strangled in the upper notes" of the arias during the first half. But the critic also wrote, "Miss Valiant possesses a true adjunct to success, in that both by voice and gesture she lends drama to whatever she sings," especially the popular songs in the recital's second half, where "she gave free vent to her expansive temperament." After this concert, Margaret pivoted away from opera, later saying it was for many reasons—the mixed *Herald* review helped her see that her strengths lay elsewhere, and she also became ill with a serious bout of pleurisy. Doctors said she had severe lung damage that was likely the result of a childhood in poverty and would make a career in opera impossible. She stayed in Europe for the next year, spending part of the time recovering as a guest at her friend Margaret Sanger Slee's villa on the French Riviera.

Margaret returned to New York by boat from Genoa, Italy, on May 31, 1927, and less than a week later she married Edwin Mims Jr., a Rhodes scholar originally from Memphis whom she had met in Paris. The couple stayed in New York, and in April of the following year, Margaret made her Broadway debut in a small singing role in Ziegfeld's *The Three Musketeers*, also serving as the understudy for the show's star soprano, opera singer Yvonne D'Arle. She later recounted how she got the part: "Ziggy lined us all up on the stage to look us over," and, after surveying her long legs and what she called her "pretty good" looks, he said, "You'll do." The show ran until the end of 1928, and after the stock market crash of 1929, she felt lucky to find work in fashion design and modeling, drawing on her long-abandoned experience making her own clothes and on some modeling work she had done in Paris. She even sold some of her designs to the high-end department store Bergdorf Goodman. Edwin did some editing for Yale University Press, but he struggled to find work amid the growing financial disaster in New York.

Margaret later wrote that her marriage was just like her singing career: "short and swift—perils throughout." But she gave few details about her relationship with Edwin, or about any aspect of her private life. (Near the end of her life, when asked during a radio interview if she had ever been married, she replied curtly, "Yes. Next question.") Strangely enough, her government personnel file now serves as one of the few sources for insight about her marriage, since the RA's Personnel Division specifically asked her references to comment on her marital status. Edwin Mims Sr., who Margaret likely listed as a personal reference knowing that the subject of her divorce would be relevant to her hiring, wrote that the end of Margaret and his son's marriage "was an unfortunate affair—but in no way due to any impropriety on her part. It was a case of incompatibility by two brilliant people. That is all there is to it." They separated amicably, and Margaret would stay in touch with the Mims family throughout her life.

Between 1929 and 1935, Margaret continued traveling back and forth to Europe, calling the Madison Square Hotel home when she was in New York City. In Europe, as she wrote in her government job application, she studied "folk singing, dancing, painting, and designing." Other than this description, Margaret left almost no written record of her life in Europe. She was fluent in French and Italian and could also speak German and Spanish, perhaps leaving clues about where she lived and visited. Margaret later said that she gave concerts of lighter material and became popular in Italy singing the traditional American folk songs she had learned in childhood. She learned to play the guitar in Naples and recounted fond memories of the day she left, when "all these marvelous friends came down to see me off with their guitars and singing." Margaret seemed able to make her way merrily in any situation through a combination of charm, skills, and a chameleonic ability to adapt to new surroundings—all talents that would later come in handy in her government work.

◈

It was aboard the *Red Star*, the ship that brought Margaret from Cherbourg to New York in November 1931, that Margaret met Ruth Crawford. The two women had much in common. Born in the same year as Margaret, Ruth had left home in Jacksonville, Florida, to study piano at the American Conservatory in Chicago. Although she had planned to stay for one year to complete a teaching certification, she decided to remain indefinitely. Finding a supportive group of mentors and teachers, she discovered her talent for composing and eventually earned her master's degree in composition despite little support for the idea of a woman becoming a composer. In 1929, she moved to New York and became part of a group of "ultra-modernist" composers known for their experiments in atonal music. When Margaret met her on the *Red Star*, Ruth was returning to New York from her own musical adventures in Europe, having spent the past year in Berlin and Paris on a Guggenheim composition fellowship—the first woman to receive the award. Margaret later described their arrival in New York, where Ruth was met by Dr. Charles Seeger, "a very learned and elegant New England scholar" wearing a dark coat, derby hat, and pince-nez—perhaps not "a totally romantic figure in the popular eye," Margaret said later, but her new friend Ruth was clearly smitten.

Charles Seeger—or Charlie, as he was known to his friends—was fifteen years older than Ruth, a musicologist and composer who taught part-time at both the Institute of Musical Art (which would later become Juilliard) and the New School. He had been her composition teacher, and the two had fallen in love in the months before she had left New York for her Guggenheim fellowship. Ruth and Charlie married in 1932, when Pete Seeger—Charlie's youngest son from his first marriage—was thirteen. By then, Ruth and Margaret had become good friends; when

Ruth became pregnant the following year, Margaret designed maternity clothes for her.

During this time, Charlie and Ruth became increasingly involved in connecting music to left-wing politics. Charlie wrote for the communist *Daily Worker* newspaper under the pseudonym Carl Sands, declaring in one of his columns, "Music is propaganda—always propaganda—and of the most powerful sort." Ruth composed several revolutionary songs, including "Sacco, Vanzetti," with lyrics by the leftist poet H. T. Tsiang that were so radical that the soprano chosen for the concert refused to sing them, forcing Ruth to find a last-minute replacement to perform the song's 1933 premiere.

Charlie became the leader of the Composers' Collective, a group of left-wing avant-garde composers who attended regular meetings in various loft spaces in lower Manhattan, paying their weekly dues of twenty-five cents and playing their compositions for each other on an old upright piano that was likely rented for them by the Communist Party. They wrote a series of atonal "workers' songs" meant to be used in labor protests, believing spare modernism to be the best representation of the proletariat. As Carl Sands, Charlie wrote dismissively of folk songs as "complacent, melancholy, defeatist" and declared, "The revolutionary movement will have its own music." Among the Collective's members were a few well-known New York composers, including Aaron Copland, Henry Cowell, and Marc Blitzstein, who would later incorporate many of the songs he wrote for the Collective into his musical, *The Cradle Will Rock*.

One of Charlie's contributions typical of the collective's style was a song called "Pioneer Song: Who's That Guy?" which he wrote in 1933 and published under his pseudonym Carl Sands. With a spare piano accompaniment, leaping atonal melody, and irregular rhythms, the song would have been difficult for anyone to actually sing. The lyrics started with the words from a poem by Tsiang, beginning with an exclamation ("Lenin! Who's that guy?") then extolling his virtues ("He leads the workers to break the world and shape the sky"). Charlie wrote new lyrics praising Stalin and conveying skepticism about Hitler ("his Nazi thing is bound to die, spouting theories that can't get by") before criticizing Roosevelt's National Recovery

Administration (NRA) for not doing enough for workers. He ended with a warning to the president and his administration that referenced the NRA's well-known blue eagle logo: "But America's workers will cook his blue bird by and by. / So the Brain Trust, the economists, and all the nuts / will yell and cry, oh me, oh my! / Roosevelt! Goodbye!"

Perhaps unsurprisingly, and despite these composers' best intentions, their workers' songs were not embraced by the people—likely because their musical language was made up of atonal melodies and complex asymmetrical rhythms that were too difficult, dissatisfying, or just plain odd-sounding to workers' ears. *Daily Worker* columnist Mike Gold blasted the Collective's output as "full of geometric bitterness" written for "an assortment of mechanical canaries."

This failure of the Composers' Collective's efforts was just one of several factors contributing to Charlie's growing embrace of folk music as the true music of the people. Ruth introduced him to her friend Carl Sandburg's *The American Songbag* anthology and had visited his Julliard music history classes to talk to his students about folk music. In the early 1930s, the radical union activist and folk singer Aunt Molly Jackson came to New York from Harlan County, Kentucky, on a tour to raise money for striking coalminers, and by 1933 she had settled in an apartment on the Lower East Side and become a favorite performer among the left-wing intelligentsia. Her songs featured fierce pro-union lyrics set to traditional melodies she had grown up singing, including Baptist hymn tunes and Appalachian folk ballads. In the winter of 1933, Jackson sang a few of her songs at a Composer's Collective meeting and listened to a few of their compositions, to mutual bewilderment. The composers cringed at her raspy singing of her National Miners Union anthem, "I Am a Union Woman," and she was unmoved by their atonal creations. Although Charlie had previously been dismissive of folk music's merits, hearing Aunt Molly's songs in contrast with the Collective's modernist creations helped him understand the appeal of using familiar songs as vehicles for protest. He began to recognize that "the people could sing her songs and they couldn't sing our songs. . . . We were all on the wrong track." Another influence on Charlie's growing awareness of the power of folk music was Lawrence Gellert's work collecting Black protest songs in the South, which appeared in the prominent left-wing magazine *New Masses* beginning in 1932, and which Charlie expressed an interest in publishing in the first issue of the *Music Vanguard* magazine a few years later.

Around the same time, the painter Thomas Benton invited Charlie to play guitar for an impromptu folk-music concert at the dedication of Benton's new mural at the New School, where both men taught. Benton had taught himself harmonica and put together an "urban hillbilly" band called the Harmonica Rascals, with his wife Rita on guitar, his young son on flute, and a group of his art students (including Charles Pollock and his younger brother Jackson, Bernard Steffen, and Manuel Tolegian) on additional harmonicas and the occasional jaw harp. Benton had grown up on the western edge of the Ozarks in Missouri, and though perhaps not himself a true member of the rural "folk" (his father was a congressman, his uncle a senator), he held a special appreciation for rural folk music. In addition to depicting folk musicians in his paintings of rural scenes, Benton had amassed an extensive collection of bluegrass and other "hillbilly" folk records.

Charlie, Ruth, and Margaret (when she wasn't in Europe) became regulars at musical gatherings that Benton hosted in his tiny walk-up apartment on West 8th Street—the living room eerily illuminated with blue light bulbs Benton had installed for the living room's daytime function as his painting studio. Benton's gatherings were somewhere between a bohemian Greenwich Village hangout and a back-porch country jam session, listening to records from Benton's collection and playing along with the Harmonica Rascals to folk songs like "Cindy" and "Ida Red." It was here that Charlie and Ruth both found a deeper appreciation for this particular brand of folk music. For Margaret, who already knew and loved this music, Benton's gatherings were like coming home. Although they couldn't have known it at the time, these sessions were, in many ways, the birthplace of what would come to be known as the Music Unit.

By the summer of 1935, Dornbush had been freed from his temporary economist role at the RA to serve as director of the new Special Skills Division. The vaguely named division had several dimensions, the most public of which was as an internal design studio and laboratory, with a staff of "artists, designers and craftsmen at Tugwell's call for anything from designing furniture and building hardware to illustrating resettlement reports." But Dornbush's new job description emphasized another goal to be carried out on the homesteads themselves: "to establish, encourage and extend individual and group activities (on an educational, recreational or economic basis) in fine, applied and expressive arts (particularly painting, sculpture, weaving, printing, ceramics, wood and metal working, drama, poetry and music)."

Dornbush's direct supervisor for this work was Grace Falke, who, at twenty-nine years old, had worked with Tugwell longer and more closely than anyone else at the RA. Born in the Bronx, her first job after high school had been as a stenographer in Columbia University's Office of the Secretary. After Tugwell served an interim role in that office and observed her competence firsthand, he arranged to have her transferred to the economics department, where she became department secretary as well as his personal assistant, since he was then department chair. When he left Columbia to become Undersecretary of Agriculture in 1933, he convinced her to come with him to Washington.

Having already served as secretary to Columbia's Office of the Secretary, in March 1933 Falke assumed her first government job, as private secretary to the Assistant Secretary in the Department of Agriculture's Office of the Secretary. By the end of 1933, she had been promoted to become the confidential secretary to the Assistant Secretary. These repetitive titles point out the absurdly opposite (and gendered) meanings of the word "secretary" at both the top and bottom of an office hierarchy, but on some level, Falke's role appeared to encompass both meanings. With wavy dark hair and intelligent eyes, she may have checked the expected boxes of a female assistant, as a note in her government personnel file described her: "an attractive young woman sitting to the left of [Tugwell's] door at a desk piled high with letters." But her work had long transcended such expectations. In the summer of 1934, she went on an extended trip with Lorena Hickok, a former AP reporter hired by Harry Hopkins as a field investigator for FERA. Falke sent regular reports back to Tugwell from mining towns and rural areas as they traveled through Tennessee, Alabama, Mississippi, Colorado, and the Imperial Valley in California. By December 1934, she was working with congressional staffers to amend legislation with language related to agricultural labor conditions.

At the RA, Tugwell put Falke in charge of overseeing five of the agency's smaller divisions: Special Skills, Public Health, Procedure, Information, and Labor Relations. Her ascent was part of a larger trend noted by historian Susan Ware—more women held positions of power in the New Deal government than in any previous administration. Falke and her RA leadership role were mentioned in a newspaper column at the time listing the growing number of women "shifting to executive and administrative positions of high authority rather than the legislative grind." Eleanor Roosevelt played an important role in supporting this new network of women in government, regularly inviting them to White House events. Falke's White House appointment card shows what this looked like, filled with neat columns of handwritten dates when she attended luncheons, dinners, receptions, and a yearly tea for women administrators that the First Lady hosted on the White House lawn.

In addition to supervising Dornbush's efforts in Special Skills, Falke oversaw the Information Division, where Tugwell's former Columbia colleague Roy Stryker was creating the Historical Unit, sending documentary photographers out in the field to show the American people the horrors of the Depression and what the RA was doing to help. Falke has since been called "the driving force behind the Resettlement Administration's involvement with the arts," but she summarized her role as a kind of peacekeeper among the five division heads who reported to her. "Of course," she said, "they were always having squabbles with each other, and they all centered in my office, and my real job was to keep everybody happy."

The RA's Rural Resettlement Division inherited almost sixty government homestead projects that had been started by two previous New Deal agencies—thirty-four communities from the Department of the Interior's Division of Subsistence Homesteads and twenty-five from FERA—all in varying stages of planning and construction, very few of which had been completed. These homesteads were intended to help three types of stranded populations: unemployed miners and other industrial workers living in desperate poverty in remote areas with no opportunities for work after mines and factories had shut down; unemployed workers living in cities, scraping by on government relief, waiting in bread lines and hoping to avoid living on the street; and farmers on submarginal land that would no longer sustain them, leaving little choice but to resettle elsewhere.

Nearly half of these projects were concentrated in the South, with a handful of others in the West, Midwest, and Northeast, representing twenty-five states in all. The Special Skills Division chose to concentrate their work at a cluster of homesteads in the Appalachian region and the South, relatively close to Washington. That included four communities for stranded miners and lumber workers (Westmoreland Homesteads in Pennsylvania, Cumberland Homesteads in Tennessee, and Tygart Valley Homesteads and Red House Farms in West Virginia); two communities for the urban unemployed (Cherry Lake Farms in Florida and Pine Mountain Valley Farms in Georgia); and one for displaced farmers (Dyess Colony in Arkansas). In the summer of 1935, the division dispatched its first group of field instructors to these communities to lead activities in painting, weaving, woodworking, and ceramics.

But just a few months later, the Special Skills Division was already in trouble. Early efforts to create arts and crafts activities were undermined by low morale and discord among the new homesteaders. They had already been hard hit by the Great Depression, and now they had uprooted their lives to move to homesteads that—in many cases—were still under construction. Given that the promised feeling *of settlement* was largely absent in these new communities, perhaps it should not have been surprising that most of them had little to no interest in communing with their neighbors.

Special Skills staffer Katharine Kellock was tasked with visiting these homesteads to determine what could be done. In a report to Dornbush, she wrote that it would have been ideal to have sent recreation leaders as soon as the residents had arrived, "in order to bind the homesteaders into harmonious social units." As it was, Kellock reported that the clubs and activities that had been designed to improve the social problem had instead become "hotbeds of discontent" as participants inevitably slid toward "a serious contemplation of their economic problems which they had no power to solve." After speaking with homestead leaders and residents and observing the situation for herself, Kellock said the solution was clear: Special Skills needed to send in music leaders "to help meet the need of the emergency situation, as well as the long-term plan." She explained, "In every one of these colonies, project managers and educational supervisors told me of the desperate need for recreation to keep up morale and carry the homesteaders through the present pioneer period. Without exception, they regarded musical leadership for the adult homesteaders as the first important assistance that Special Skills could give."

Dornbush's search for a music leader to fill this emergency role is what led back to Thomas Benton's Greenwich Village jam sessions from a few years earlier. Benton's former student (and Harmonica Rascals member) Charles Pollock was among the first painters Dornbush had hired to join Special Skills in the summer of 1935. Pollock remembered Charlie from those sessions and suggested him for the music job. When Kellock interviewed Charlie in early October, she was clearly impressed, nearly gushing in her report that "Mr. Seeger's professional reputation is so high that this interview was almost unnecessary." She described his appearance as "the typical lean, gray New England scholar; his manner is dry and business-like," and concluded, "The number of professional people with Mr. Seeger's training, experience and outlook is so very small, that it seemed to the interviewer that a special effort should be made to get his services for this division." Three weeks later, Dornbush sent Charlie a night telegram informing him that his appointment as technical assistant in music had been approved and asking him to report to Washington as soon as possible.

For Charlie, this was welcome news. By the fall of 1935, he had lost his teaching job at Julliard and was struggling to find work, while Ruth devoted her time to caring for their growing family in their cramped Manhattan apartment. (Michael was two, and Peggy just a few months old.) His misgivings about the Roosevelt administration had softened along with his musical aesthetics, mirroring the overall shift of the Popular Front, which encouraged a left-wing embrace of both American folk culture and the New Deal beginning in 1935. Charlie promptly accepted Dornbush's offer and said he could start the following week. Margaret, who had returned from Europe a few months earlier and was unsure what she would do next, didn't need much convincing to join the Seegers in leaving New York, even without a job in hand. In November 1935, she found herself squeezed into the back seat of Ruth and Charlie's car, with Peggy and Michael on her lap and surrounded by all of their possessions, as they made the drive south to Washington.

On November 12, Charlie reported to the RA's headquarters in the Barr Building, a Gothic Revival office tower with spires rising eleven floors above Farragut Square. That week, Katharine Kellock gave him a full report on the urgent need for music in the homesteads she had visited. Of Cherry Lake Farms, Charlie was told that the homestead manager "is very eager for musical assistance as soon as it can be given," and that he had specifically requested a woman music leader because they wouldn't have had anywhere to put a man. With the homestead still under construction, the only housing they could offer was a bunk in a barracks-style building already occupied by two female schoolteachers. Kellock also warned of a general bitterness toward northerners coming to Florida to take their jobs and suggested a few names of Floridians that should be considered as music representatives.

But Charlie already had someone in mind for the position, and a few days later, he brought Margaret into the office for an interview. In his report, he made no indication that they knew each other but made a strong case for her candidacy, describing her as a "young woman of old southern family, brought up in the country and knows country people." He praised her musical ability and training but made a special note that she lacked any "affectations that country people sometimes find objectionable in people who have lived in cities or travelled extensively."

Unlike Charlie's appointment, which was approved in a matter of weeks, Margaret waited more than a month without hearing if this government job would come through. Finally, in the first week of January 1936, she was directed to report to the Special Skills Division's new headquarters in a former factory building at 2216 M Street in northwest DC. Beginning on January 7, she would be the newest member of the RA's Music Unit, a field instructor assigned to Cherry Lake Farms.

Charlie provided two weeks of training and detailed written instructions for new music staffers, outlining his vision for the unit's work and what would be expected of them in the field. Upon arriving at their assigned homestead, field representatives were to follow two basic principles: "First," Charlie instructed, "he should make friends." This would allow the representative to find the musicians among the homesteaders, as well as anyone willing to participate in musical activities. Charlie urged his representatives to think of themselves as the "village musician"—a fellow practitioner, not a strict music teacher, despite the word "instructor" in their job titles.

Their second priority should be to determine what kind of music the homesteaders liked—or, as Charlie described it in characteristically dense prose that may have been more at home in an academic treatise than a government memo, "to have a keen sense of the values of the various ingredients that go into making up the musical currency of his locality." Charlie reasoned that the homesteaders' music of choice, which he thought would likely include the kind of folk music that he had recently discovered at Thomas Benton's, would be the most effective vehicle for their purposes. He told his new staffers that in making choices about the music to incorporate into their work, they should go beyond its immediate, practical functions—for dancing, or marching, or listening—to consider its larger social *use* in facilitating feelings of cooperation and community. In providing this guidance for his field representatives, Charlie articulated the Music Unit's overarching goal: "To regard music as a social function, to direct it towards certain definite social goals as an activity of masses of people rather than merely of isolated individuals—these should be his main concern." After just a week of orientation in the DC office, Margaret was deemed ready to report to her assigned homestead.

In the months since they had first arrived in Washington, the Seegers had settled into a small rented brick house in Clarendon, Virginia, just over the border from DC, and Margaret had found an apartment of her own on K Street, only a few blocks from the new Special Skills office. As she packed for her trip south, she was secure in the knowledge that she would be returning to her city life in a few weeks. It may have been difficult to imagine what items from her New York/Paris wardrobe would be suitable, but she was certain, at least, that she would need her guitar. On January 14, 1936, Margaret boarded a train for Madison, Florida, unsure what she would find at Cherry Lake Farms—a place that might feel familiar from her childhood in the rural South, but within a government experiment unlike anything she had experienced.

CHAPTER 2

IN THE SLOUGH OF DESPOND

On May 11, 1935, FERA administrator Julius Stone Jr. addressed a crowd assembled on a warm Florida afternoon. "This thing is fraught with possibilities," he announced. "If it succeeds there is no telling how far it will go. Working together, we can show the country what honest American citizens can do with the help of the government." Stone could have been giving this speech to citizens of Key West, but instead he was at the island's geographical opposite: landlocked, rural Cherry Lake, just a few miles shy of the state's northern border. Stone stood on a makeshift wooden platform alongside Florida governor David Scholtz to inaugurate a new project: Cherry Lake Farms, where they would build a brand-new community from the ground up, what one journalist called "the second of the government's unique Florida experiments in bettering humanity," after Key West. John Mick, one of Cherry Lake Farm's first new residents, made a short speech on behalf of the project's homesteaders, asserting, "No one here can say we would be better off anywhere else." At that, loud applause broke out from the crowd of about three hundred people, a mix of farmers from the surrounding areas and newly arrived homesteaders.

Cherry Lake Farms was part of FERA's nationwide effort to create new planned communities for those on government relief who had no job prospects where they lived. In FERA's decentralized system, state offices were given full control over decision-making and management of the agency's programs in their state, whether by establishing these new communities, providing direct relief grants and loans to struggling farmers, or purchasing submarginal land and retiring it from farming through conservation.

In Florida, Stone and his fellow FERA administrators decided to build what the agency called a "rural-industrial" hybrid community for Florida's urban unemployed, a radical government experiment in urban relocation and cooperative living. In Jacksonville, Tampa, Miami, St. Petersburg, and other cities, married men on relief who had at least one child were invited to apply for a spot at Cherry Lake. A rigorous selection process followed—including home visits, letters of reference, and credit checks—and those men selected were brought to Cherry Lake for a two-week trial period. Historians have pointed out these strict selection criteria highlight a fundamental disconnect within the RA between its goals to help the poorest families most in need and its desire to choose those most likely to bring the project success, as Wayne Flynt concludes, "Although noble in conception and sometimes successful in execution, the resettlement communities merely skimmed the top off the bottom class." At Cherry Lake, those admitted included office clerks, sailors, housepainters, at least one doctor, a jeweler, and a few journalists.

Tragically, one strict rule guided homesteader selection in all Florida cities (and across the RA): Cherry Lake Farms would be Whites-only, as state FERA officials followed local Jim Crow segregation practices to exclude Black Americans from living in the community. This kind of racism was baked into the New Deal from its beginnings to appease southern Democrats in Congress whose votes the administration needed to implement any reforms. New Deal programs ceded control to state and local officials, who limited Black participation and upheld discrimination while federal administrators turned a blind eye.

Cherry Lake's beautiful farmland, rolling hills of red clay punctuated by copses of trees, was also marked by its darker history. An abandoned plantation manor built by enslaved people was renovated to serve as the homestead's office headquarters, a stark repurposing of a violent past by a project that was itself built within the confines of Jim Crow. Scattered shacks used as temporary housing for Cherry Lake's homesteaders had once housed Black tenant farmers, whose expulsion may have been an unintended consequence of New Deal programs. Before the RA was established, the Agricultural Adjustment Administration's policy of paying landowners to reduce farm acreage resulted in widespread evictions of tenants and farm laborers. Although the RA's main purpose was to provide direct help to these tenant farmers and sharecroppers, historians have since shown that the agency evicted Black tenants to make way for White homesteaders on projects in Louisiana and Mississippi. Even a progressive agency like the RA—which one historian called "the one bright spot for the black community" in the New Deal—struggled to make a difference in the Jim Crow South.

As in all of FERA's rural-industrial communities, cooperatives were at the core of Cherry Lake Farms. According to historian Paul Conkin, all of the New Deal's planned communities were centered on "the idea of co-operation, which was to replace competition and extreme individualism." He notes that "no more concerted public effort was ever made in the United States to develop co-operatives of all kinds." At Cherry Lake, this meant cooperative farming and dairy operations, a cooperatively owned power plant, and cooperative industries that included a commissary and grocery store, furniture factory, and canning operations. New residents bought their homes and supplies on credit; in return, homesteaders worked on the community farm or in the other cooperative enterprises, with any surplus food being sold to FERA's relief agencies. Of course, these cooperative communities were easy targets for conservatives, many of whom fumed that such "Communistic and socialistic influences" would eventually "destroy American ideals and the self-respect of millions of our citizens." One journalist living on the homestead pointed to Cherry Lake's capitalist ties in its defense: "Is this local socialism? Surely it is not communism, as some hint. Private property, business and other cherished American ideals are not suppressed."

Beyond the literal cooperation in its cooperative farm and its various enterprises, other signs of community were beginning to show themselves among the homesteaders, such as a Cherry Lake Self-Governing Club, a Women's Club, and a Boy Scout troop. Boxing had become a regular pastime for the men living in the homestead's barracks, who built a makeshift arena and held regular bouts in their spare time. As the crowds of spectators for these matches grew among homesteaders and locals, the project architect designed an arena with eighteen hundred bleacher seats.

The homestead also provided some needed relief efforts to the entire region, hiring many local residents to work the homestead's farm, sawmill, and factories, and opening a community grocery store that specialized in goods from local farmers and artisans. Unlike its segregated residential policies, these hiring practices extended to African Americans, who made up more than half the population of Madison County, 90 percent of whom were tenant farmers or sharecroppers with few opportunities for work.

In December 1935, homesteader and canning plant employee Margaret Watkins wrote a glowing article in the local Madison paper about her experience at Cherry Lake Farms: "All are cheerful and happy," she wrote. "We owe this to the dream of Mr. Roosevelt, and we wish him a very Merry Christmas."

Despite the rosy press coverage and seemingly utopian community feeling, cracks were beginning to show in Cherry Lake Farms' shiny surface. Optimism had abounded at the inauguration ceremony in May 1935, where the stage was set up on the first foundation laid for the community's new homes. Architects developed six different designs for two- and three-bedroom homes to be built from local Florida cypress. Each would be equipped with electricity, running water, a phone line, furniture from the homestead's cooperative factory, two palm trees in the front yard, land for a small farm, a mule, and a chicken coop. Yet it wasn't until September that the first home was finished and ready for occupancy. Construction was slow due to delays in federal appropriations and a lack of skilled workers to build and supply lumber, as well as planning that prioritized launching cooperatives over building housing.

In October, Kellock visited Cherry Lake and reported that only fifteen houses were finished, though there were by then ninety-seven families living on the homestead, "chiefly in shacks and houses that were built to care for flocks of chickens, yet to be bought." Kellock saw this not as the result of bad planning, but a lack of coordination with state relief agencies. The plan had been for the men in each family to move to Cherry Lake first to help build their homes and work on the homestead, while the women and children would stay in the cities and continue to collect relief funds until their homes were ready. But as state relief funds dwindled, Florida relief offices had begun to cut families from city relief rolls if anyone in the household worked or was involved in a government work program. For families selected for Cherry Lake, this presented a real problem, leaving them no choice but to join the men on the homestead, even if it meant somehow getting by in their chicken coops.

Men whose families hadn't yet arrived lived in temporary barracks, which were themselves the source of numerous complaints: they were too hot, had been tracked full of dust and mud, had bad air circulation, and left no place to play cards after lights out. Other disgruntlements soon emerged from homesteaders who lamented that the roads were bad, there were too many bugs, the trading post closed too early, the cooks in the mess hall were rude, and the food was "too much starch and greasy stuff." The Cherry Lake Self-Government Club had become so contentious that they couldn't even agree on how to hold their meetings, debating whether they should be open to all or closed sessions. Homesteader H. R. Mattox seemed to think it didn't matter much, since "they don't do anything but argue with one another at the meetings anyhow." Kellock agreed with Mattox's sentiment, reporting that the club was dominated by "rebellion and complaint."

Chaotic shifts in governance were also roiling the leadership at Cherry Lake. In the spring of 1935—right around the time of Cherry Lake's inauguration ceremony—the Roosevelt administration had undertaken a huge reorganization of its New Deal agencies: FERA became the Works Progress Administration (WPA), with a heightened focus on job creation, and its rural-industrial communities were transferred to the newly created

Resettlement Administration. Yet on the ground, the shift did not play out as smoothly as on paper, with FERA offices continuing to operate separately from the WPA through the end of the year. These changes appeared to spark a leadership churn in Florida, with Julius Stone leaving Florida to assist Harry Hopkins at the WPA's headquarters in Washington and Cherry Lake's original community director departing to take a state-level position in the WPA.

Cherry Lake's new director, Paul Vander Schouw, arrived from the WPA's St. Petersburg office in October 1935, and with him came a raft of changes to fix what the agency's national office saw as poor planning from the homestead's beginnings. Vander Schouw, in his late thirties, described himself as "a man of action, not words." Hoping to build all of the remaining houses by June, he halted plans for a new sugar mill to focus their efforts on home construction. Following directives from the WPA's national office, he also made plans to move the homestead's trading post, grocery store, and homestead offices away from the main highway to a newly built community center that would soon also include a new school building, post office, and community hall. For the homesteaders, these plans brought hope of finally moving out of temporary barracks and chicken coops, but the physical move of their community's center and the scaling back of cooperative industries also seemed to undo much of what they had worked toward since the project began.

Adding to the tumult over leadership, Cherry Lake Farms was one of a handful of communities that the WPA did not hand over to the Resettlement Administration. Instead, the WPA retained control of all but a few aspects of community management, including education and recreation, which it delegated to the RA. Decisions in the governance of Cherry Lake thus often needed to go through several layers of approval within the WPA's state and national offices, not to mention the RA's Special Skills and Education divisions in Washington. To manage the activities that were now under its purview, the RA sent in an educational supervisor, C. B. Loomis. In addition to his background in adult recreation programs (most recently in Leonia, New Jersey), Loomis seemed to have what Kellock called "a good supply of tact [and] diplomacy," which was especially critical in navigating the tensions bubbling under the surface between state-level WPA officials and the RA's Washington office. One major source of resentment came from the RA sending in northerners to fill positions at Cherry Lake, including Loomis and his assistant, Carl Rude, who was originally from Wisconsin. Loomis made sure to tell Special Skills staffer Katharine Kellock that "there was real feeling in Florida about the introduction of further 'Yankees' in a state that has great employment difficulties because of the influx of jobless northerners."

All of this helped explain why it took so long for Margaret's job to be approved that fall, since her appointment needed to wind its way through the hiring bureaucracies of both the Florida state WPA and the RA's Washington office to gain approval. Charlie's decision to hire her also went against Kellock's recommendation to consult with the state WPA office to hire a local music representative of their choosing. Clearly, some negotiations with the state WPA office were needed to justify the RA's choice to bring yet another outsider to Cherry Lake, though Margaret's southern roots likely helped her cause.

Despite all these logistical woes and political tensions, Cherry Lake seemed to hold great potential for the kind of program envisioned by the Music Unit. In addition to recreational leadership from Loomis, Vander Schouw understood the value of community programs, having served as director of the Detroit Public Recreation Department before moving to Florida ten years earlier. Music programming had become a particular area of interest, as Kellock wrote, "Mr. Loomis and all other administrative personnel are eager for a leader of musical activities as soon as possible."

Buy-in for music on the homestead also came from the homesteaders themselves, a group of whom had formed an Arts and Crafts Committee that Kellock said was most interested in promoting music programs. The committee leader was Clarence H. "Red" Stevens, a red-headed electrician from Tampa who had already organized a "tin-pan orchestra" that played in the evenings on the steps of the community store. Red played lead on his accordion accompanied by whatever other homesteaders could find to play—usually a couple of guitars, with percussion supplied by a washboard, a kettle, and a board rubbed with sandpaper.

⁂

For her trip to Florida and her first day in her government job, Margaret decided to wear her best shoes and suit to make a good impression—even if Cherry Lake Farms itself appeared to make no such effort. She arrived on January 15, 1936, a cold, rainy morning, after a nearly twenty-hour train trip from Washington and a harrowing car ride from Madison on the project's washed-out roads. She reported to the administration's headquarters in the old Hinton mansion, and the project secretary led her to get settled in her new living quarters, as Margaret later described in an unfinished memoir:

> Still shivering, I left with her, and, absentmindedly, stepped off the porch of the administration building into a Red Sea that came up to my ankles, ruining my good shoes and splashing my only suit. "I'll carry you over in the station-wagon," she offered colloquially, "No one walks in this weather—unless they have boots."

Margaret reported a somewhat dismal impression of Cherry Lake in her first dispatch to Washington: "The physical aspects of the place; of that section which houses the offices and personnel, are, at first glance, unattractive, though the rolling country surrounding, with pines and moss-festooned live oaks, is nice." She continued that the living quarters, "long narrow one-story white painted barracks, about thirty feet apart . . . are woefully uniform in their austere simplicity." She later described the project secretary's brief orientation in her barracks room that first day:

> "You can get a bath, if there's some hot water, and light a fire, if there's any wood. Gets cold, 'specially at night. Supper, and all

meals, are served in that other barracks." I followed her finger across the bare fields to another lonely structure, then back to the tin stove and iron cot, on opposite ends of the cubicle which was to be my home.

Despite the inauspicious start, Margaret wasted little time getting to work. It soon became clear that most adults on the homestead assumed she was there to provide free music lessons to kids and nothing more. In her meeting with project director Paul Vander Schouw on that first day, he hinted that she should "proceed slowly and through the children." She reported that when the three young schoolteachers in her barracks said they were "crazy to have the kids have music lessons, I didn't commit myself other than to indicate a Spirit of Smiling Cooperation." As she summarized, "I gather from my conversation with local administration and other teachers that my musical approach to the adults must be through the children—a sort of 'salting the calves to get the cows.'"

On her first full day on the homestead, she spent the morning at Cherry Lake's school, observing classes from first through eighth grades and talking with teachers about how to incorporate weekly music instruction. That night, she gave a presentation about music at the PTA meeting, introducing her "Music for Everyone" program, which would involve both children and adults. She met with the education director, C. B. Loomis, who told her that adult musical activities had stalled completely. That Sunday, when she held her first weekly music meeting, just two home-steaders came. She concluded her first week's report, "I gather the going will be slow and rough."

Margaret realized the situation required going beyond Charlie's advice about making friends—she needed to build a team of allies, finding musi-cians and music lovers who would join the homestead's music committee and help to sell her planned music program to the rest of the community. Her first ally was also the first musician she met on the homestead—the accordion-playing electrician Red Stevens, who, as head of the music com-mittee, offered his full support for her plans. She began to gather names of others said to have some musical connections and, given the state of the roads and her lack of appropriate footwear, made arrangements to visit them by horseback.

In one of the shacks serving as temporary housing for homesteader families, she spoke with Anna Mae Skirvin, who played piano for the Sunday school and had come to Cherry Lake from Miami with her husband James (now the homestead's school bus driver) and their four young children. Anna Mae seemed a bit skeptical of Margaret's plan, expressing her doubt that any of the other homesteaders would get "stirred up" about music, but she agreed to join the committee. Zelma Priest, described by Margaret as "young and attractive, also living in a shack with three small children," had come to the homestead from Jacksonville, where her husband Granville had been a railcar operator. Eager for planned music activities, she said she would "be crazy about anything that has some life to it," but she wasn't sure she could participate, partly because of Granville's new schedule (leaving for his job at the cooperative dairy at 3 A.M.) and partly because he strongly disapproved of any entertainment that was not religious. "That was something of a problem to answer," Margaret wrote, but she left the invitation open.

At the barracks, Margaret tracked down a man who she had been told was a good singer. "Lady," he responded, "I've been separated from my family for a year, with promises of my house being built, and I'm no nearer having a house now than I was then—how do you expect me to feel like singing?" To this, Margaret wrote, "I could only say that I didn't wonder, but that if he spent an evening singing, he might sleep better and it would cost less than going on a binge."

In response to her reports of all of these obstacles, Charlie encouraged Margaret to take a broader view, writing, "I know this is a hard situation, perhaps the hardest in all of the six communities in which we have music workers, but if we remember that it is not entirely the peoples' fault, but rather that of the general cultural collapse which is beyond their control, we can bolster them up by patience." He also offered her a note of encouragement: "While I sympathize with you in regard to the difficulty of stirring things up, I feel quite confident that if you go at it slowly and persistently, you will succeed where most other people would fail."

Charlie's confidence proved to be well-placed. That Sunday, more than fifteen homesteaders came to her music committee meeting, including the dispirited singer from the barracks. In addition to committee chair Red Stevens, members now included Anna Mae Skirvin and Zelma Priest, as well as Pierson W. (Bill) Carr, who worked on the transportation crew; Larry Roffe, who ran the gas station; and J. L. Doolittle, the plumbing warehouse bookkeeper who, at fifty-seven, was among the oldest of the homesteaders. The assembled group sang for an hour then reviewed Margaret's typed "Music for Everyone" program plan. Activities for children at the school would include weekly group singing for each grade, a glee club, a school band, music appreciation, public performances, and music memory contests. The adult program had four components: (1) community sings "in which everyone participates, to be made a part of every gathering"; (2) an adult glee club and quartets; (3) music appreciation groups; and (4) the Cherry Lake Orchestra, under the direction of Stevens. Much to Margaret's delight, the committee's "enthusiasm kept them on from 3 until 7" that afternoon, and they ultimately decided to hold biweekly orchestra rehearsals and to form the adult glee club as the first steps toward bringing the music program to life.

Following her strategy of "salting the calves" to lure the adults, Margaret focused her early efforts on the school program, where enthusiasm was high, with more than thirty kids signing up for group lessons in piano and guitar. But the cows proved more difficult to reach. To gauge interest in the various activities for adults, she sent home a printed copy of the music program with each child on the bus, but most parents did not understand that it was the adults in the household who were to sign up, not the children: "The first two I saw had 'music appreciation' written out clearly as the choice, above unknown signatures. I was delighted at this discriminating adult taste and hastily inquired who the signers were. I was informed that they were two very small boys in the second grade."

Margaret's next target was the crowd of high school students and young adults (ages fifteen to twenty-five), whom she called "easily the most difficult lot on the project." She threw a "musical party" for them on the last Friday evening in January, held in the bare school assembly room, which she tried to liven up by decorating with maple and pine branches. To her surprise, nearly forty young people came. She devised a set of elaborate musical games meant to help them all get to know each other and to build a sense of fun. As they arrived, each person had to whistle, sing, or (for those too shy) simply name a "theme song," the tune of which Margaret notated next to their name. Then she divided the group into two teams, and as she played each person's theme song on the piano, they had to go up to the front and write a musical note on the staff she had drawn on the blackboard. Once each team had finished their melody—most of them having never before written a note and having no idea what it might sound like—she improvised an accompaniment and played the two compositions, asking three latecomers to serve as judges. "They loved it," she reported back. "I've been told by everyone, including the teachers, that it was the most fun any of them ever had in the community. When I suggested meeting every other Friday, they demanded, 'every Friday' and I agreed."

Certainly, this night displayed Margaret's unique set of musical and interpersonal skills—not everyone could notate a warbled tune or devise a piano accompaniment on the fly for a random melody, or do any of it with the easy warmth that had always helped Margaret win friends wherever she went. As one of her job references had gushed in a letter to the RA personnel office, "Her personality is the kind I would give my eye to possess." Margaret was thrilled by their enthusiasm, but she concluded her handwritten report with a reminder of the hardships that came with her assignment: "I regret having no typewriter in my room where I am trying to recover my voice, keep warm in bed, and forget flooded corridors and burst pipes in the bathroom."

That same week, Loomis sent his own effusive report back to the Special Skills office in Washington:

In my last report I named three "needs." The first was for a music supervisor. Two weeks ago today Margaret Valiant arrived, a flesh and blood answer to our prayer. And what an answer. In a meeting of the Music committee one of the homesteaders called her "a gift from Heaven." She has captivated the group, children and adults. Music like chicken pox is breaking out all over the place. They camp on her doorstep from dawn until midnight. At this stage of our psychological depression (we've been rather deep in the slough of despond), nothing could have meant more than a chance to harmonize, and it is hard to conceive of a person more adequately equipped with both music and personality to do the thing which is so needed to be done here.

Despite any effect that Margaret's presence may have had on the homestead's overall mood, the "slough of despond" continued to be expressed in Cherry Lake's weather: after more than a week of intense cold, days of steady rain washed out the roads yet again, and many residents (including Margaret) became ill. To her great relief, she escaped in mid-February for a week of meetings at the Washington office, sleeping in the comfort of her own little apartment on K Street, with heat and hot water. But when she returned, she discovered that her absence had caused a loss of momentum. She was able to resume activities easily enough with the children but found it much more challenging to begin again with the adults. Still, at her first music committee meeting, the same man who had earlier responded incredulously that he couldn't possibly feel like singing now told her "that both the Glee Club and the Sunday afternoon sings had died out while I was gone, 'and for God's sake start 'em up again!'" So they met to sing together that evening and made plans to expand the string band and schedule rehearsals.

In early March, Margaret wrote to Washington, "This week has been, in some ways, the most exciting of any in developments." It started with a return visit to the home of Zelma Priest, who had begun offering her hairdressing services to the women of Cherry Lake, to have her hair set:

As it happened the husband had just arrived from his vigil at the dairy and was waiting for breakfast before he went to bed. I helped get breakfast, drank a cup of Postum with them (a Field Representative learns to take anything from blizzards to Postum) and then gave Madame a guitar lesson and sang hymns and talked with Monsieur while my hair dried.

"Afterwards," she admitted, "it seemed an expensive ordeal, I being out half a dollar and two hours of time, besides having my hair look awful." But it proved to be a sound investment. That night, Mr. and Mrs. Priest were among the forty homesteaders who attended the first joint meeting of the music and dramatic committees. It was, she said, "the largest and most enthusiastic of any group gathered together so far for any purpose other than considering the physical problems of making a living." Sitting on wooden benches in the school assembly room, "they were all there then—the various dissenters; the dramatic group leader who wanted to play Emperor Jones and was opposed to any attempt at writing our own play; the red-headed electrician who said he didn't see any connection between music and acting and he'd 'rather stick to one kind of playing.' And there were plenty of hecklers and wisecrackers."

Margaret began by asking the dramatic leader to explain that they had discussed having the homesteaders write a play based on their own experiences, as she sat on a small bench at a table, ready to write down their ideas: "As it gradually dawned on people that this was an opportunity for some cracks at the staff and that I was zestfully putting them all down, everyone seemed to catch the idea and the excitement, so that for two hours I listened, wrote, suggested and revised as rapidly as I could." The agreed-upon theme had come from a contingent from Tampa, who suggested they do a "Gasparilla" play based on the Carnival-like festival held there every year, which involved a reenactment of the eighteenth-century pirate Jose Gaspar's legendary (and possibly fictitious) invasion of the Florida coast. The homesteaders' Gasparilla play would imagine Gaspar and his crew arriving at Cherry Lake, as Margaret described it, "a united effort based on local daily life, combining music and acting, seriousness and comic relief, and designed to require no expenditure for costumes or settings, and a minimum of rehearsals." Margaret ended that week's report with two additional comments: "I forgot to add the climax of the evening. Mr. Priest, the praying dairyman, contributed many of the best digs and is cast as one of the principal homesteaders"; and "If this doesn't seem exciting to you, I can only say that it would if you had been here for the past month."

But it wouldn't last. The next week, she reported that meetings had been poorly attended, and she had to cancel their second Amateur Night for lack of applications (in contrast to the first successful and lively event). She sought answers for this sudden decline from the staff and her allies on the homestead. First of all, the accelerated building program meant more families were finally moving into their homes—wonderful news for the community that proved to have negative effects on music participation, as homesteaders became busy with getting settled. This activity, she was told, combined with the beginning of the spring planting season, left many of the men too worn out to come to evening meetings. Plus, she learned that spring baseball had started up on Sunday afternoons, conflicting with music committee meetings. "Finally," she wrote, "there is the explanation of the 'novelty wearing off.' This latter explanation I have and shall refuse to accept despite continuous reiterations, though there is some evidence of its truth." That week's joint meeting with the dramatic committee drew only six people, and, Margaret noted sadly, "Our recently converted (I thought) religious dairyman did not attend." She soon found that Red Stevens shared her disappointment, calling his fellow homesteaders a "glum lot," and telling Margaret that "he didn't intend to stay here among them if they didn't show more spirit." In response, she told him "that it was up to him and me to show them what could be done. But I confess I was talking as much to convince myself as to convince him."

In his training materials, Charlie had stressed that the music representative's goal should be to lead homesteaders toward music performances that enacted the RA's broader collectivist vision—group music, drawing on the folk songs that most of them knew, as "an activity of masses of people rather than merely of isolated individuals." However, he left it up to his staffers to determine how to make this happen, and Margaret felt unsure how to proceed. Her own goals were less theoretical and more practical, with an emphasis on helping the homesteaders through the hardships they faced, as she later explained, "It was my job to stimulate them into hope for better things, and by paying attention to their own folk arts . . . to give them a sense of belonging and of their importance to the country." She saw instilling pride and confidence as a key first step toward achieving a more community-oriented mindset: "Because if you take pride in yourself, and in whatever you can do," she wrote, "then we all move on together." But how could she even begin if people already felt too skeptical and worn out to participate in her musical activities in the first place?

Hope seemed easier to find among the children, who were beginning to rehearse their Easter play. "Though this is the first attempt many of them have made in mime or dance, their efforts are valiant," she wrote, then concluded with a less cheerful assessment for her third-person self: "So much cannot be said for the Field Representative who feels, this week, valiant in name only."

CHAPTER 3

MUSICAL ENGINEERING

B ack in November 1935, in one of the many newly built simple frame houses dotting the Western Allegheny Plateau, Charlie had met his first employee. It was his second week on the job as director of the Music Unit, and he had traveled to Westmoreland Homesteads, just south of Greensburg in southwestern Pennsylvania, to meet W. Jefferson Simmons, a local musician and music teacher who had already been hired by project leaders to serve as the homestead's field instructor in music. Charlie expressed his deep disappointment in his report to Dornbush:

> He has had a rather second-rate musical training and has lived a professional life of a narrow and provincial sort—the sort that imitates the New York fashions of a lower order—but has no first-hand familiarity or knowledge of them. He has been working in a small radio station that relays the imitations of the imitations of big town stuff in music just as the local department store in Greensburg might relay the imitations of the imitations of Paris fashions. He is a regular run-of-the-mill public school teacher in music who has had a rather hard time getting along. . . . All creative spontaneity, sense of adventure, curiosity and imagination has been, it seems permanently, squashed. In

its place sits educational routine enthroned on a foot-stool—and "music methods work"—i.e., I believe, something lower than anything known in the whole depressing, old-style educational bag of tricks. In addition, he is practically completely ignorant of the developments in music during the last fifty years and has a most superficial knowledge of music history and literature.

The unrestrained snobbery of Charlie's report—his shuddering at what he calls "narrow," "lower order," "provincial," "imitation," "run-of-the-mill," "ignorant," and "superficial"—shows that he clearly hadn't yet shifted gears from his previous life among New York's avant-garde elite, teaching composition and musicology at Juilliard and writing atonal workers' songs in the Composers' Collective. He hadn't yet embraced folk music as the musical language of choice on the homesteads, and more than that, he showed little understanding of what life was like for the actual "folk" themselves.

None of this should come as a surprise, given Charlie's background. He was born (in 1886, making him more than a decade older than most of the other Special Skills staff, and five years older than Tugwell) into a wealthy New England family, studied music at Harvard, conducted in Europe, and served as head of the music department at the University of California in Berkeley. His previous experience with rural working-class life had been brief, when he and his first wife Constance, a violinist, had hatched a plan to drive from Charlie's parents' estate in Patterson, New York, to California, earning money by giving violin and piano recitals that would bring "good" classical music to people in rural areas. They started out in November 1921, driving their Model T Ford with their three sons (the youngest, Peter, was two) and pulling a trailer with a pump organ, an iron pot for laundry, and a set of hand-lettered signs. But they only got as far as Pinehurst, North Carolina, before they discovered that the country roads they planned to take became impassable in winter weather. Spending a few winter months giving concerts in Pinehurst, Charlie was surprised to discover that locals actually had their own music and were not impressed by the Seegers' introduction of Bach and Beethoven. After that winter, he headed back to New York, and he would begin to appreciate folk music only when it came to him, brought to Greenwich Village by Aunt Molly Jackson and Tom Benton's jam sessions.

Charlie ended his report from Westmoreland with an almost audible sigh of resignation about his new staff member: "Nevertheless, I think he will do us no particular discredit. He will be accepted by the homesteaders as a regular guy, I suppose. . . . His presence in Westmoreland is better than having no one there—at least I hope so. He will do a routine job. We cannot expect composition of any value."

In a separate report to Katharine Kellock written a few days later, Charlie articulated what he saw as his ideal music representative, perhaps with a background similar to his own:

> Above all, he will regard himself as a creative worker: first, in composition, or second, at least in what we may call *musical engineering*. On the one hand, he may make new music for the people in his community, locality or region, using the idioms familiar to the people there and introducing such material as may seem practicable to him; or he may stylize this idiom or its repertoire for composition of a more professional sort, through which he may hope to gain for the community or region, a favorable notice in other places.

Charlie's elevated vision for his staff representatives as high-level creative workers was quite far from what project leaders on the homesteads wanted, which was simply a competent leader of musical activities that would bring the homesteaders together—no "musical engineering" necessary. In the coming months, he would make an extended field trip to visit all six of the Music Unit's representatives in their assigned homesteads, a trip that would help him understand what was truly needed, and what they were up against.

When Charlie returned to Westmoreland in March 1936, his opinion of his field instructor remained unchanged. The project staff seemed satisfied with Simmons's music program for children in the school, but Charlie still found it to be "very ordinary run of the mill public school routine, devoid of any substantial value." The homestead's music program for adults—which was the unit's central goal—had "flopped completely." In his own reports, Simmons told of leading group singing and folk dancing at a Cooperative Youth League meeting, and of his glee club having a "really good turn-out" of thirty people, including some adults. But the only musical activity Charlie saw as successful was initiated not by Simmons, but by J. C. Cooley, a cooperative specialist from the RA's Education Division who managed adult education programs at several RA homesteads. Cooley felt that "the musical factor in co-operative education is considerable," and he had already put together a small songbook that he used in group singing at his cooperative study meetings.

Even as Charlie remained unimpressed with the homestead's music program, he concluded his report on a positive note: "The co-operative idea is catching on in Westmoreland. My landlady and her husband are 'sold' on it. Things seem to be moving." This cooperative ethos seemed to run especially deep at Westmoreland. In addition to Cooley's regular cooperative education sessions for adults, Westmoreland hosted a youth conference on cooperation for participants from several homesteads. Homestead manager David Day, a twenty-nine-year-old Quaker farmer from Indiana, saw cooperation as central to the project's success and emphasized that those chosen to live there needed to be "eager to cast their lot with others in building a new and cooperative community." Day established the Westmoreland Homesteaders Cooperative Association, which gave residents a say in project governance and its cooperative industries, and he created cooperative study clubs and social organizations, including a youth club, a mothers' club, a theater production committee, and an active homestead newsletter, the *Homestead Informer*.

But just as Katharine Kellock had seen, managers found that these clubs seemed to do less to facilitate cooperation than to provide a forum for "gossip" and criticism—of which there was plenty. Disgruntled home-steaders had circulated a petition protesting a 50 percent pay reduction that Day said should be viewed as a contribution "for the benefit of the community," which the *Greensburg Tribune* gleefully reported as a battle of the protesting homesteaders' "rugged individualism" against the oppressive "socialism" and "collectivism" of Westmoreland's leaders. In addition to these ideological differences, Kellock had also found deep cultural divisions among the homesteaders at Westmoreland. All the RA communities she visited had used Christianity as a requirement in its application process, with most specifically requiring membership in a Protestant church and proof of Anglo-Saxon heritage. But at Westmoreland, nearly half the homesteaders came from the large population of Slavic, Catholic immigrants who had worked in the area's mines for decades, and Kellock heard that the Anglo-Saxon Protestant group had "an active distrust of 'the foreigners that do only what the priest tells them.'" Overcoming such ideological, political, religious, and cultural rifts seemed like a lot to ask of Simmons's thirty-person glee club, but the Music Unit would certainly continue its efforts.

From Westmoreland, Charlie traveled about seventy miles due south to Reedsville, West Virginia, the birthplace of the New Deal's entire homestead enterprise. Its roots began in the summer of 1933, when FERA field investigator Lorena Hickok visited the mining area known as Scotts Run in West Virginia. Harry Hopkins had hired Hickok to bring her approach as a former reporter to help him understand what the Depression meant for real people. "I don't want statistics from you," he told her. "Tell me what you see and hear. All of it. Don't ever pull your punches." When she arrived at Scotts Run, Hickok was shaken by the brutal poverty, describing it simply as "the worst place I had ever seen," black with coal dust, with broken-down shacks, filthy water, and "everywhere, grimy, undernourished, desperate people."

Rather than simply filing her report with Hopkins's office, Hickok decided to take action. She invited her friend Eleanor Roosevelt, now acknowledged to have been her lover, to come see this suffering for herself, knowing something must be done. The First Lady drove to West Virginia (by herself, with no Secret Service detail, in her convertible) and was as horrified as Hickok by what she saw. She learned of an effort by the American Friends Service Committee (AFSC) to move the miners to a planned farm community, following a "Quaker model" of rehabilitation that valued cooperation, self-help, respect for personal dignity, and a focus on cultivating a strong sense of community.

When Eleanor returned to the White House and told President Roosevelt about the horrible conditions and the AFSC's project, he agreed that the government needed to lend its support. An agrarian at heart, FDR had long believed in the benefits of such homesteading projects—he had advocated for them as governor of New York and discussed their potential in his first meeting with Tugwell, before he launched his 1932 presidential campaign. The Roosevelts' affection for the idea of government homesteads has roots in their support for the back-to-the-land movement, a doctrine with a somewhat romanticized view of self-sufficient farming that had taken on mythic proportions in the 1930s as a response to the Great Depression. Tugwell later said that FDR "always did, and always would, think people better off in the country." President Roosevelt soon created a new Division of Subsistence Homesteads (DSH) within the Department of the Interior, which in the fall of 1933 announced a new community to house two hundred miners and their families—Arthurdale, the New Deal's first subsistence homestead.

Eleanor Roosevelt took on Arthurdale as her own project within the administration, making frequent visits and involving herself in decisions down to choice of house décor. According to her biographer Joseph Lash, "All Eleanor's executive ability, her doggedness, and her influence were now placed at the disposal of the fledgling project, for she firmly believed that what was done in a single community might show the way to a nation." But instead of being welcomed as a model, Arthurdale quickly became infamous for its well-documented blunders as planners worked to get it finished as quickly as possible, such as choosing prefabricated houses that could not withstand a West Virginia winter. Predictably, the new homestead became a ready target for the administration's critics, who claimed it was part of a Communist takeover, its industries were undercutting private enterprise, and Mrs. Roosevelt was wasting millions of taxpayer dollars for her "West Virginia commune." Even some within the administration privately expressed concern about the cost, as Secretary of the Interior Harold Ickes wrote in his diary: "Mrs. Roosevelt took the Reedsville project under her protective wing with the result that we have been spending money down there like drunken sailors." Eleanor's insistence that homes should include electricity and indoor plumbing was condemned as an expensive extravagance, which one reporter slammed as spending taxpayers' money on "electric curling irons for hillbillies." Nevertheless, the First Lady persisted, and Arthurdale became the model for all the other homestead projects that the Resettlement Administration inherited from the DSH and FERA.

Tragically, the Arthurdale model reinforced the racist practices of the Jim Crow South. The Washington DSH office declared that Black and White citizens should participate equally in the homestead program without discrimination but also determined that homesteaders should be chosen "according to the sociological pattern of the community," a decision that resulted in de facto discrimination based on the biases of local officials and the homesteaders themselves.

Even Eleanor Roosevelt could not persuade Arthurdale homesteaders to allow African Americans to live among them. Westmoreland Homesteads admitted exactly one Black family—Helen and Chauncey White—but only after Helen White sent a complaint to the First Lady when the homestead's cooperative association denied their application on racial grounds. Eleanor shared the letter with President Roosevelt, who wrote back to say there would be no discrimination on government homesteads. DSH officials wrote a stern letter to project manager David Day stating that homesteaders with racial prejudices would be asked to withdraw from the project, and Day supported this policy, all of which convinced the homestead's cooperative board to grant Helen and Chauncey White a place on the homestead. Admitting just one African American family had thus required the deter-mination of Helen White, the authority of the White House, threats from

DSH officials, and support from the local homestead manager to implement the change on the ground. But the alignment of these factors—especially a willingness to fight prejudice and segregation at the local level—proved to be quite rare. All told, of the more than 150 rural resettlement projects that would be managed by the Resettlement Administration, there were just 13 Black-only communities in nine southern states, and 26 projects that included both White and Black families. Despite Eleanor Roosevelt's strong beliefs in racial equality and her ability to harness the power of the FDR administration, her beloved Arthurdale continued to bar Black families from participating.

The Music Unit's programs were especially bound up with the segregation that persisted on the RA's homesteads. These homesteads essentially served as physical manifestations of what historian Karl Hagstrom Miller has called a "musical color line," an artificial segregation of White and Black music in the South that erroneously designated "hillbilly" music as White despite the contributions of Black string band musicians, not to mention the African and African American roots of the banjo. This segregation of sound depended, in part, on a misguided view of Anglo-Appalachian folk music as the purest expression of a "traditional" American folk culture, as Sonnet Retman has described, segregating Black music as an "exotic, domestic 'other'"—just as Black families were excluded from the RA's homesteads. This view of Appalachian folk music has roots in the English folklorist Cecil Sharp's discovery that old British ballads (often called "Child ballads" in reference to Francis James Child, the nineteenth-century folklorist who catalogued them) had miraculously survived the existential threats of popular culture and commercial media and were alive among White people living in the region's remote areas. The myth of the so-called purity of White Appalachian culture—and the idea that it needed to be preserved—was one of the forces that shaped not only the Music Unit's work, but the entire resettlement program in the area.

Even before the RA took over—and long before the Music Unit was created—Eleanor Roosevelt was known to enjoy folk music and often joined homesteaders in square dancing when she visited. As summarized by Joseph Lash, folk music preservation was one of her main priorities for Arthurdale from the beginning: "She wanted it to have the most advanced educational system, a model public-health service, producer and consumer cooperatives, and a program of handicrafts and music that would preserve the folk culture of Appalachia." Because of the First Lady's interest, Arthurdale already had its own music and folklore educator in place with credentials that rivaled Charlie's: Fletcher Collins, an expert in English ballads with a newly minted PhD from Yale. As part of his role as director of music and drama at Arthurdale's progressive school, Collins built a folk music program for adults with the express purpose of building community and a sense of ownership at the homestead. In July 1935, Collins mounted a music festival (attended by Eleanor, of course) featuring a fiddling contest, jig dancing, ballad singing, mouth harping, and a square dance contest.

After paying his respects at Arthurdale, Charlie continued his tour at Tygart Valley Homesteads, just outside Elkins, West Virginia. Tygart Valley was established in 1934 as the DSH's second homestead project, this one primarily for stranded lumber workers, with sturdy A-frame houses set on both sides of the river running through the valley. An early Special Skills report on Tygart Valley took special note that "the morale of the people is breaking down," with much "discouragement and unrest" among the homesteaders. But Katharine Kellock had also found "more interest in music among the homesteaders than in any other single social and cultural activity," with several fiddle and guitar players among the lumberjacks living on the homestead, and her recommendation for Special Skills was decisive: "The one clear and definite need is for leadership in music to provide cultural diversion and unite the homesteaders into a harmonious unit." The music representative sent in by the division before Charlie was hired was Rene Van Rhyn, a recent immigrant from Holland who had been working at a music recreation program in New Hampshire. Initially, Van Rhyn and the homesteaders had trouble understanding one another—literally, because of his accented English, and also because he was a cultural outsider in the extreme. Attendance at his scheduled musical events was low until he rebranded one chorus rehearsal as a "music and gardening meeting," which attracted a large crowd.

In his visit to Tygart Valley, Charlie had a lukewarm impression of his representative, who continued to focus his program around classical music even as it proved not to resonate with homesteaders: "Mr. van Rhyn is rather inflexible: new ideas come hard; but they do eventually penetrate somewhat," he reported. "I am inclined to give him credit for having done more than the average man could have done in two months." Of his integration into the community, Charlie noted, "The people do like him—nobody denies it. But he is caught in a rather peculiar situation here: there are five distinctly foreign people in conspicuous positions on the staff. This is too much for a West Virginia community and should not have been allowed to happen. But here they are."

Still, Van Rhyn did have some success when he connected to the homesteaders' musical talents at an amateur music contest night, held outdoors in the absence of a community hall (his written description reflecting some of his struggles with idiomatic English):

> Most of them arrived with some instrument—naturally guitar players galore—then a few violins, mouth harmonicas and ukuleles. When I arrived they were sitting around—their usual reserve and seeming cold wave, but I know and have learned by now that this is only the surface and that underneath their frigid attitude they are deep lovers of music. Before long I had them one by one, or in groups of two or three, do their musical stunts which were really quite remarkable, and once you have them started you cannot stop them.

"This was," Van Rhyn concluded, "the most amusing evening I have had since I came to the Homestead."

Charlie continued his southward trek to his next field representative, assigned to Pine Mountain Valley, about seventy miles south of Atlanta. If Arthurdale was the First Lady's pet project, then Pine Mountain Valley

was the president's, situated among the rolling red-clay hills and pine for-
ests adjacent to his beloved retreat, known as the Little White House, in
Warm Springs, Georgia. In December 1935, the president gave an address
to Pine Mountain Valley residents, declaring the community "like a dream
come true" that should serve as an example for local governments to follow.
Georgia's state FERA office built the rural-industrial community, like
Cherry Lake Farms in Florida, for former farming families living on relief
in Atlanta and other cities in the state, advertised as a new kind of living
where "the farm and the city are so amalgamated as to be one inseparable
whole." It included urban amenities—community centers, running water,
and telephone and electric lines—built around farming, small agricultural
industries like canning, and arts and crafts enterprises. On his visit in
the spring of 1936, Charlie noted that the Music Unit's field representative, Robert Wallace, "has made a real hit." Wallace had studied
opera at the Cincinnati Conservatory and was an ornithology expert,
and Charlie noticed that people admired his "spunk and ingenuity" in
navigating the homestead's tricky terrain despite his paralysis due to
polio. "People like him," he observed. "He has clear blue eyes, a regular guy
physiognomy and a winning smile."

But Wallace's music program brought out the New York snob in Charlie.
"Musically, he is even smaller-town than Simmons. His 'selections' for
programs exhibit a baseness of taste that I had thought perished from the
globe. . . . I am not sure that he has ever heard of any 20th century composer. It is unbelievable. He has practically no creative ability or interest in
anyone else's creative ability." Still, Charlie advised that they keep Wallace
at Pine Mountain, "in spite of his terrible musical work."

Cumberland Homesteads, the DSH's third community for stranded
miners, lay on the mountain plateau outside of Crossville, Tennessee.
Grace Falke had visited the area on her road trip with Lorena Hickok in
the summer of 1934, almost a year before she or Tugwell were involved
in managing government homesteads. She took a special side trip to the
homestead because, as she wrote presciently, "I don't think it will harm
us to know all we can about these projects." She found the mountains

"breath-takingly beautiful" and was also quite taken with the homestead itself, which she described in some detail: "The houses are just about perfect. Native stone quarried right there on the land and timber from their own woods are used exclusively. The homesteaders are miners, lumbermen, and destitute farmers, and they are doing the actual building themselves. The houses are large, practical and really very lovely."

As at other homesteads, Cumberland project leaders had already hired a local music teacher to direct its music programs before Charlie arrived. Leonard Kirk had been a junior high music teacher in Knoxville, but even if he fell into the "general type" of school music instructor that Charlie had deplored in his Westmoreland representative, Kirk proved to be an able representative. Other than suggesting "more extensive use of American material," Charlie had only positive things to say, noting Kirk's "very charming manner" and concluding, "Everything seems to be going well here. He is limited in his capacities; but what he does is well done."

At this point, having been on the road for nearly a month, the excitement of his field trip had worn off for Charlie. "I'm tired of colonies, folk music and business," he wrote home to Ruth. But he had one remaining stop—and happily, it would involve something of a reunion. To fill the vacancies for representatives not already chosen by the homesteads or assigned by the Special Skills office before he arrived, Charlie had hoped to convince several of his colleagues from the Composers' Collective to ride out the Great Depression working as music representatives at RA homesteads. These would have been his ideal "musical engineers," familiar with twentieth-century composers and meeting his standards for musical creativity. But only one of these composers was willing to give the Music Unit's rural experiment a try: Herbert Haufrecht. At twenty-four, Haufrecht had thus far lived only in cities, having grown up in a Jewish household in New York and studied composition at the Cleveland Institute of Music and Juilliard. He certainly knew twentieth-century composers, and out of all of the RA's music representatives, he came closest to Charlie's ideal of a field composer and musical engineer. But he knew next to nothing about the people who would soon be his neighbors on the homestead—their lives, where they came from, or the music that they cared about.

Charlie assigned Haufrecht to Red House Farms outside Charleston, West Virginia, built on six hundred acres of a two-thousand-acre tract in the western part of the state, on farmland once owned by George Washington. Red House—named after the nineteenth-century brick building that served as its administrative headquarters, not as a sign of its nefarious ties to Communism as its critics claimed—was one of FERA's first rural-industrial communities and the only one built for stranded miners, following the model set by the DSH with Arthurdale, Tygart Valley, and Cumberland. FERA's emphasis on cooperative farming meant houses were built close together on smaller plots, with small houses of plaster over cinder blocks that were more utilitarian than the larger homes built on more expansive DSH homesteads from native lumber and stone. But Haufrecht fondly described his new home at Red House: "They gave me a little bungalow, a nice place. The architects made wonderful private homes in different designs, . . . and they had space between; it was in a beautiful semi-circle with a field in front of it. And two or three rows, concentric circles, of houses." Haufrecht took to heart Charlie's instructions to find the musicians in the community and identify the kind of music they liked, later describing a miner who played blues guitar, a psalm-singing carpenter, a group of young men who formed a "hillbilly" string band, and an ex-boxer who loved to sing hymns in the Southern shape-note style. It was all new to Haufrecht, but he had some success in winning over the community's musicians, who gathered at his small house for musical activities six out of seven evenings each week. Still, Charlie urged Haufrecht to "get busy" with his own creative work, suggesting he compose an operetta with a libretto provided by Mr. Cooley's cooperative education staff.

Part of Haufrecht's duties were to organize the community's regular square dances, which sometimes required him to drive as far as forty miles away to find a dance caller. He had just learned how to drive (which hadn't been necessary in his previous city life), and navigating the hill country roads proved to be quite an adventure. Years later, he remembered one outing to fetch a homesteader's uncle to call that night's dance, when the road disappeared into a stream. "He had to go by foot over the hill," he explained. "I had to stop at the car. So I was waiting a half hour. His uncle finally came with his fiddle, his wife, his daughter, her kids. There [were] about eight people in my little Chevy, just loaded to the gills."

If square dances had become a powerful venue for community building at Arthurdale, they almost seemed to serve the opposite purpose at Red House. It was built deep in "Republican country," and a serious political rivalry had taken root in the community, among both homesteaders and staff, as Republicans had taken on leadership positions in an attempt to undercut the Roosevelt administration's project from within. This included the community manager, Don Healey, who seemed to view square dances and all the music work on the project as "simply one more of those foolish extravagances of the New Deal." One night, Healey's assistant and a group of "boozed up" Republicans crashed the square dance and tried to break it up—a violent episode that Haufrecht reported to RA headquarters, resulting in the assistant's dismissal. In his confidential report of his visit, Charlie wrote, "The split among the homesteaders, which has made so much trouble, is getting worse and worse. Mr. Haufrecht has kept clear of it and is regarded well by both factions." As Haufrecht later described the political rift, "They had secret societies. They met at night. They had passwords. There [were] almost lynching parties and all that sort of thing." He added, with a laugh, "And I was supposed to soothe all this with music."

During this trip, after his dispiriting observations of Simmons at Cumberland and Wallace at Pine Mountain, Charlie came to a new conclusion about his field representatives, one that clearly pained him:

> I want to put on record that better men *must* be put in these places if any approximation of our program is to be carried out in music. Where we are to find them, I cannot say. Perhaps we shall have to train them. Unquestionably, however, the items are: first, personality; secondly, musical ability. For me to have to

make this concession is a contradiction of a lifetime of holding the opposite. But in RA communities there is no escape from it.

Seeing that Simmons and Wallace were so well-liked on their home-steads helped Charlie to truly recognize the importance of his own first rule for field representatives—to make friends. Yet he still struggled with the idea that this quality might come at the expense of the kind of music program he had envisioned.

The gendered language throughout Charlie's reports can easily be attrib-uted to the accepted language conventions and casual sexism of the time. But his call for "better men" seems particularly poignant here, written before he visited Margaret just south of the Georgia border at Cherry Lake Farms. He knew what to expect, as he noted, "Miss Valiant's activities are well enough known to the Washington office through her reports." So Charlie's use of "men" could have simply drawn on the widely understood meaning of the word at the time—or it may have hinted that, unlike the men, the Music Unit's only woman field representative was doing just fine.

CHAPTER 4

COOPERATION IS OUR AIM

B ack in Washington, Charlie seemed to have gotten himself into a bit of trouble. In April 1936, his frequent use of the phrase "confidential" in his memos and reports drew concern from the director of the Business Management Division, perhaps worried about the security clearances required for confidential government files. Charlie explained—not particularly convincingly—"I have marked a number of my reports 'confidential' purely for the reason that I have noticed that in our office, unless this is done, that reports, etc. are apt to lie around a bit openly, and I was enclosing material that should be kept covered. If you think this marking is unnecessary or that I should not deal with such material, please let me know." Yet despite this apparent willingness to change his confidential ways, the use of the word within the Music Unit's reports and memos remained pervasive, and it is clear that the Special Skills Division wanted to keep their musical activities below the radar.

Any arts-related program within the agency would have been seen as frivolous, as Tugwell wryly reflected later, "Congressmen just loved to make fun of all kinds of projects of a cultural sort." Back in October 1935, word appeared to have gotten out about Special Skills, though its purpose was not necessarily well understood, as an AP article reported that the division was created as "a cultural uplift campaign," tasked with "elevating standards of taste in the backwoods." The following week, a more pointed critique appeared in the *Buffalo News*, which warned its readers, "Many persons will look with ill-concealed disfavor upon the tap dancing, painting, song-writing and play-producing activities carried on under the auspices of the Rural Resettlement administration's 'special skills' division."

Such criticism showed the RA's arts activities to be an easy target for the agency's critics. This concern may have inspired an almost covert instinct where even Dornbush's bimonthly letters to field representatives were marked confidential. These efforts appeared to pay off, as the division's arts programming largely faded into the agency's massive structure and out of the public eye. The Music Unit may have taken the need to stay below the radar especially seriously because of its close ties to the RA's ideological underpinnings. As Dornbush explained, "The music and dramatic activities of the division are not engaged in as ends in themselves, but rather as means by which larger social aims may more readily be achieved." Any music activities on the RA's homesteads would have been ridiculed, but a folk music program invested in spurring an ideological shift toward collectivism among the rural poor could seem downright dangerous.

The most vociferous criticism of the RA went beyond the usual complaints of New Deal overspending to condemn it as "Communist in its conception" and "modeled on the collective farms of Soviet Russia," or, at best, "semi-Socialistic." Tugwell was used to such criticism, having been targeted in the same way for his progressive views ever since he had come to Washington. In his previous life as an academic, he had been accustomed to nuanced argument rather than politically prudent sound bites, and the conservative press loved to use his past words and deeds against him to paint him as a dangerous revolutionary, evoking his visit to the Soviet Union in 1927 and past statements taken out of context to sound menacing. "Business will logically be required to disappear," he once said, and privately held land must be "controlled to whatever extent is found necessary." The complexity of Tugwell's views did not translate to this new political realm—he believed in "planned capitalism" that fell somewhere between the laissez-faire and the socialistic, and in a collectivism tied to democracy, without the "regimentation of opinion" of the Soviet system. This was close enough for his adversaries to label him a Red, and he quickly became the acknowledged whipping boy for the FDR administration. It didn't help matters that he didn't care what people thought of him, exuding what his friends saw as a kind of gallant confidence, but others chose different adjectives: "disdainful, contemptuous, supercilious, arrogant, pompous, haughty, imperious, conceited."

By the time Tugwell took the helm of the RA, he had already solidified his whipping-boy role by championing a bill to prevent false advertising for food and drugs, unleashing a coordinated campaign against him from powerful food, drug, and advertising trade groups, with a stated goal to "discredit the bill by calling it the Tugwell bill and calling him a Red." Tugwell later reflected, "I made the mistake of attempting too much at once—of undertaking battles on more fronts than were necessary or could be successfully fought; and once engaged, I could not or would not withdraw. So I would become not so much a symbol of progressivism as a kind of crackpot radical. . . . By the end of my first year I was confirmed as a notorious character."

So with a target already on the agency's back, the Music Unit did its best to stay hidden from view, its collectivist goals certain to raise alarm bells (not to mention if word had gotten out about Charlie's Bolshevik-adjacent past, composing songs meant to spur workers to revolt). But now, with his representatives busy at their field assignments, Charlie turned to the central question of what *kind* of music would best serve the RA's deeper purpose of building community.

&

In January 1936, Charlie began the first music memorandum to his field representatives by declaring (in the third person), "The Director wishes you to have on hand a small reference library of works on American traditional music," followed by a list of four books he planned to send them, which lends some insight into his thinking at the time. The first was J. T. Howard's *Our American Music*, a six-hundred-page textbook that would have fit in comfortably on a class syllabus (but likely less so on a government homestead), with its historical focus on composers of psalms and art music. Next was George Pullen Jackson's *White Spirituals of the Southern Uplands*, a book of folk hymns in the shape-note tradition that had been published just a few years before and that both Charlie and Ruth later pointed to as critical to their growing awareness of folk music; they were shocked that they hadn't known about this living folk tradition with its "subversive harmonies" and "vigorous, disciplined beauty" in line with their own musical aesthetics.

The last two books represented the two schools of American folk music studies that would deeply impact the Music Unit's approach: academic folklore in Cecil Sharp's *English Folk Songs from the Southern Appalachians*, published in 1932; and the public approach of John Lomax's *American Ballads and Folk Songs*, published two years later, which dispensed with many academic conventions and included more recent songs from varied sources to appeal to a wider audience. "Frankly," Lomax admitted, "the volume is meant to be popular." Still, both Lomax and Charlie had spent enough time in academia to absorb Sharp's approach to folklore, and neither man could completely abandon placing high value on the age of a song or perceiving folk music as a dying art in need of preserving. As Charlie wrote, "To keep this widespread and deeply rooted rural American culture alive by capturing it wherever found and increasing its circulation, and to put it to work as the integrating social force it can become, is the job of Special Skills." For Charlie, a folk song with a long history that was still in use was the best vehicle for fostering social cohesion, as he wrote:

> If singing together is a means to this end, which nobody will deny, then singing an *old* song which has meant much to many generations is better for this purpose than singing something composed for rural consumption by a mediocre urban composer. And if singing any traditional song is good, singing the songs which have acquired the flavor of the American spirit is better.

As Charlie continued to move away from his previous stance against folk music, he aligned himself with many folklorists of the day in positioning American folk songs as an endangered art that needed to be "preserved" and "captured." However, the RA's interest in the social *use* of music set them apart not only from academic folklorists but also from other public folk-music collectors like Lomax, whose goals were focused on dissemination through song books, concerts, and recordings.

One week after he sent this list of books, Charlie seemed to have settled on a slightly more practical goal for his music representatives' libraries, requesting one thousand copies of a twenty-cent compilation called *The New American Song Book* to be distributed to his six staffers in the field. Still, he wasn't satisfied that even this songbook was quite up to the task. Although some folk songs were included, homesteaders could easily pass them over for sentimental popular songs or classic hymns. Even the folk songs included in the book failed to project the collectivist messages that Charlie felt necessary to truly build a collective consciousness among the homesteaders. For Charlie, it seemed the only way forward was for Special Skills to create its own song-sheets to distribute on the homesteads.

Dornbush saw this song-sheet project as a central piece of the Music Unit's work, with the potential to become "a songbook of the American people." They would choose folk songs that had the power to "build renewed respect for our common heritage of American tradition and so to build up a feeling of security in our present capacities to help ourselves. The emphasis of our day, however, will be upon group action, where in former days it was upon the rugged individual." This ideological intent brought them into more complicated territory, as he defined their goal: "A collection of American material," he wrote, "some of it perhaps one out of four 'genuine antique,' the rest is mostly material adapted to some definite aim—call it propaganda, if the word can be made respectable."

It was up to Charlie to find songs that could be considered respectable propaganda. While still on his spring field trip, he took another look at the cooperative song pamphlet Wallace and J. C. Cooley had created at West-morelands and was alarmed to find its songs to be "distinctly the wrong type." He explained in a letter to the Music Unit's assistant, Judith Tobey, "I do not mind a good vigorous push behind the co-operative movement. But any songs or operettas designed to further this movement *must be specific* in their content—specifically co-operative, not mere borrowing of vaguely socialistic songs of protest." He warned that they needed to prevent word from getting out about these songs: "Personally, I think they will make a terrible row for RA if they ever get around." To show he was serious about keeping them quiet, he sent this letter to Dornbush's home address rather than to the office, since he didn't have Tobey's address. He seemed to have felt uniquely prepared for this moment from his time with the Composers' Collective, as he concluded, "I think I know just how to handle this situation. I have made a special study of propaganda songs in [the] USA."

About a month earlier, Charlie had met someone who seemed similarly qualified to help them find what he felt were the right type of songs for their purposes. On February 19, 1936, Rupert Hampton (who went by his last name, or "Hamp" to his good friends) had been directed to Charlie's office by Education Division director Agnes King Inglis, who also oversaw the Cooperative Education unit. "She would like to use me," Hampton confided in a letter a few days later, "but would be afraid of getting me past personnel, and thought that perhaps as a special skilled man I could get through." On the surface, it wasn't clear why this twenty-five-year-old pianist from Nebraska, with a degree in sacred music from Union Theological Seminary, would have trouble getting past personnel. But in the fall of 1933, Hampton had been among the founding teachers at the Highlander Folk School in Monteagle, Tennessee, which ran workshops teaching union organizing strategies to workers and the unemployed from nearby towns, including miners, woodcutters, textile workers, and farmers. He taught piano, led group singing, helped to create plays and puppet shows, and—most important for the Music Unit's purposes—collected labor and folk songs to use in workshops. Not surprisingly, conservatives assailed the school as a dangerous threat, with one anti-union speaker calling it "the Highlander Folk School of Communism" and charging that its theme song was "Keep the Red Flag Waving."

Perhaps Agnes Inglis saw it as easier to "get through" personnel from Special Skills because the division kept quiet about their connection to cooperative education and thus were less prone to scrutiny. Whatever the reason, her prediction proved correct. Personnel Division staffer Charles Peck deemed Hampton "probably a first rate candidate for Special Skills. Has had fine practical experience of the right sort. Knows the ropes of rural teaching and how to get along with rural people." (On the same interview form, Peck rated Hampton's personality "excellent" and his appearance "satisfactory"—second from the top on a scale with a high of "attractive" and a low of "impossible.") In recommending him for the position, Highlander School director Myles Horton was less vague about why Hampton's practical experience would be a good fit for Special Skills: "He has many friends in the mountains and among organized labor groups in neighboring towns and southern cities. . . . His past experience in this section of the south enables him to reach individuals and groups otherwise difficult to reach."

On May 4, 1936, Hampton reported to the Special Skills headquarters on M Street as the Music Unit's newest staff representative. But instead of being sent to work within one RA homestead, he was given a "special assignment in song collection in the field," which Charlie explained in his signature dense prose: "This work would be part of the general study of and preparation for work on such a scale as to weld into one effective unit the music culture off and on the RA communities, as it has been, is, and can, though our efforts, become." In other words, they wanted to know what songs homesteaders already knew, assuming those would be the ideal vehicles for social unity. But it wasn't just any songs—Charlie thought Hampton's experience with labor union songs could be very useful for the Music Unit's work in communities with stranded industrial workers who had been involved in union activism and strikes (many of whom lost their jobs and were blacklisted as a result). For example, in 1934 several union leaders and fired workers had found refuge at Cumberland Homesteads in the violent aftermath of failed strikes at the nearby Wilder-Davidson coal camps and the Harriman Hosiery Mills, assisted by Highlander staffers and sympathetic government officials to find a place among the original group of homesteaders.

Many union protest songs sung by striking workers used traditional folk melodies with added protest lyrics that gave them a new potency, which Charlie saw as a unique opportunity for the Music Unit:

> These homesteaders know a musical activity that they dare not participate in with their governmental guides and friends. It is the most vivid that most of them have known. It can and should be sublimated and utilized in pushing the co-ops and the general amalgamation of the heterogeneous collection of "selected" families that make up the new communities. If the music representatives know these songs and have an understanding of their functional use, they can get at the bulk of the homesteaders and their natural leaders in a manner that no other thing can give them.

Hampton knew some of these songs and "better still," Charlie wrote, he "knows how to get at more."

The Music Unit's new regional representative's field assignment would involve collecting songs within the mountain communities surrounding the RA's homesteads in Tennessee and West Virginia. Officially, his assignment was quite broad: "to build up a body of data regarding the songs current along the western slopes of the mountains in Region 4 by consulting such representative people as Y.M.C.A. Secretaries, C.C.C. Camp personnel, ministers, school teachers, labor leaders, folk-singers, etc." Charlie explained that this was needed to understand "the music-historical processes operating among stranded worker populations." But he remained most enthusiastic about the union protest songs, which to him were something new, as he wrote separately to Special Skills assistant director Robert Van Hyning: "No collection of material of this sort has ever been made in this country. Even aside from the use to which we may put it, it will have very great value." In addition to Hampton, Charlie wanted to hire Lawrence Gellert to "do similar work with the negro agricultural workers," showing the continuing influence of Gellert's work on Charlie's approach, as he noted that "Gellert has been collecting work songs for almost ten years and has unsurpassed contacts."

Before Hampton left on his field assignment, he spent a few weeks training in Washington and helped Charlie generate a list of potential songs to include in the song-sheet project. On May 18, Charlie announced, "We are ready to start the making up of the song-sheets." He laid out the general plan: "The first selections would be definitely such as would advance the Resettlement idea, the co-operative projects, etc., and make good feeling at meetings. Later, ballads and love songs that are worth preserving could be used." They decided that instead of simple mimeographed sheets, they would print a folded pamphlet with an illustrated cover, which Pollock (the Special Skills painter who had recommended Charlie for the music job in the first place) agreed to create. The idea was that the pocket size and cover art would "appeal to the people as something they want to take home with them and keep." Following the social realistic style of art that he had studied with Tom Benton, Pollock was instructed to "design the covers in harmony with the spirit of the song itself, using scenes and figures and situations that will appeal as directly to the singer as the song itself—something within common and immediate experience."

Charlie and Pollock worked quickly to put out the first two songs in the summer of 1936. The cover for their first song-sheet conveys a bleak scene in pen-and-ink—a man in overalls and a straw hat with his back to us, a woman looking downcast as she sits in a wagon tied to two skinny mules. A feed store sign juts out above them, and above that the song's title, "The Farmer Comes to Town," is emblazoned across the top, with the word "farmer" in all caps (in case the focus hadn't been made clear). The inner two pages feature a simple melody with three verses, with the words written in a pleasing hand. (Charlie wrote the musical notation, and Powell wrote the words). This song seems a smart choice for the RA's inaugural song-sheet—the lyrics clearly connect to the rural setting of the homesteads, and the explanation on the back page shows it to have deep roots in American history, dating from the 1860s. The tune manages to be both melodically interesting and easy enough to sing, with dotted rhythms and an up-and-down melody in the verse that seem to mimic the slow movement of a broken wagon, followed by a rousing chorus.

The song (and the RA's explanatory text, nearly word for word) came from Carl Sandburg's *American Songbag*, where it sits somewhat uncomfortably among the cowboy songs in the "Great Open Spaces" section. Ruth had created harmonizations for some of the other songs in this book during her time studying piano and composition in Chicago, so she may have known about "The Farmer" and suggested it to Charlie. But a later memorandum indicated that Hampton contributed the first four songs in the series, and a close look at the lyrics shows some differences from Sandburg's version that likely came from Hampton and give the song more of a protest edge. For example, the song-sheet's third verse, which is completely absent from the Sandburg version, ends with what sounds like it could be a veiled strike warning from a farmers union: "It would put them to the test if the farmer took a rest, then they'd know that it's the farmer feeds them all."

The second song-sheet makes no attempt at subtlety in connecting to the RA's larger goals. On the cover, two men in overalls—one young, one old—stand together, facing front, each resting a hand proudly on two waist-high sacks that stand between them. Framing the men are two vertical poles they hold on either side, attached to a banner that stretches above them declaring the song's title like a protest slogan: "Co-operation Is Our Aim." In case the meaning was somehow missed, the official Twin Pines cooperative symbol decorates their sacks and appears above the music on the first page. The obvious message conveyed in the song's title, with lyrics borrowed from several different cooperative association publications, must have seemed important enough that Charlie was willing to overlook aspects of the song that he would have found less appealing: its melody was from the British drinking and college song "There Is a Tavern in the Town," which was often included in popular song books and had been made newly popular by a Rudy Vallee recording in 1934.

Notably missing from these song-sheets is any indication of who produced them—no government logo or Resettlement Administration imprint appears, only a note on the back covers that they are part of "a series of American songs rarely found in popular collections." An artful use of the passive voice dodges the question of provenance: "Additional verses to this song will be welcomed, as will be also suggestions for future issues of the series." At the time, Charlie claimed that this lack of attribution was an attempt to keep the song-sheets informal, and Dornbush explained that agency designation wasn't necessary since they were meant to serve as "in-house" publications. But it seems clear that this anonymity was part of the larger pattern of secrecy for the Special Skills Division in general and the Music Unit in particular, as Charlie later admitted they kept them quiet because "we had at least that amount of political sense: the program would have been stopped sooner."

In her detailed reports from Cherry Lake, Margaret made no mention of the RA's new song-sheets, though she noted making use of the *New American Songbook* at a PTA community sing. For Margaret, the content of the songs seemed to be less important than the act of making music together, with whatever song was available—the only song titles she mentioned using as vehicles for group singing were "He's a Jolly Good Fellow," "Billy Boy," and "Yankee Doodle," all likely chosen because they were widely known, making entry into the group appealing and not intimidating anyone who might be on the fence. But the song-sheets may have simply seemed less of a priority in her work at Cherry Lake, as she increasingly focused her efforts on the stage.

CHAPTER 5

NEW WINE IN OLD BOTTLES

O n the morning of Cherry Lake's Easter pageant in April 1936, Margaret had lost her voice again, this time because she had worked all week despite being sick. But the long hours seemed to have paid off, with all the preparations ready for the performance: "The boxing green gorgeously festooned and garlanded, its three sides thickly banked with trees and its fourth ingeniously filled in by two painted doors—decorated to represent the covers of a history book—was as completely transformed from its former fistic aspect as Gene Tunney was after he read 'Lady McDuff,'" she wrote, referencing the former heavyweight boxing champion's well-known love of Shakespeare. Some children were already in costume, excited for the performance. But, she continued,

> Then came the rain—a deluge with wind and all the trimmings. Result: We hastily assembled a few surplus palm branches (begged by me from the nearby Court House authorities when I noticed the palm trees there were being pruned) and decorated the school assembly. What costumes remained dry (they were made of paper) were collected, repaired and hurriedly supplemented. But Apollo, the Sun-God, and the Prince of Darkness were drenched and their costumes melted in an alarming way.

I wrapped them in sheets while I rushed to concoct other costumes; the show must go on in an hour. One of the teachers had a black cape, another a black bathing cap; the Prince of Darkness was provided for. My orange evening cape, a yellow pleated skirt, and orange pajamas twisted around his head for a turban produced a resplendent Sun-God. And so on.

Then several of the principal actors did not appear; ill or rained out. Worst of all, the chief character, the narrator, who was to "turn back the pages of History" and recount the story as it was pantomimed, did not appear and at the last moment I, with the aid of an amplifier, had to pinch-hit.

The play, as Margaret had conceived it, would tell the origin story of Easter by depicting spring celebrations throughout history and from different countries: ancient Mayans and Aztecs, Greeks, and Romans in the first half; Christian Easter traditions in France, Germany, England, and the United States in the second. For music, in addition to the children singing together "at strategic points," she played phonograph records related to the play's themes—including "Hymns to Apollo," a Gregorian chant, and Handel's *Messiah*—which she had secured from the University Library Lending Service. (Luckily, she had been successful in persuading regional FERA officials to send her a phonograph player after Charlie informed his representatives that the RA purchasing department would not approve any requests for music equipment from Washington.)

Despite the last-minute scramble and the loss of their outdoor stage, painted set, and costumes, Margaret reported, "The morning performance for the children held them rapt. It was the first thing that has been given, including the movies, in which we haven't had to ask for attention or quiet." But she wasn't sure their parents would be so enthralled:

The performance in the evening was given to a packed if somewhat puzzled house. They had come, I imagine, to see the children dressed as angels, carrying lilies and singing hymns.

We opened with a sacrificial dance which was distinctly pagan. Screened by palms, as I narrated through the amplifier, I saw them consulting their programs and their neighbors, but at the end they gave their unqualified approval. To one of the fathers who expressed his interest afterward, I explained that we thought this was the kind of pageant best for children; it taught them history and geography and customs as well as history of music. "Yes, it taught us grown up children too," he answered. Another father (noted for his bigotry) said to me, with a puzzled air: "I never thought there was so many different ways of being religious." . . . The best part of it all was that the children, many of whom—especially the boys—were loathe to be in any kind of a play ("that's for girls and sissies") showed remarkable poise and dignity, and because no one laughed they want to be in "lots more plays."

Margaret felt triumphant. "Today I am full of rejoicing," she wrote. "First that it went off so well, but mostly that there is a week of Easter vacation during which time I may recover my voice."

When she returned from her week off (spent "by the sea-shore in the sunshine"), it seemed her absence might have contributed to a familiar drop in momentum for community programs. Both the "Gasparilla" play and a planned craft and hobby exhibit had already been postponed twice because of construction delays for the new trading post, resulting in lagging attendance at play rehearsals and low interest in contributing handicrafts for the exhibit. As Loomis and Margaret worked "to sweep back the invading flood of indifference," the construction department asked for a third postponement. But this time, Loomis and Margaret appealed to homestead director Paul Vander Schouw, who authorized them to use the large community hall—an impressive space with enormous hand-hewn beams and thirty wagon-wheel chandeliers hanging from the ceiling—which was deemed complete enough to finally host the two-day event celebrating the trading post's opening on April 24th and 25th.

Margaret, Loomis, and one volunteer from the music committee spent the morning of Friday's event driving across the entire homestead in the school bus collecting entries for the exhibit. Many people said they had nothing to contribute, but Margaret persisted: "With the belief that psychologically the effect of exhibiting would increase the self-confidence and community spirit of the homesteaders, we made a point of trying to discover something in each place, even if it were only, as in one home, an ingenious door-prop made of a Sears-Roebuck catalogue." When they were finished, they brought everything back to the hall: "A more heterogeneous collection you couldn't imagine. There was everything from a tanned cow-hide, snake skins, stuffed fish and cured meat to furniture, canned goods, vegetables, handwork, pictures and flower arrangements—232 separate entries. . . . The quilts alone, hung like tapestries on the walls from the beams, were so numerous and varied and handsome that we had to classify them in three groups for judging."

Margaret arranged the exhibit and decorations mostly by herself (given the lack of enthusiasm from volunteers), and while she was holding a last-minute rehearsal for one of the nervous performers in the play, a man from the construction staff stormed in. "I'm sore at you," he exploded. "I never liked the idea of this building being used until everything was finished, and I like it less now." With that vote of confidence serving "as a reviving cocktail," she headed back to her barracks to change.

A few hours later, the hall was full, with cars arriving so fast they needed to quickly find volunteers to direct traffic. After a few cast members turned up missing and hasty substitutions were made, the play finally went on, mostly following the original script but with "much spirited ad-libbing" that elicited howls of laughter from the crowd. Scenes were punctuated by a few solo singing performances, ending with a final, rousing chorus that almost everyone joined in. The play was followed by informal music and dancing late into the evening. For Margaret, "the high spot of the evening was when the staff member who had voiced such hearty disapproval in the afternoon came up and said again before everyone: 'I must tell you I've never been so wrong about anything in my life. This is the most important thing that ever happened to the Community. I've been here eighteen months and this is the first time I've seen these people happy.'"

Saturday night brought even bigger crowds from nearby towns and across the state line for more entertainment, ending with a barn dance. It was here that Margaret produced her "trump card" in the form of fiddler Russell Wise. He had been working as a cab driver in Jacksonville when Margaret discovered him and maneuvered ("with difficulty") to hire him as a music worker at Cherry Lake. Though down on his luck and playing music only at Jacksonville's beer joints at the time, he had won the county fiddling contest the night before, and he brought the event to a triumphant close with his virtuosic playing.

Just as the new trading post itself represented a new era of stability for Cherry Lake, this opening event marked a different sort of turning point. "If it comes within the scope of a Staff Representative to make a challenging declaration," she wrote in early May, "this one would like to go on record as saying: Community is awake!" Margaret's word choice here—not "the community," but "Community" with a capital C—can be found throughout her reports when referring not only to the group of people living at Cherry Lake but to the concept of community, a kind of shorthand for cooperation. Historian Paul Conkin takes note of something similar to be true throughout the RA, that "the very word 'community' became a synonym for a form of collectivism."

During that first week in May, Loomis had asked Margaret to provide music for an auction fundraiser for the baseball team, which they thought would be "a good way to get the county politicians out here to spend some money." She agreed to help if half the proceeds would go to the orchestra, arguing persuasively that they needed money for baseball uniforms in the spring but needed music all year. The program featured a wide range of performers Margaret had found at relatively short notice: tap dancing, dramatic skits, card tricks (by the mess hall cook and a dishwasher), songs, and solo violin, followed by dancing led by the new fiddler Russell Wise, Red Stevens, and the other five members of the Cherry Lake Orchestra. "I even persuaded the County Superintendent of Education to do his 'break down' to the tune of 'Chicken Reel,'" she reported with pride. "Everyone had a hilarious time, and it looks as if we are even in a position now to get up something on short notice and have it a success—Hence my opening sentence." Community was awake.

Music did appear to be gaining a central place on the homestead. More and more homesteaders signed up to perform at Amateur Nights—a recent event featured a duet between a boy and his dog ("howlingly funny"), a tap dance performed by a ten-year-old girl (that night's winner), an acrobatic act, and a magic show, concluding with singing and dancing by the large audience, led by the orchestra. Attendance increased at Margaret's music memory contests, where she asked participants to identify the title, composer, and nationality of a classical piece she played on the phonograph. Music at a PTA meeting in May included one of these music memory sessions, a concert where she accompanied Russell Wise on guitar, and group singing.

The Cherry Lake Orchestra had become well-known enough off the homestead to be invited to perform on a radio amateur hour at a nearby city. The program featured a few tunes by the full orchestra, an accordion solo, a fiddle solo, and a few singers accompanied by Margaret on the piano, including Bill Carr, an original member of Cherry Lake's music committee, who turned out to have an astonishingly low basso profundo voice. She reported proudly that "it was said by the announcer and studio hangers-on to have been the best amateur programs given by that station," and that "the announcer said over the air that these performers wouldn't be in the amateur class long; he appeared quite astounded by the low C of the basso." Once unleashed, their music apparently couldn't be contained, as Margaret described their trip back to Cherry Lake: "We stopped by our favorite honky-tonk for a sandwich and a glass of beer. Feeling good, we put on a performance and were immediately offered an opportunity to perform there every Saturday evening."

Another critical step toward capital-C Community occurred when the planning and execution of the Community Players' next performance came entirely from the homesteaders themselves. One homesteader came up with the idea for the show, which was to be another fundraiser split between the baseball team and the musicians. Members of the baseball committee, the orchestra, and the music and drama committees sat up far into the night working out the structure of the play. They chose a homesteader to serve as director and formed a committee for every detail: script, program, advertising, publicity, costumes, and props. "The whole thing has proceeded in a workman like way with no hurt feelings," Margaret wrote. The orchestra, flush with funds from the last benefit event, agreed to advance the money that would be needed for costumes and wigs. Red Stevens handled the lighting, four volunteers decorated the set, and the head of construction put together an extra team of workers to have the stage and auditorium completely finished before the performance. "Heretofore, I would have been dismayed by all there was to be done," Margaret reported, "but this time there was cooperation."

At last, here was that magical, sought-after moment of cooperation, the goal not just of the Music Unit but of the entire RA enterprise. Yet this performance also represents an ugly stain on the Music Unit's work that reflects on the RA and the New Deal itself, because the play that Cherry Lake homesteaders so enthusiastically thought of, planned, and performed was a minstrel, done in blackface. Since the term "Jim Crow" comes from a stock character within nineteenth-century blackface minstrelsy, a minstrel show performed on an all-White government homestead serves as an unignorable staged incarnation of the racism in the Jim Crow South. It was also a nasty byproduct of the Music Unit's goal of focusing on the "musical currency" of the segregated community, whatever it may be. In her reports, Margaret seemed to distance herself from the content, emphasizing instead what the project meant for the community: "Another small triumph to be recorded: The idea for the minstrel came to me from one of the homesteaders—not *from* me, as everything heretofore." When, during their late-night brainstorming session, someone proposed a title that included her name along with the familiar racist tropes of blackface minstrel shows ("Margaret Valiant's Community Hot Chocolate Drops"), she "hastily proposed adjournment on the ground that we were all too sleepy by this time to know what we were saying." Her reflections after the show focused on its scale and audience reception rather than its worth, calling it "mammoth, colossal and stupendously successful." She noted only that "the gags were mostly of the 'That's no lady, that's my wife' vintage, but they were delivered with gusto for a not too exigent consumption, and the singing was tops." Her final assessment focused on the opinions of unnamed experts and on the community's involvement in mounting the production: "Although I am delighted that it was considered good entertainment—some of the authorities said it was as good as any professional Minstrel—the important thing to me was that it was really directed by a homesteader. We had committees—of homesteaders—for every detail."

So it may be that Margaret and the rest of the Special Skills staff did not necessarily approve of the practice of minstrelsy but saw it as a necessary evil to achieve their goal—just as the RA allowed regional offices to enforce segregation on the homesteads, and the New Deal as a whole capitulated to Jim Crow in order to earn support from Southern Democrats in Congress. However, many White government staffers—even progressive ones like those who believed in the RA—may also have viewed minstrelsy as an accepted part of American culture. Black activists and their allies had protested against the evils of blackface for decades, but it remained an entrenched component of American popular culture into the twentieth century. On some level—and perhaps especially during the Great Depression—the practice continued to function as Wesley Morris describes at its origins: "Paradoxically, perversely, minstrelsy's grotesquerie deluded white audiences into feeling better about themselves," its racist caricatures of Black people drawing "a comforting contrast with a white person's sense of honor and civility, with a white person's simply being white. *No matter how bad things might be for us, at least we're not them.*" Although its use had waned since its height of popularity in the nineteenth century, blackface performance in the twentieth century became fused with an insidious nostalgia for a false, dangerously romanticized view of the old South. Throughout the 1930s, star performers appeared in blackface in films with a nostalgic lens: Shirley Temple in *The Littlest Rebel* (1935), Fred Astaire in *Swingtime*

(1936), Irene Dunne in *Showboat* (1936), and Judy Garland and Mickey Rooney in their first let's-put-on-a-show musical, *Babes in Arms* (1939).

Historian Rhae Lynn Barnes writes that amateur blackface performances like the one performed at Cherry Lake (and depicted in *Babes in Arms*) remained pervasive across the US during the Jim Crow years, persisting through the mid-twentieth century. Commercial how-to manuals about mounting a minstrel show were readily available for anyone to buy, a resource ubiquitous enough that Margaret reported taking a quick trip to Jacksonville to find "a book on producing a minstrel" that would provide "the authority of the printed word" in guiding Cherry Lake's production. Barnes traces the prevalence of these amateur shows to the blackface tradition within the Elks Club (often referred to as "the burnt cork brotherhood"), the largest fraternal order in the country, with many politicians and presidents among its members—including FDR. In fact, she argues that amateur blackface minstrelsy came to assume "something akin to an official culture" within the US government up through the mid-twentieth century, specifically noting that minstrels were performed in schools as part of plays and music chosen by the WPA.

In June 1936, Margaret and C. B. Loomis held the first official meeting of the Cherry Lake Community Players, a dramatic club that would put on regular shows beyond what the music and drama committees had been able to pull together thus far. The group of about thirty participants elected officers and chose Red Stevens as the director for their next play. Margaret had some misgivings about this choice since he already directed the orchestra, but, she wrote, "it was felt—aside from his fitness—that he should have the honor because of his animating cooperation in all undertakings. As a matter of fact he was elected in his absence, being momentarily occupied with making the lemonade." Indeed, his election seems an appropriate symbol for the new enthusiasm for drama on the homestead, since despite his general cooperativeness even Red had been skeptical about drama before the Gasparilla play.

Early that summer, the Special Skills Division sent Bernard Steffen, a field representative in painting, to join Margaret at Cherry Lake. Happily, the two already knew each other from Thomas Benton's music sessions back in New York. As a student in Benton's studio, Steffen had played harmonica in the Harmonica Rascals alongside Pollock, who later recruited him to join Special Skills. After his arrival at Cherry Lake, Margaret wrote to Dornbush expressing "appreciation of Mr. Steffen and his spirit in entering into the whole life of this place." She clearly enjoyed having him at Cherry Lake as a colleague, and the homesteaders seemed glad to welcome him into the community, as Margaret described with her usual wit, "On Sunday our painting representative and I were invited on a picnic with about fifty homesteaders, and for a few hours we were both Staff Representatives (literally) in the field." As a musician, artist, and friend of Margaret's, Steffen was a welcome addition, and he would not only teach painting at the homestead's summer school but would play an important role in the Community Players' attempt to mount their first full production.

On short notice, Margaret was asked to plan a program for a dedication ceremony that would mark the long-delayed completion of the community building, to be held on July 8. It would need to be simple—a children's choir, a ceremony to present a certificate of appreciation to the director, speeches from dignitaries, followed by a square dance accompanied by the orchestra—since "nothing more seemed possible in so short a time." But when the ceremony was (perhaps predictably) postponed to July 22, Margaret saw an opportunity. The extra two weeks might give the Players time to write, rehearse, and perform a play she had long wanted to help produce: "The Rehabilitation of John Doe," which would tell the story of Cherry Lake through the lives of the homesteaders themselves. "I do believe it can be impressive and an authentic document as well," she wrote to Dornbush, "if we can get people to talk of their actual experience without restraint." When homestead director Paul Vander Schouw gave his enthusiastic approval, Margaret outlined the general idea at that night's Community Players' meeting, "followed, and interrupted, by an open discussion." In describing the dissenting opinions that emerged from this discussion, Margaret outlined her hopes for the play:

> There are two chief dissenters who expressed themselves as being opposed to a calling-up of that trying and humiliating relief period; but we tried tactfully to explain that there were two constructive purposes in so doing. First, that by getting a perspective on those recent years of trial we might get a more detached analysis of their causes, thereby aiding those who follow to avoid the same mistakes; and second, that such a work, based on natural experience, would be, in a modest way, a historic document. In that light, we were able to convince one of the dissenters (who later took one of the chief roles and contributed many ideas). The other departed, saying "it was all a punk idea."

The players decided they would rehearse every night for the two weeks before the event, setting up a grueling schedule after the homesteaders worked what Margaret called "a full man's or woman's job during the day." The cast shared their personal experiences for Margaret to gather as dialog into an official script, then they met the following night to try out the material and decide where to go from there. That meant Margaret taught summer school music classes in the mornings and spent the afternoons "constructing and reconstructing the play from the previous evening's developments." She quipped in her report, "Rehearsals resumed around eight o'clock and continued until unconscious."

This would be their first full play—not a pantomime like the children's Easter play, or an ad-libbed extended skit like Gasparilla, or a formulaic minstrel drawing on racist stereotypes—it would be a play of their own creation, that told their own story. It had a cast of eighteen, which included several original music committee members along with many new faces, both adults and children. Red Stevens had apparently convinced his wife Mary to join the cast, as did Bill Carr, whose wife Freda played the female lead. Steffen designed the sets and joined the cast as an extra.

Now titled *New Wine* (after the bible verse quoted in the script and on the program, "No man putteth new wine in old wine skins"), the play told the story of Cherry Lake through the experiences of Mr. and Mrs. John Doe, with Act I set in their Tampa living room in March 1935. It begins in classic melodramatic style, with a villain in the form of Mr. Burke (identified as a "slick collector" in the program) coming to collect the money due on their refrigerator, even as John Doe is laid off, their young daughter Irene has fallen ill, and his wife Ivy reveals that there is another baby on the way. Surrounding them are Gramps (John Doe's father, a rabble-rousing labor leader) and their neighbors, the Miltons and the Johnsons. The second scene takes place six months later (September 1935), the script indicating, "Same set, only not so comfortable." The Doe family has gone on relief, and Mrs. Milton brings the caseworker Miss Love over to sing the praises of Cherry Lake Farms, "one of the most wonderful places in Florida." By the end of Act I, the Does, the Miltons, the Johnsons, and even Mr. Burke have all been convinced to apply.

Act II begins three months later, as the Doe family moves into an empty shack at Cherry Lake, joined onstage by the other characters, who have all by now relocated to the homestead. Complaints abound—"All the modern inconveniences," the pessimistic Mrs. Johnson snipes. "Sun porch for the children, with mosquitoes for playmates." Her final assessment: "I'm going to get what I can before this place goes bust." But Ivy and John are not swayed. "Well, we are no worse off than we were," Ivy says, with John adding, "At least we have got the country." Soon appears a more seasoned homesteader, the kindly Aunt Joe, offering them fresh milk from her cow and telling them about the homestead band, whose members then appear for a rehearsal as the others dance. Things seem to be looking up until little Irene collapses, and the scene ends with her being taken to the hospital. In the second scene of Act II, the script indicates, "Same scene, little more livable. An air of healthy skepticism reigns" (though it seems unclear how such an air would be portrayed onstage). The stage directions describe an idyllic moment in the Doe household: "John is clearing up supper—Ivy is out to movies." Little Irene has recovered after a long stay in the hospital. The other men enter, discussing the new homestead director and whether his plan to build one hundred houses in ninety days will actually happen, and Mr. Burke announces he's leaving ("to get away from this filth and a bunch of bums!").

Act III moves into the present day (June 1936) as Ivy and John prepare for a housewarming party in their newly completed home, but they are dismayed to learn that the money for finishing the community buildings and paying workers on the homestead has run out. Still, the talk is full of their shared community life: Ivy is president of the PTA, John president of the Cherry Lake Players, Gramps secretary of the Homesteaders' Club; they talk about evening classes for adults at summer school and how they got help when Irene was in the hospital. They've heard that mean Mr. Burke is now stuck in Jacksonville without a job. Finally, someone runs in with the "swell news" that the government sent a new appropriation—"half a million bucks!"—their jobs are safe, and construction on the new school and community buildings can begin. Everyone shouts with joy, and the orchestra plays "Happy Days Are Here Again" to end the play.

This play, while certainly highlighting the benefits of community and serving as the kind of "respectable propaganda" the Music Unit strived to create, was also powerful because homesteaders saw their real experiences presented onstage, including the struggles they had overcome, in a narrative arc that brought them to a happy ending in the present—represented by the real-life $550,000 appropriation the project had just received from Washington. After its performance at the dedication ceremony on July 22, Margaret reported proudly that the play "went off triumphantly. Its effect was far beyond our fondest hope."

She ended her report making sure "to designate to just what extent this play was a cooperative effort," knowing that it was the process of creation as much as the final product that mattered to their work in Special Skills. "The original conception was mine, but I had invaluable assistance and stimulus in the beginning and throughout from our educational director." It was Loomis who suggested the quotes included in Gramp's fiery speech defending labor protests as part of the American way in Act I:

Gramps (reading): "Whenever the American people grow weary of their existing government they can exercise their revolutionary right to dismember and overthrow it." I suppose Bolsheviks said *that*. Well, they didn't. Abe Lincoln said it. Now listen to this: "The spirit of resistance to government is so valuable on certain occasions that I wish it always to be kept alive. It will often be exercised when wrong but better so than not to be exercised at all." I suppose Bolsheviks said *that*, too. Well, Thomas Jefferson said that.

Margaret also reported that "John Doe's speech was actually taken down by me (and integrated) from animated suggestions offered by three members of the cast when they felt more punch was needed to close Scene 2 of Act II." That speech comes after the other men are complaining about the pace of construction and other headaches, when John pounds on the table and jumps up:

John: Lissen, you guys! You been doing all the talking, I haven't said much. Now you lissen to me a while. Of course there are mistakes, but the guy that don't make mistakes don't do nothing! Put that crabbing on the shelf and use some of that energy to build up instead of tear down! What did you come here for; just to find something, or did you bring something with you; what have you got to offer? What do you want here? It's for you (pointing to audience) to decide.

Margaret said she welcomed their suggestions, "not only because they were good theatre, but because they were spontaneous and voluntary." She concluded this final report, "The actual writing of the dialogue was done entirely by me at the urgent request of the players, but this fact should not, I feel, lessen the communal character of the whole undertaking."

With *New Wine*, Margaret had now found more roles—playwright and director—to add to her already long list of talents: pianist, singer, clothes designer and model, music teacher, choir director, event planner. Music did not take center stage in this play, with the orchestra only appearing twice. The only tune named in the script was not the kind of folk music Charlie had envisioned, but "Happy Days Are Here Again," a song from a Broadway musical that had become a well-known campaign song—perhaps the oldest musical incarnation of respectable propaganda in American political life—for FDR's successful presidential bid in 1932. But if folk music had slid from the center of Margaret's program at Cherry Lake, it certainly remained the focus in Washington, aided by a few new arrivals at the office.

CHAPTER 6

DELIGHT IN WHAT IT IS TO BE AMERICAN

P lans for the Music Unit's new phase of work began quietly. In what seemed to be a run-of-the-mill accounting of planned equipment purchases in early February 1936, Dornbush reported, "An order was placed this week for an Electrograph portable sound recording apparatus, which will be used both in the laboratory and field, for the making of special records for use in the music services of this division."

Charlie and Dornbush had decided—with Falke's approval—that it wasn't enough to send music staffers like Hampton out to collect folk songs by writing down the lyrics and notating the melody. They needed recordings of the songs as sung by the folk themselves. Dornbush described it simply: A music representative with the recording machine would "dig out the folk music and then turn it back into active singing and dancing programs." For Charlie, the machine also served a larger purpose of preserving the folk songs and dance tunes that, he said, "belong to the people who are now homesteading on Resettlement communities." He saw it as a core responsibility of the Music Unit "to keep this widespread and deeply rooted part of American culture alive by capturing it wherever found (by means of the recorder)." More than that, "The recorder should—and can—be of great help as a tangible proof of the importance of this culture in the eyes of the Federal Government."

In March, more than six weeks after having first placed the order for their new recording machine, Dornbush alerted Charlie that their request continued to work its way through the RA's purchasing and budget offices, and that a ten-day bidding process would cause further delays. "However," he continued with a note of optimism, "there should be no further obstacles in the way and you can make your plans for field work in that connection." Unfortunately, Dornbush underestimated the government's capacity for further obstacles. It was around this time that Charlie received word that all equipment ordered for his field representatives was being "held up indefinitely." Another month went by with no sign of the unit's hoped-for equipment, but the office soon received a visit from someone who would prove just as essential as the recording machine to its future plans.

Sidney Robertson had not come to Washington looking for a job. She was staying with friends on a farm in Maryland while she waited for a berth to become available on a freighter that would bring her back home to San Francisco via the Panama Canal. But as the wait dragged on, she began to spend more time in the city, visiting the Music Division of the Library of Congress to try to answer a burning question she had: What was *American* about American folk songs? She met up with an old friend of hers, George O'Neil, who worked in the RA's Education Division under Agnes Inglis (whom Sidney referred to as his "lady boss," the same person who had sent Hampton to the Music Unit). O'Neil told her he had heard about a man running a folk music program somewhere in the RA and suggested that Sidney go and find him.

That's how, on April 15, 1936, she ended up in the Special Skills Division's converted factory building on M Street, with its noisy woodworking shop on the second floor, tracking down Charlie's office. Sidney, in her early thirties, was gregarious and outspoken, always ready to engage in witty repartee, with intense, observant eyes behind her glasses, chin-length brown hair framing her round face. She found the Music Unit's corner of the office only to learn that Charlie was away on his extended field trip to the homesteads. Still, she had a nice chat with Judith Tobey and, following her suggestion, filled out an application with the personnel office. She followed up a few days later with a letter of five single-spaced pages addressed to her new friend Miss Tobey. (Sidney's writing style tended to be as voluminous as Charlie's was dense.) She expounded on her varied experiences related to American folk music and group music-making and apologized for the letter's length, joking, "I seem to have included everything but what I had for breakfast!" On the final page, she wrote something that seemed sure to catch Charlie's eye, if he made it through to the end: "My interest in music is secondary to my interest in people and their development," she wrote. "I feel music has a definite role to play in bringing about the sort of group expression which is indispensable to democracy."

Charlie returned from his travels the following week, and when he and Sidney finally met, they discovered that they had a good friend in common—the avant-garde composer Henry Cowell. Impressed with her background, Charlie told her about his plans for the eagerly awaited recording equipment and said that he would like to hire her. "Seeger, the music boss at the Resettlement office was so swell," she wrote to her mother a few days later. "I feel life is greatly simplified." That long-awaited berth on a freighter was seeming less and less necessary.

Sidney had come to Washington from New York, having lived and worked for nearly a year at Henry Street Settlement House on the Lower East Side. Henry Street was part of a larger settlement house movement in which workers and volunteers lived in the low-income communities they served, as neighbors rather than outsiders. The settlement house movement in the United States was dominated by women, offering independence and an alternative to marriage for college-educated women for whom there were few other career opportunities.

Sidney would soon travel a well-worn path from the settlement house movement to the New Deal's resettlement efforts. The "settlement" roots of the RA went beyond the similarities in their names, as they also shared an emphasis on addressing individual needs and a commitment to "moral and material uplift of the poor"—an ethos that permeated the New Deal as a whole. High-ranking New Dealers like Labor Secretary Frances Perkins and WPA director Harry Hopkins had previous connections to settlement houses, and several others had worked at Henry Street, including Treasury Secretary Henry Morgenthau Jr. and Brain Truster Adolf Berle. Historian David Kennedy calls these reformers "middle-class missionaries," describing them as "earnest, high-minded, and sometimes condescending," possessing "both the courage and the prejudices of their convictions." Eleanor Roosevelt had volunteered as a young woman to teach dancing and calisthenics at Rivington Street Settlement House, an experience that built her dedication to public service and gave her—and her husband—an awareness of the individual suffering wrought by poverty. When Franklin accompanied Eleanor to visit a sick child in a tenement near the settlement house, he was aghast at the living conditions he saw and reportedly said, "My God. I didn't know people lived like that." According to Eleanor, those visits would continue to have a powerful impact on the president, and they certainly shaped her own approach at Arthurdale and the government homestead program.

Katharine Kellock, the Special Skills staffer whose reports had a strong influence on the Music Unit's development, also came to the RA from Henry Street Settlement House, where she had worked as the assistant to its founder, Lillian Wald. Like Eleanor Roosevelt, Kellock seemed to have been deeply influenced by the settlement house movement's use of recreational clubs and activities—including music—as a mode of assimilation for new immigrants and to bridge differences within the community. Social music programs offered participatory music to people of all skills and backgrounds, with the express purpose to "ease relationships among members of the community through music."

Since its founding by public health pioneer Lillian Wald in 1893, Henry Street Settlement House had become a catalyst for all kinds of social initiatives aimed at improving the lives of the immigrant poor and working class living on the Lower East Side. The list of programs bears a striking similarity to Eleanor Roosevelt's stated priorities for Arthurdale: a visiting nurse program, the city's first public-school nurses and special education teachers, the first public playground (in the building's backyard), child care and kindergarten, summer camp, vocational training and English-language instruction for adults, music lessons, school tutoring, social activities, and performances. Henry Street's community was a mix of ethnic European immigrants (mostly Jewish, but also others from Eastern and Southern Europe) and African Americans who had come north as part of the Great Migration from the Jim Crow South. Wald was known for her progressive views on race and was among a multiracial group of reformers who created the NAACP, with the founding conference taking place at Henry Street Settlement in 1909. Henry Street was thus among a handful of settlement houses that included both Black and White residents and volunteers, though many of its programs remained segregated.

After Sidney had moved into a room in one of Henry Street Settlement's red brick tenements in July 1935, she began her work as a volunteer. She taught in the settlement's preschool ("great fun") and helped with events for adults in the evenings, which included rooftop folk dancing and community singing sessions. She also helped arrange classical concerts by outside performers. In September, she was hired to direct Henry Street's large social music program, working with the WPA's Federal Music Project and Federal Theatre Project offices to coordinate the settlement house's eighteen social music teachers. She tracked down Yiddish speakers among the settlement residents and asked them to teach her Yiddish folk songs, which she then taught to the WPA song leaders to use in their community singing sessions—following a strategy that the RA Music Unit would pursue among its homesteaders. In the job application she submitted to the RA, her description of her work at Henry Street shows the diverse but largely segregated nature of most of its activities: "I led a negro chorus and 'social club,' a group of 125–200 unemployed (men and women, negroes and whites mixed), a special group of Jewish women, some children's classes, a negro children's carol group, several boys' clubs (ages 18–22)." Her five-page letter to Tobey gives more details, including a description of her work with the settlement's Black community that illuminates a tiny piece of what was missing on the RA's Whites-only homesteads—since they were "struggling to extend their culture by exploring their own past and that of other races, . . . we started discussion groups and hunted the spirituals through to discover the hidden meanings of slavery days, and undertook the study of folk-songs of peoples all over the world."

By the winter of 1936, Sidney was suffering under the demands and long hours of her busy job, and she came down with bronchitis so severe that in early March 1936 she was admitted to the hospital. The doctors there said the bronchitis was a response to the cold weather of her first New York winter and urged her to go back to California. Sent to convalesce for a few weeks at the Valeria Home in upstate New York, Sidney made plans to stay with her friends in Maryland while waiting for a passenger berth back home to San Francisco.

But the idea of heading back home may have been half-hearted from the start. The week before she found the Music Unit's offices at the end of April, she wrote, "I'd love to come west: I miss my friends there very much. But on the other hand, now is my chance to get unique experience, almost anywhere I set my hand. I don't want to spend more than 2 or 3 years all told in the east," she concluded, "but 1 year isn't quite enough."

Sidney was born in 1901, the oldest of four children in a wealthy San Francisco family, living in a large house in the southwestern part of the city. Her mother came from a well-to-do Louisiana family and felt strongly that Sidney should participate in an eclectic array of lessons befitting a girl of privilege: ballet, horseback riding, piano, botany, fencing, French, and sewing. She was sent on tours of Europe led by her English piano teacher, trips she said brought her to a series of remarkable experiences: a playdate with the royal children of Italy, attending the premiere of Stravinsky's *Le Sacre du Printemps* in Paris, seeing the young Jascha Heifetz perform in St. Petersburg, venturing off the tourist track to view the controversial paintings of the French Impressionists, and becoming stranded in England when the Great War broke out.

In college at Stanford, Sidney continued her activity-filled life as a reporter at the *Stanford Daily* and a member of the swim team, the freshman women's basketball team, the tennis club, the French club, the English club, the Wranglers Society debate club, and the music club. She became one of two women within a close group of male friends, most of whom were young World War I veterans on education grants returning to college after army service, including the novelists John Steinbeck and Archie Binns.

A few days before her Stanford graduation in 1924, Sidney married Kenneth Gregg Robertson, a graduate student in philosophy, the son of Scottish immigrants who had settled in Oakland. Sidney later said he had "telegraphed our future" on their first date at Sticky Wilson's fountain at Stanford, where not only had Sidney paid for their sodas, but Kenneth had absent-mindedly pocketed the change afterward. With financial help from Sidney's parents and a doting aunt of Kenneth's, the couple moved to Paris in the summer of 1924 (coincidentally, the same period when both Margaret and Dornbush were in Europe). Sidney studied music theory and piano while Kenneth began studying psychiatry, but after a few months they both dropped their studies and escaped to a quieter life in Montpelier. In the spring, they travelled to Zurich to participate in a rare seminar conducted in English by the pioneering psychoanalyst Carl Jung, now viewed as a pivotal event in the history of analytical psychology.

When the couple returned to Palo Alto a year later, Sidney found a job teaching music at the Peninsula School of Creative Education, a progressive school that had recently taken over a rambling, purportedly haunted Victorian mansion in nearby Menlo Park. She later said the Peninsula School is where she first discovered the power of American folk music. The children had seemed to like the British folk songs that she taught, but when she introduced "Home on the Range" from Lomax's *Cowboy Songs and Other Ballads*, she said, "I had a revolution on my hands, for the song became an obsession and was to be heard almost non-stop all over the school for weeks," played by impromptu bands of penny whistles, mouth harps, and harmonicas procured at a nearby Woolworth's.

By 1930, Sidney and Kenneth had divorced amicably, and she had become the music department director, a position that ended when the Depression forced the school to make cuts in 1932. Desperate for work, she took what was meant to be a two-month stint as a live-in governess for a wealthy family in Pebble Beach, just south of Monterey on the California coast, but ended up staying in the job for two years before moving on her own to nearby Carmel-by-the-Sea.

At that time, Carmel was a seaside artists' colony largely shielded from the effects of the Great Depression, a cozy retreat for those who could afford it, streets dotted with adorable fairy-tale cottages given quaint names like "Hansel & Gretel" and "The Secret Garden" rather than street numbers. In the fall of 1934, Sidney had moved into The Gray Goose, a one-bedroom cottage on Casanova Street that she shared with her cocker spaniel Sis, two cats, and two pianos—a Steinway grand piano, which she nicknamed her "great-grandmother," and a sturdy Baldwin. She was a frequent attendee of avant-garde music and art events at the Denny-Watrous Gallery, and her social circle was also populated with writers—her college friends John and Carol Steinbeck, left-wing journalists Lincoln Steffens and Ella Winter, and the poet Robinson Jeffers, as well as occasional visitors like Gertrude Stein and Langston Hughes.

In early 1935, Sidney found a promising job as the music editor at the *Pacific Weekly*, a new left-leaning journal based in Carmel that she described as "a sort of western *New Yorker*, with a faintly radical tinge to it." She reviewed classical music concerts and recordings, commented knowingly on national and international music news, and reported back about the avant-garde performances at the Denny-Watrous Gallery.

She also served as an occasional book critic at the *Pacific Weekly*, a role that seemed to contribute to her growing awareness about the state of the world beyond Carmel-by-the-Sea. A few years later, she would proudly confide to Charlie that she wrote book reviews for a "radical mag" under the alias Robin Howe. As Howe, Sidney reviewed *Waiting for Nothing* by Tom Kromer, a realistic, autobiographical novel about the hard life of a vagrant traveling west. She wrote, "The impact of this book is like nothing that has been written out of individual experience of the Depression. It is stark as a winter tree; no pathos, no plea, no art intervene between you and the facts of Kromer's experience." She included a warning of sorts for those who minimize or rationalize the painful effects of the Depression—perhaps

82   A CHANCE TO HARMONIZE

as she herself did: "If you have evolved anything resembling that cheering philosophy of the depression which tells you that hard times are good for us all, an asset to character, and that things were too easy and we needed some discipline, then let this book alone; you're much more comfortable as you are." In reflecting on this period later in her life, she said, "The Depression crept over the country slowly, and in California you didn't hear about it too much. But I began hearing things and decided I was having much too privileged a life."

On April 24, 1935—the same day the *Pacific Weekly* published Robin Howe's searing book review—Sidney put her escape plan in motion by writing to Helen Hall, the director of the Henry Street Settlement House in New York City, to ask for a job in their social music program. A little over a week later, Hall replied that Sidney was welcome at Henry Street for the summer and possibly longer, and Sidney soon prepared to head east. She very quickly made up her mind that driving herself across the country was an excellent idea. She assured her mother, "A transcontinental trip sounds wild but after all it is only the trip from Carmel to San Francisco multiplied 20 times in various ways." Leaving her cocker spaniel Sis, her orange cat Oliver, and the majority of her belongings in San Francisco with her mother, Sidney packed her car for the longest drive she had ever taken.

In 1935, a cross-country drive was not as easy an undertaking as it is on today's interstate highways—less than one-quarter of US roads were paved at all, and only 3 percent could have been considered "high quality." Still, in 1909 Alice Ramsey had shown it was possible when she became the first woman to drive from New York City to San Francisco, as a promotion for the Maxwell-Briscoe car company. Sidney had fond childhood memories of accompanying her father on business trips by car—she said he was rarely as severe with her on trips as he was at home, and she loved what she called "the perpetual emergencies of automobile travel," stopping to help others on the road and brainstorming quick fixes to their own car trouble. As a student at Stanford in the early 1920s, Sidney was given use of her family's Packard but said the car made her feel self-conscious, so she bought a 1914 Buick that she named Emmaline for driving herself and her college friends around. Later, she bought a Ford coupe that allowed her to travel the Bay Area as she pleased. As a single woman, owning her own car gave Sidney an independence that was available almost exclusively to the wealthy, since fewer than one in five Americans owned a car at the start of the 1930s. A car could mean freedom, for a woman who could afford one.

On June 15, 1935, Sidney set off from Carmel to New York City in her trusty Ford, with another young woman, a friend of a friend relocating to New York, as a passenger helping to pay for gas. Her regular postcards to her mother describe stops at the Grand Canyon and in Flagstaff. ("This is beautiful country. All goes smooth as glass & cheerful.") On July 3rd she wrote with humor about some minor car trouble in Wheeling, West Virginia: "This road goes more places we never suspected! Practically all the bolts in the car were loosened in Arizona over her corduroy washboard roads—so small bits of the car keep falling out. Nice mechanics work over it with a wrench for an hour or two & then say: 'Fifty cents, please.'" The next day, she wrote from Harrisburg, Pennsylvania, "We're 189 miles from N.Y.C.—a mere nothing to us!" She ended this last postcard with the same phrase she had used in one of her first, her admiration undimmed even after a long drive: "Such beautiful country." The adventure of a cross-country drive clearly suited Sidney. She later wrote that this road trip had been her first step toward shedding what she called her sentimental ties to Europe and acquiring, for the first time, "knowledge and delight in what it is to be American."

CHAPTER 7

WHAT ARE PEOPLE SINGING NOW?

T he recording machine finally arrived at the Special Skills office during the third week of May 1936—a huge brown case with a small handle on the side, called "portable" despite weighing in at around 150 pounds. When the latch was opened, the top cover swung up to reveal a turntable with a heavy silver stylus to cut the blank aluminum discs that came in a matching case, not quite as big or heavy as the machine itself but still stretching the idea of *portable*. After their lengthy bidding process, the RA purchasing department had approved a model designed by Walter C. Garwick, an electrical engineer who had created a similar machine for John Lomax a few years earlier, rather than going with a (likely more expensive) machine from the Presto Corporation, which had developed a lighter acetate disc and was rapidly becoming the industry standard for portable recorders.

A few days after the machine's long-awaited arrival, Sidney wrote to her mother with her own good news:

> Yesterday I got a letter from Seeger at Resettlement saying would I please come in at once. . . . When I arrived early and sat

down outside, the group around the corner hailed me cordially on in, & Seeger asked me whether I'd be willing to defer going out into the field until Sept. or so & work as his assistant in the meantime! Nothing would please me better, as I'll get trained in the process & will go out knowing exactly what is expected of me.

She added, "To my great delight, one of my jobs will be acquiring skill in managing the recording machine which is taken out into the field to record folksongs. Just think what sport!"

Much later, Sidney enjoyed telling the story of how the approval for this equipment had come all the way from the top:

> After repeated requests for a recording machine and repeated refusals for it from the budget director, who was understandably puzzled by the need of such a thing—or by anything to do with folksong at all, for people whose first need was money for food—Adrian Dornbush . . . took the problem to Mrs. Roosevelt, who spoke to her husband, and FDR then said to the budget director, "Oh, hell, let them have their recording machine!"

Eleanor Roosevelt certainly had a soft spot for anything related to the RA's homesteads, but she and the president also shared a special appreciation for folk music. In 1933, she signaled this interest publicly by attending the White Top Folk Festival in Virginia, where she said in a short speech, "Historically as well as esthetically, these folk songs, stories and dances are of value." Even this tepid statement represented a change from previous administrations, since the Roosevelts were perhaps the first White House occupants to show even the slightest interest in folk music. In addition to Eleanor's love of square dancing at Arthurdale, she said FDR was "particularly fond of American folk tunes," and he often invited string bands to Warm Springs. As Alan Lomax later told it, "He fell in love with all of the old fiddlers, and they used to get drunk together on moonshine, and he loved fiddle tunes." The Roosevelts brought folk music into the White House as well, with Eleanor dancing the Virginia reel and the president often serving as the caller at White House press parties.

This New Deal interest in folk culture went beyond the Roosevelts. Vice President John Garner and FDR's advisor Tommy Corcoran often entertained the president by playing traditional tunes together (Garner on fiddle, Corcoran on accordion). Other high-up members of the administration—including Tugwell and the Secretaries of the Interior (Harold Ickes), Agriculture (George Wallace), and the Treasury (Henry Morgenthau)—were all known to appreciate folk music, which "rang out at house parties all over Washington." Historians have taken note of how New Dealers embraced folk culture as a true representation of "the people," as well as of a documentary impulse that characterized American culture in the 1930s. All pointing toward a general inclination, to paraphrase FDR, to just letting the Music Unit have their recording machine, even if no one was entirely sure why.

When the recording machine arrived, Sidney said Charlie "hovered over it like a duck with one duckling," too enamored with his new toy to part with it. On June 2, 1936, Charlie held the Music Unit's first recording session—not out in the field, but in a makeshift recording studio in the Special Skills building. He assembled a reunion of sorts from Tom Benton's musical gatherings, bringing in Pollock and Steffen to play harmonica duets from their days in the Harmonica Rascals, their interconnected melodies fitting tightly together to create the sound of one collective accordion.

Charlie also invited a new friend to attend this first recording session: John Lomax, who came in and out of Washington as the (unpaid) honorary curator of the Archive of American Folk Song at the Library of Congress. Lomax was a generation older than Charlie, and the two men must have made a funny pair—tall, slender, and bespectacled Seeger next to Lomax, who had an image as a "big round bear of a man" given his bald head and girth, but at about 5 feet 10 would have seemed quite short in comparison. Sidney later said their backgrounds and political orientations seemed opposite as well, since Charlie was a "New England Connecticut aristocrat" and Lomax "a kind of Texas roughneck who wished he were a plantation owner." She thought Charlie tolerated Lomax's coarse racism and intolerance for tactical reasons typical in Washington, considering that the older man would be a powerful ally given his position at the Library of Congress and his national profile. Charlie may also have felt genuine admiration of Lomax as a pioneer of American folk song collecting, and the two men discovered that they had been at Harvard at the same time—Charlie as an undergraduate music student and Lomax doing graduate studies in folklore in the English department. Lomax's biographer also noted similarities in their temperaments, writing that "each held himself in high regard and had scant tolerance for fools." Now, having finally received the new recording equipment, Charlie had practical reasons for cultivating a friendship to learn from the more seasoned folk collector's expertise. The day before the Music Unit's inaugural recording session, he had accompanied Lomax on a collecting trip in Richmond, Virginia, for the Library of Congress, observing and practicing for his own venture into life as a public folklorist.

At that first session in the Special Skills building, Lomax sang a few songs and likely helped troubleshoot any technical issues with the machine, but neither he nor the Harmonica Rascals was the focus of the session. The main performer was Rebecca (or Becky) Tarwater, a pale young woman with long brown hair from Rockwood, Tennessee, who brought along her banjo and was joined by her younger sister Penelope (nicknamed Nippy). "We were hillbillies," Becky said later, "and in our family, everybody sang. . . . My grandmother taught me the most beautiful songs, like 'Bonnie Annie Laurie' and 'Barbara Allen.'" It isn't clear how they had found the Tarwaters, and Charlie left no detailed report or field notes describing how the session came to be or what transpired during it. Still, the recordings capture the moment. The two singers seem to have started with "Skip to My Lou," singing in the sweet, close harmony only sisters can achieve. But the recording levels were too high, distorting their voices, and some sort of technical glitch interrupts the melody toward the end. Luckily, the Garwick machine allowed for instant playback (using a lightweight needle made from an actual thorn rather than the heavy stylus), so it is easy to imagine the two sisters, Charlie, Lomax, Steffen, and Pollock gathering around to listen.

Charlie showed the most enthusiasm for Becky's singing of the famous Child ballad "Barbara Allen," creating a spoken introduction on a separate track as if in anticipation of sharing it with others later. His interest shows he hadn't entirely abandoned academic folklore's preference for ancient ballads, but he would later note that her version was "not, strictly speaking, typical of traditional country singing" but more like "what the average urban concert-goer would consider 'good singing.'" Overall, the Tarwaters' matching soprano and alto voices, both with a hint of vibrato, were clearly trained in a high-art Western classical tradition, and their recordings sound like polished concert performances, with coordinated changes in dynamics and tempo for maximum effect. Their sound is very different from the flinty, grittier timbre of most traditional Appalachian singers—what the members of the Composers' Collective had found so bewildering when they first heard Aunt Molly Jackson's singing.

If Becky Tarwater was a hillbilly, as she had said, then it was a kind of highborn hillbilly, similar to Tom Benton. It was the kind whose family owned factories and entire factory towns. They sent her to private school in Philadelphia and then to the King-Smith Studio School in Washington, DC, which taught music and dance but for many students functioned more as a finishing school, including instruction on how to set a table for a banquet. This school, where Becky studied and then taught for several years, had taken over four elegant houses next to one another just on the other side of Dupont Circle from the Special Skills office—perhaps an easy trip for the Tarwater sisters to take down New Hampshire Avenue for the recording session on that Tuesday in June. The recordings show that the assembled group clearly had fun playing music for each other, with Rebecca laughing after she took a banjo solo and the harmonica players joining in to accompany her singing of "My Horses Ain't Hungry." (Soon after this session, Charles Pollock's younger brother Jackson fell in love with Rebecca Tarwater after Steffen introduced them at a party, so that she—and the

Music Unit's first recording session—sometimes make a brief appearance in biographies of the famous artist.)

This first RA recording session was still early in Charlie's journey toward a full appreciation of folk music and its role in the lives of everyday people. At that point, he seemed most at ease within this urban-transplant, elite hillbilly culture that he had first encountered at Tom Benton's, among those who shared his wealthy background and appreciated folk music as a form of art, at a comfortable distance from its hardscrabble roots. A few weeks after this first session in Washington, he brought the recording equipment to Arthurdale for the community's annual music festival, but he recorded just three discs, "comprising some fair fiddling, mouth-harp, and one ensemble," he described succinctly in his report. "The singing," he concluded, "was not worth recording." But in her syndicated "My Day" column, Eleanor Roosevelt described her experience of the same festival's music competitions with a diplomatic appreciation for the role of music in the lives of the homesteaders. This was the purported focus of the RA's Music Unit, but Charlie was not yet inclined to value it above overall musical aesthetics. The First Lady wrote, "There were moments when I felt that volume and action represented the whole aim and object of some of the contestants, but on the whole, the spirit expressed to me by one of the judges was prevalent throughout. Said he: 'For thirty years I never missed a day of practicing on my fiddle. Life without music wouldn't be worthwhile.'"

Back in Washington, Sidney was adjusting to her new life as a New Dealer. By the end of June, she was still living with her friends in Lanham, Maryland—commuting three hours a day into Washington—and worrying she might be wearing out her welcome as a guest of now more than two months. Even though she had begun her new position immediately at the end of May, she wasn't yet on the RA payroll, agreeing to work on a volunteer basis. As she gushed to her mother, "The delay in getting me on the payroll is partly because this is a new job specially designed for me, ahem!!" But it was difficult to retain such enthusiasm as several weeks passed with no pay, and in Sidney's next letter home she asked her mother to look into selling the first edition of Lomax's *Cowboy Songs* that she had left among her things in San Francisco. When Sidney had met John Lomax, he had mentioned that it was out of print and could fetch $100. "I need new shoes very badly," she wrote. "Mr. Lomax would be tickled to think he'd got them for me!"

Sidney's gossipy letters home fill in the details of life beyond the office that are missing from the division's reports and official correspondence. She described her first day: "There is a swell gal in the office, Judith Tobey, who looks exactly like [the actress] Ruth Lee. . . . She & I took to each other very much. She's another sort of ass't to Seeger—I met about 20 people this p.m. & haven't got it all straight yet." On July 1, Sidney moved into a rambling farmhouse near Alexandria, Virginia, with new friends from the Special Skills staff, "all delightful people." Her housemates were Tobey and her six-year-old son Christopher, along with Whitney Atchley, a ceramicist who managed the Special Skills laboratory, and his wife and young daughter.

Sidney's first months in the office coincided with one of the busiest periods for Margaret at Cherry Lake, as she worked to put on the *New Wine* play on short notice. But even meeting briefly when Margaret was able to get back to Washington, the two women discovered they had much in common—both were in their thirties, divorced with no children, had classical music training and spent significant time in Europe, and came to DC after living in New York City. While Margaret left scant details about her personal life in her own letters and reports, Sidney's chatty letters to her mother shed some light on Margaret's central place within the Special Skills Division's social scene in Washington. On July 8, Sidney wrote from Margaret's apartment on K Street:

Margaret and I are giving a party tonight . . . to which Florence Kerr, Nina Collier (daughter-in-law of John Collier of Indian Bureau), and Leon Henderson, among other people are coming. Tomorrow night, ditto, with Antonia Brico and God he knows who all else: It's Tugwell's birthday and 6 birds are being killed with one stone. Margaret is of course meeting all the expense, as I am still checkless; I hope soon to be able to return her what I owe her. You will be amused to know that the plans for dinner tonight include a bust of Roosevelt which is at present in Aubrey Williams' office but is coming home at 4:30 today in the car wrapped in my sleeping bag. (Sounds like part of the menu but is only décor!)

The guest list for these parties shows that Special Skills staffers had joined a lively group of New Dealers involved in the WPA's arts and cultural programs—Kerr was a regional director of women's activities, Collier an early administrator of the Federal Art Project, and Brico an orchestra conductor working for the Federal Music Project. The group also included progressive New Deal leaders like Tugwell and Aubrey Williams, who had recently left his position as WPA deputy director to lead the National Youth Administration.

The day after this party, Sidney's work life would take an unexpected turn when John Lomax invited her to accompany him on a collecting trip to North Carolina. She sent her mother an urgent message asking her to send $25 right away, the telegram's typical capitalization and lack of punctuation seeming to convey the same breathless excitement as an all-caps text message today: "OPPORTUNITY TWO WEEKS TRIP CAROLINA MOUNTAINS WITH VETERAN FOLKSONG COLLECTOR EXPENSES PAID EXCEPT FOOD." In a letter to Lomax, Charlie specified the terms of her apprenticeship: "We have authorized her travel with the explicit understanding that she is to be engaged solely in acquiring valuable experience and training under your guidance in a delicate and complicated task. It is hoped that in return for this, she will be of real assistance to you."

Sidney confided to her mother that "the trip seemed *very* important to me because with the experience it will give me I shall be qualified to do far more interesting work here than otherwise" and admitted to already feeling some restless boredom in the office. "I am on the verge all the time of being set at a long-winded piece of bibliographic research work that I don't want to do—my particular skill being with people first & books second." She made plans to take a night train from Washington, DC, to Blowing Rock, North Carolina, on July 12, 1936, to join John Lomax, "my swell old Texan friend, who has collected folksongs all his life. He is 125% a comic & sentimental character—we get on in a funny joking fashion."

Lomax had been invited to North Carolina to accompany Duke University professor and well-known folklorist Frank C. Brown in collecting Anglo-Appalachian ballads sung by elderly residents living near his summer home in Blowing Rock, a quaint mountain town about ninety miles northwest of Asheville. The two men had known each other since the early days of the American Folklore Society in the 1910s, when Lomax served as president and asked Brown to form a North Carolina chapter. Back then, both collectors used a portable Ediphone wax cylinder recorder, but unlike Lomax, Brown continued to rely on this machine even as the technology became antiquated, replaced by instantaneous disc-cutting machines, with much better sound quality and disc-copying abilities. By the mid-1930s, Brown was undoubtedly curious about the newer technology and wanted to see it for himself. However, a tension over territory and control rippled beneath the surface even before Lomax arrived, as Brown remained intensely protective of his sources and his songs, and Lomax wanted to add the recordings to the Library of Congress's collection in his role as curator of its Archive of American Folk Song. Brown insisted that Lomax sign an agreement to seal these recordings in the Library of Congress for five years, ensuring that they would not be published or otherwise circulated among folklorists until Brown could lay claim to them in his own book. (Only after Sidney agreed to be bound by the same agreement did Brown allow her to come along.)

The two men may have viewed each other as leaders of opposing factions of folklorists. Professor Brown was ensconced in academia, following the traditional collecting methods laid out in the previous century, based on classifying texts and tunes. Lomax was a lone cowboy pioneering public folklore, focusing more on what would sell than on academic method-ologies. Brown was slimmer than Lomax and professorial in dress and demeanor, with short-cropped silver hair. He was usually dressed in a dark suit jacket and dress shoes, regardless of the terrain, and he was known to smoke a pipe while recording. Now in their late sixties, both men were used to being in control and having their own way, and Sidney's trip would be as much about navigating their egos as it was learning to operate the recording machine. In a note to a Special Skills colleague, Charlie remarked with mild admiration that Sidney's experience with the two collectors "reveals a flair for diplomacy."

One can imagine that these men—both born in the previous century—didn't quite know what to do with a woman like Sidney. As Sidney described in her report, "Once Mr. Lomax recovered from the notion that a woman is a fragile thing, to be waited on hand and foot, I was able to relieve him with the driving and recording and lugging odds and ends about, recharging batteries, etc." Lomax also appeared to misunderstand their business relationship, making a few awkward romantic passes at her in their off time in Blowing Rock. Sidney easily deflected his advances, but about a week into their trip she asked Charlie to send a telegram urging her back to the office that she could present as an excuse to leave if she wasn't able to "manage the gent without offense." As for Dr. Brown, he could only view Sidney as filling the traditional role of secretary, taking notes for him and driving into the village several times a day to bring him a cold Coca Cola from the tobacco shop icebox.

In addition to learning how to operate the recording equipment and navigate "the rough-and-tumble of folksong collecting under the wing of a veteran in the field," Sidney saw it as equally important "to get training and experience in contacts with what I had been led to believe were difficult and strange folk: the mountain people." But upon meeting the people who lived in these North Carolina mountains, she found that their "social grace is as perfect as anything I have ever seen" and noted, "I felt almost everyone spoke his or her mind to me freely." Still, she found it important to distance herself from her identity as an urban Yankee. "I was several times glad I had left my cigarette case and lipstick at home! and that I could claim a parent from Louisiana and residence in Old Virginia. It all helped." Sidney's strategies to mask her identity underscores a fundamental issue for the Music Unit: attempting to bridge the cultural divides along class and urban/rural lines between many of its staffers in Washington and the people on the southern RA homesteads that they were meant to serve.

Sidney loved to enliven her reports with anecdotes and details about the people she met, told with affection but sometimes leaning uncomfortably close to making fun. She was amused when the husband of an elderly ballad singer appeared to be on a first-name basis with President Roosevelt, underlining his comment, *"Franklin is certainly doin' the best he could!"* But she also found much to appreciate. In the town of Silvertone, they recorded Mrs. Leander Wilson, who said she was seventy-five but seemed much older, her voice weakened by a chest ailment that was unfortunately quite common among the older singers they encountered. As Sidney wrote to a friend, "Her singing was extremely introverted and quiet, and very beautiful. . . . I wanted her to repeat her songs again and again." Later, Sidney described how she drove Mr. O. L. Coffey, a man in his fifties known throughout the area as a talented banjo player, from his home in the tiny town of Shull's Mills to Blowing Rock for a recording session, since his wife disapproved of him playing at home. "Good banjo picking on a 5-string banjo is one of the briskest, danciest kinds of music I ever heard," she wrote that night, "and we had such a gay and lively evening that I now can't sleep for the noisy tunes running through my head and am sitting up writing you despite the imminence of tomorrow's daylight start." She ended reflecting on the gorgeous scenery: "I wish you could see the view that will be spread out below my room when I get up in the morning—row on row of deep blue peaks, receding south and deeply cleft just below me."

Sidney reported happily that Lomax eventually "made every effort to divorce himself from the machinery so I could have a shot at it." After nearly a week of ballads, Lomax brought Sidney along on a side trip to collect songs from the Black prisoners at a segregated state prison camp about ten miles north in Boone, North Carolina. Both Brown and Lomax subscribed to the traditional notion that folk music could exist only in isolated areas, which for Brown meant the physical isolation of the mountains. But for Lomax, it was the state-sanctioned isolation imposed at segregated prison camps, one of the most nefarious institutions in the Jim Crow South, where he said he could find songs "in their near purity among the most completely isolated Negro convicts."

Their travels through the Carolina mountains appeared to delineate the segregated Jim Crow South along both geographical and musical lines. Brown's balladeers not only sang songs rooted in the so-called pure Anglo-derived folk tradition, but they lived in all-White towns, with one White resident of tiny Estatoe, North Carolina, proudly telling the collectors a chilling story of the violent removal of Black residents by freight car—all except the two Black families who owned their land. At Boone, Sidney found evidence of racial violence appearing as an "incontrovertible fact . . . written out on the blackboard behind a glass door." Referring to whippings administered the day before, the board read "Stripes, 39, Friday the 17th." Later, she said she felt appalled by Lomax's domineering, patronizing treatment of the men at Boone, where he seemed to enjoy the role of "the big White man." She was incredulous at how Lomax "rather ostentatiously" gave the captain eighty cents to distribute among the nearly twenty singers they had recorded: "Four cents per man?"

On the surface, the work songs, blues, and spirituals sung by these men were quite different from Dr. Brown's Child ballads, but even in a Black prison camp that violently upheld Jim Crow segregation, a complete segregation of sound proved impossible. Sidney made special note that one of these spirituals, "Brother Are You Ready?" was classified as "an old white camp-meeting song" in the *Sacred Harp* by George Pullen Jackson and also included in Nathaniel Dett's *Religious Folksongs of the Negro*.

Of course, these spaces were also segregated by gender, with Dr. Brown tending to visit many older women thought to be the keepers of traditional ballads, while the prison camp was defined by masculinity. When Lomax asked whether he could bring Sidney along, the captain of the camp said, "If you're going to bring a lady don't come until after three o'clock so I can make everybody take a bath." Sidney found this amusing but did not seem particularly alarmed, as she had always been comfortable in the world of men, perhaps foreshadowed by her traditionally male given name of Sidney William. At sixteen, she chose to leave Castilleja, an all-girls boarding school, to study engineering at San Francisco's Polytechnic High School, where most of her classmates were boys (though she soon shed her engineering ambitions and wrote for the school's literary magazine and newspaper instead). When she was at Stanford, admissions restrictions capped the number of female students at five hundred, resulting in a ratio of roughly four men to every woman. Reflecting on her comfort in the male sphere later, she said her interest in the recording equipment and her ease in discussing it with men meant she was "sometimes included in conversations with small male groups in ways that women in those days were not." Still, among the prisoners at Boone, Sidney was careful not to make eye contact, knowing how dangerous the presence of a White woman could be for Black men in the Jim Crow South.

Sidney and Lomax returned to Blowing Rock and another week of ballad hunting with Dr. Brown, from which she took away several practical lessons about collecting. "I came to the conclusion that the collector's visit to make records should be a social occasion, never a business one," she wrote. "All the social amenities should apply with particular force. In general, I think it is best to avoid any suggestion of being in a hurry; and anything like a crispt [sic] businesslike manner smacks of the city and will defeat one's end. Dr. Brown always called to make an appointment a few days ahead of time no matter how arduous the trip, and I feel this should be the invariable rule." She approved of Dr. Brown's method of paying musicians by discreetly tucking a dollar in their hands on his way out (unless another amount had been worked out), and Lomax told her to expect collecting to take an average of about one record per hour (allowing time for driving and chatting).

But much of what Sidney learned on the trip seems to have been by negative example, especially in terms of how to treat people. On several occasions, she took note of how the collector's behavior affected the musicians. She quoted Mrs. Burkett, who was clearly annoyed when Dr. Brown insisted she sing a song that she had told him she didn't know: "You goin' to get me into a *snap* here in a minute such as I won't sing more fer yo' a-tall."

WHAT ARE PEOPLE SINGING NOW?

She noted that the banjo player Mr. Coffey "resented the over-long session Dr. Brown insisted on, . . . although he was too well-mannered to be rude."

She thought more attention needed to be paid to a musician as a human being, not simply a carrier of songs. "The collector is after all in the position of one making a favor, and he should be alert to the fatigue of singer and player and return another day if necessary," she wrote. "Nothing worthwhile ever came our way when insistence had passed the bounds of good manners. At this point music-making becomes a business and the collector has defeated what should be his primary aim: the continuance of a live folksong tradition." For Sidney, the interaction between collector and musician should never be merely transactional: "While music is being recorded I felt that the collector should listen and enjoy it to the full, and avoid fiddling unnecessarily with his gadgets. In one way or another he *must* manage to seem to participate in the performance, not only to profit from it—if only by sharing the feeling of the performer about the music." She continued, "The collector should definitely take on the responsibility of preserving the love of music-making for its own sake. He can do this if he will see to it that he doesn't so cut himself off from the performance as to become 'audience'—someone observing something from the outside which is of no real importance to himself." Sidney's view of the collector as a participant in a musical experience certainly fit in with the RA's focus on the collective, as well as the Music Unit's interest in the social use of music.

In many ways, this trip helped Sidney clarify her understanding of the Music Unit's goals in collecting folk music. Their interest in the social *use* of music set them apart from Lomax and Brown, who may have differed in their approaches but were both focused on capturing and classifying remnants of a static history rather than on the role of music in contemporary life as something to be practiced, performed, and shared within one's community. As she wrote in her report: "Dr. Brown's classifications of 'folksongs' doesn't give us the faintest hint along the lines that are important to us: What are people singing now? What are people singing most? Where is the live current, as contrasted with the antiquarian one? . . . His whole contact with contemporary life is that of a man with his head over his shoulder toward the imagined perfections of the past."

Sidney got a bit worked up thinking about the importance of the Music Unit's work in framing folk music as a living tradition that held value in and of itself, concluding in a poetic tone not usually associated with government reports: "And here we are," she declared, "struggling to make our way into the main current of contemporary culture, which we conceive as dynamic and alive, drawing its force from a thousand tributaries which flow forward with a perpetual meeting of the waters, in the future!"

CHAPTER 8

LOOK DOWN THAT LONESOME ROAD

The end of Sidney's adventures with Lomax and Brown coincided with Margaret's triumphant production of *New Wine* at Cherry Lake, an event that served as a turning point for the community. The performance had been just one part of the dedication ceremony marking the long-delayed completion of the community building and the groundbreaking for the project's school building. In essence, it served as a celebration of the community itself, a sort of bookend to the inaugural event where Julius Stone and Governor Sholtz had spoken nearly two years earlier. But rather than that makeshift stage of a plank set atop an unfinished house's foundation, this ceremony took place in the soaring new community hall, its auditorium now complete with two dressing rooms equipped with makeup tables and bathrooms. WPA administrator Lawrence Westbrook traveled down from Washington to address the audience of nearly one thousand, including homesteaders joined by residents from nearby Madison, Quinman, and Valdosta. "Ideas used in such projects as Cherry Lake will in the future affect millions of people for a long, long time," he told the crowd. It was a model community, one of the country's "most outstanding social experiment laboratories," that was now moving from its construction phase to its operation phase, to be built on cooperative industries.

This day also marked Margaret's last at Cherry Lake, and the beginning of a new phase of work for the entire Music Unit. Charlie had written to her a month earlier, brimming with pride: "I cannot tell you what pleasure you have given both Ruth and me by the splendid way you have done the very difficult job. Of course, the whole division admires you, but since you were my appointee it is an awfully nice thing for me too." He concluded with a message strikingly similar to Westbrook's praise for the entire community: "Your work at Cherry Lake is a model of what can and should be done." In fact, her achievements at Cherry Lake became Charlie's new definition of success. He wrote in a manual created for the WPA that the main goal for any government music program was "development of the community to the point where it produces its own leaders and makes its own music expressing its own life and aspirations as a community."

Margaret's success inspired Charlie to rethink the Music Unit's structure. After she had been on the job for just three months, Charlie began hatching a plan to shift her to a regional role, and by May, he was determined to move forward. "While it is probably too much to assume that you have made yourself completely unnecessary at Cherry Lake," he wrote her, it seemed clear that her music program had "come of age." The orchestra managed their own bookings and finances and had taken charge of Amateur Night events. The music and drama committees had elected officers and were planning their own activities. Charlie advised, "If you can begin to taper off your actual direction of the work and retain a more supervisory attitude, the way will be all the clearer for the regional work which we expect to put you in by July 1."

Though somewhat surprising given the usual delays in government timelines, by the end of June, it had been decided. Cherry Lake would soon no longer be Margaret's "official station," although she could make shorter-term trips there as part of her new regional role. She was told to make arrangements for a permanent move back to her Washington apartment and to be prepared to leave Florida within the next ten days. Vander

Schouw was predictably crushed at this news. "It is with extreme regret that we must accept your new arrangement regarding the assignment of Miss Margaret Valiant," he wrote to Dornbush as soon as he heard. "She has done a most excellent piece of work and, although we feel sure that she will be of great value in your general program, we feel that our loss here will be very great." He ended with perhaps as vociferous a plea as the language of a government bureaucrat would allow: "If it is possible for you to revise your plans so that she can remain with us for a longer period, it will be greatly appreciated."

Vander Schouw got his wish for a slight delay, as the date for the dedication ceremony was postponed a few weeks and she agreed to stay on to produce her final play on July 22. The next day was her final day at Cherry Lake, the stultifying heat perhaps wiping out the memory of the freezing rain that had fallen when she had arrived—before all the homes were finished, before capital-C Community was alive. She left no record of her own feelings or any account of what must have been heartfelt goodbyes, hints of which can be found only in a letter from the Cherry Lake Community Players to Tugwell, expressing "our deep appreciation for the services and associations of Miss Valiant" and a sincere hope "that Miss Valiant can be with us much in the future." On July 23, she left Cherry Lake unsure when she would return, but she had one important stop to make before unpacking at her apartment on K Street.

The idea had come to Charlie months earlier. "There is a Folk Festival of Music in Ashville [*sic*], N.C., July 23, 24, and 25," he wrote to Margaret. "I am hoping that a number of the Staff Representatives in Music can meet us there for what may be a very profitable couple of days." Charlie had met the festival's founder, Bascom Lamar Lunsford, in March, when he stopped in Asheville on his way south from Tygart Valley Homesteads in West Virginia to Warm Springs in Georgia. In a confidential report to Dornbush, Charlie seemed almost breathless in describing Lunsford. "He is, personally, the finest kind of man," he gushed, "and excellent company." An "outstanding singer of traditional songs" and "a pretty fair banjo picker," Lunsford was also the son of a professor, a Rutherford College graduate, and a practicing lawyer. In Lunsford, Charlie had found another "highborn hillbilly" with whom he felt comfortable, one who could also serve as a powerful ally for the Music Unit. Lunsford could name the precise number of songs he sang (315) and had collected lyrics for about three thousand folk songs, priding himself on remembering the tunes by heart. Columbia University had already made recordings of all of his songs, and the success of his Mountain Folk Festival had made him a well-respected figure in folk music circles, with his Asheville festival serving as the model for the first National Folk Festival in 1934. Charlie left his visit with Lunsford brimming with ideas about how to bring him into the Music Unit: "His assistance upon the song-book project will be invaluable," and he could "get the traditional music going" on the homesteads. Lunsford told Charlie that he would give them access to all of his recordings and collected songs if they brought him on to work for the RA. So Charlie likely hoped that a field trip to the Asheville festival would have a number of benefits for his staff, deepening their perspectives on the region's music and helping them to feel more like a cohesive unit—but it would also help to cement this important connection.

For Charlie, Asheville would be more than a business trip. He and Ruth had both hoped that she could join him on his work field trips, but she couldn't escape the demands of domestic life. In addition to taking care of two-year-old Mike and baby Peggy, in April she oversaw the family's move from the outskirts of town in Virginia to a small house on P Street in Georgetown, just across the river from both the Special Skills office and Margaret's apartment. It was a frustrating time for Ruth, who needed to abandon her own composition practice and stay on the sidelines as Charlie delved into this new musical world. In one of many letters the two exchanged during Charlie's spring field trip, Ruth wrote, "Your letters don't make me sad, they make me mad—not at you, but on account of the missed experiences (together) to which I looked forward so long." The Seegers were both determined to take the July trip to Asheville together. They found child care for Mike and Peggy, and in a moment that would later become steeped in the origin story of the folk revival, Charlie invited his seventeen-year-old son Pete to join them. Pete was home for summer break, planning to attend Harvard in the fall. He had played the four-string banjo in his school jazz band ("clunk, clunk, clunk," he later described it, following the chords on the sheet music), but he couldn't figure out the banjo parts he heard on the Seegers' growing collection of folk music recordings. In folk revival lore, this story usually omits the presence of Ruth and the context of Charlie's business trip, as Pete Seeger's biographer describes it: "Charles suggested they talk it over with banjo picker Bascom Lunsford in North Carolina. A few weeks later, father and son packed up their big blue Chevy and drove south."

The Music Unit staff looked very different in July than it did when Charlie had first conceived of the idea of an Asheville staff trip back in May. Of all the original field representatives assigned to particular homesteads, only Margaret and Kirk remained. Perhaps not surprisingly, Simmons was the first to go. Charlie's visit to Westmoreland to deliver the news had him thinking about the Great War, despite the idyllic green countryside. "Mr. Simmons leaves his community *'spurlos verenkt,'*" he wrote, German for "sunk without a trace," a term made infamous by Germany's vicious U-boat campaign, which destroyed all remnants of a ship and its crew. "I could find no trace of any regrets on his part or anyone else's. He has left absolutely no music activity to carry on after him." Van Rhyn at Tygart Valley and Wallace at Warm Springs were also dismissed, having similarly left no mark on their communities. Haufrecht had been the only one of the unit's representatives to engage in Charlie's original idea of musical engineering, composing a set of songs for children inspired by the music he heard at Red House Farms. But Charlie's ideas about what constituted success had shifted—from musical engineering to sowing the seeds for a grassroots program that came from the homesteaders themselves—and Haufrecht was not included in the Music Unit's reorganized structure.

On July 23, the first day of the festival, Special Skills staffers descended on Asheville from all directions. Sidney drove west from a tiny mill town north of Charlotte, where she and John Lomax had accompanied Dr. Brown for the last recording session of their trip. Margaret and Steffen came north together from Cherry Lake. Kirk made the trip due east from Cumberland Homesteads in Tennessee, across the mountain plateau and the Great Smoky Mountains. They were joined by a small crew from the Special Skills office in Washington: Dornbush, Tobey, and Hampton, along with a few staffers from other units. Pete Seeger later remembered that first drive to Asheville with Ruth and Charlie feeling like "visiting a foreign country. We wound down through the narrow valleys with so many turns in the road that I got seasick. We passed wretched little cabins with half-naked children peering out the door; we passed exhibits of patchwork quilts and other handicrafts which often were the main source of income."

At the same time, musicians from mountain towns across the Appalachians were making their way to the same spot: McCormick Field, usually used for baseball, was transformed for the festival with a wide stage and an enormous canvas roof, its stands large enough to hold an audience of about five thousand people. As Lunsford's daughter Nelle described the scene, "The performers came for three days, some from over 100 miles, sometimes in trucks converted into living quarters. They cooked meals over open fires at the edge of the ball park, and endured many discomforts, but they held the riches that Dad had discovered." Lunsford had one major blind spot in his so-called discoveries, neglecting to invite any Black Appalachian musicians to his festival. This was an omission that simultaneously upheld the physical segregation of the Jim Crow South and the false musical color line that positioned Appalachian music as pure White, despite the generations of talented Black musicians, the African American roots of many traditional songs performed by both White and Black musicians, and the African roots of the five-string banjo itself.

A handbill for that year's event—the Ninth Annual Mountain Dance Contest and Mountain Music Festival—boasted of four hundred participants, with more than one hundred folk musicians along with the twelve dance teams and twelve mountain bands competing for championship prizes awarded on the final night. "They could sing, fiddle, pick the banjos, and guitars, etc., with traditional 'grace' and style found nowhere else but

BETTER LAND
for
BETTER LIVING

RESETTLEMENT ADMINISTRATION
WASHINGTON, D. C.

THE WORK OF
RESETTLEMENT

RESETTLEMENT ADMINISTRATION
WASHINGTON, D. C.

esettlement Administration brochures. *Franklin D. Roosevelt Presidential Library, Henry Morgenthau Papers. Courtesy: National Archives and Records Administration.*

Rexford G. Tugwell, administrator, Resettlement Administration. *Library of Congress, Prints & Photographs Division, FSA/OWI Collection.*

Grace E. Falke, executive assistant. *Library of Congress, Prints & Photographs Division, FSA/ OWI Collection.*

Adrian Dornbush (right, holding chair) with staffer in the Special Skills Division's furniture design studio. Photograph by Harris & Ewing. *Library of Congress, Prints & Photographs Division.*

Charles Louis Seeger. Photograph by Harris & Ewing. *Library of Congress, Prints & Photographs Division.*

Margaret Valiant, c. 1924. *Margaret Valiant Collection, Manuscripts Division, Archives and Special Collections, Mississippi State University Libraries.*

Sidney Robertson, c. 1929. *Library of Congress, Music Division,*
Sidney Robertson Cowell Collection.

ABOVE: Residence at the Cherry Lake Rural Rehabilitation Community, Cherry Lake, Florida, 193⁵ *State Archives of Florida, Florida Memory.* BELOW: Margaret Valiant (behind children at right) on stag with the cast of her play, *New Wine*, Cherry Lake, Florida, 1936. "Red" Stevens with accordion left. *State Archives of Florida, Florida Memory.*

Form RA-KL 3
10-30-35

RESETTLEMENT ADMINISTRATION

Special Skills Division

DAILY WORK REPORT

To be filled out daily,
and submitted to Section
Chief each Wednesday for
transmission to Director.

Margaret Valiant
Name
Special Skills
Section
Wednesday **Saturday 1/25/36**
Week ending

Sunday afternoon was spent organizing the Dramatic group. Monday morning

with the second, third and fourth grades. Monday afternoon I called pers-

onally on five people whose names were given me as likely material for mus-

ical and dramatic efforts. Tuesday morning was spent with the first grade

rehearsing them for an Assembly program. Tuesday afternoon the eighth grade

was separated into groups of those who play instruments and read music and

those who play instruments and read music and those who do not , and instruc-

ted accordingly.

Played for Assembly Wednesday morning in the interests of musical appreciation

and conducted a song. Afterward rehearsed the first grade. Attended a meeting

of the Board of Governors in the evening, at which I was presented, and talked

over ideas for a music programme. Thursday had the sixth and seventh grades.

Thursday afternoon I called on more "prospects" with the idea of enlisting

them in adult activities. Thursday evening I met the music and dramatic

groups and outlined a first performance based on Project life, which they

approved. The "Music for Everyone" programme was also submitted for critic-

ism and was approved by the committee and will be mimeographed and sent to

all homesteaders. Friday had the 3rd., 4th. and 6th. grades and at 3 P. M.

the High School students. Friday afternoon I called on homesteaders interested

in music. Saturday went with Mr. Loomis and other teachers to P. K. Yonge

Laboratory School.

Daily work report, January 25, 1936. *Margaret Valiant Collection, Manuscripts Division, Archives and Special Collections, Mississippi State University Libraries.*

ABOVE: Residence at Cumberland Homesteads, Crossville, Tennessee. Photograph by Carl Mydans, March 1936. *Library of Congress, Prints & Photographs Division, FSA/OWI Collection.* BELOW: Dancers taught by Music Unit representative Leonard Kirk. Cumberland Homesteads, Crossville, Tennessee. Photograph by Ben Shahn, 1937. *Library of Congress, Prints & Photographs Division, FSA/OWI Collection.*

ABOVE: View of Westmoreland Homesteads, Pennsylvania. Photograph by Arthur Rothstein, September 1936. *Library of Congress, Prints & Photographs Division, FSA/OWI Collection.* BELOW: Sign near Penderlea Homestead, North Carolina. Photograph by Ben Shahn, 1937. *Library of Congress, Prints & Photographs Division, FSA/OWI Collection.*

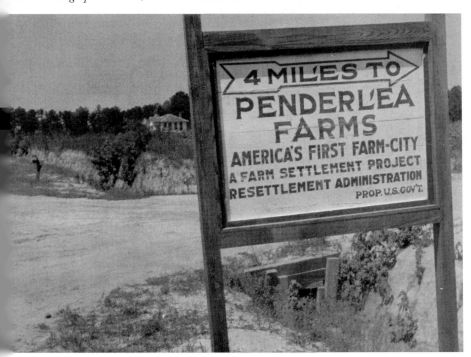

LEFT: Emma Dusenbury and her daughter Ora at their cabin door near Mena, Arkansas. Photograph by Sidney Robertson, December 1936. *Library of Congress, Music Division, Sidney Robertson Cowell Collection.* BELOW: Denoon family, Springfield, Missouri. Photograph by Sidney Robertson, December 1936. *Library of Congress, Music Division, Sidney Robertson Cowell Collection.*

In his "American Songbag", Carl Sandburg says that he heard fragments of this song in Illinois in the early 1890's. "S.K. Barlow," he says, "a Galesburg milkman, who used to be a fiddler at dances near Galva, sang it for me as we washed eight and two gallon delivery cans and quart-measure cups on winter afternoons. W.W. Delaney said, 'As near as I can remember, that song came out in the 1860's, just after the war.'"

This is number

1

in a series
of American songs
rarely found in popular collections

Additional verses to this song
will be welcomed, as will be also
suggestions for future issues of the series.

the FARMER comes to town

THE FARMER

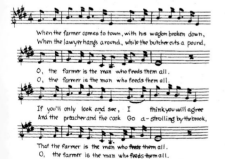

When the farmer comes to town, with his wagon broken down,
When the lawyer hangs around, while the butcher cuts a pound,

O, the farmer is the man who feeds them all.
O, the farmer is the man who feeds them all.

If you'll only look and see, I think you will agree
And the preacher and the cook Go a-strolling by the brook,

That the farmer is the man who feeds them all.
O, the farmer is the man who feeds them all.

The farmer is the man, The farmer is the man,
The farmer is the man, The farmer is the man,

Lives on credit 'til the fall;
Lives on credit 'til the fall;

Then they take him by the hand and they lead him from the land,
With the int'rest rate so high, It's a wonder he don't die,

And the middle-man's the man who gets it all,
For the mortgage-man's the man who gets it all.

When the banker says he's broke And the merchant's up in smoke,
They forget that it's the farmer feeds them all.
It would put them to the test If the farmer took a rest,
Then they'd know that it's the farmer feeds them all.

The farmer is the man, The farmer is the man,
Lives on credit 'til the fall;
And his pants are wearing thin, His condition it's a sin,
He's forgot that he's the man who feeds them all.

Song-sheet covers and interior pages, "The Farmer Comes to Town," 1936. Cover art and hand-lettering by Charles Pollock; music notated by Charles Seeger. *Library of Congress, Music Division, Sidney Robertson Cowell Collection.*

Song-sheet cover, "Cooperation Is Our Aim," 1936. *Library of Congress, Music Division, Sidney Robertson Cowell Collection.*

Song-sheet cover, "We Ain't Down Yet," 1936. *Library of Congress, Music Division, Sidney Robertson Cowell Collection.*

DOWN *in the* VALLEY

This song is also widely known as "Birmingham Jail"; but the names of other cities are found in its stead, with, of course, a countless variety of verses: as "Barbourville Jail", in Kentucky; "Powder Mill Jail", in Tennessee, etc. Upon the San Francisco bridge, in 1935, it was sung as "We're building bridges, bridges so low; Hang yourself over, feel the wind blow". Then there are the verses called "Little Willie":

> Tree on the mountain, tree in full bloom;
> Oh Willie my darling, I've loved you too soon.
> Your parents dont like me, so well do I know;
> They say I'm not worthy to knock at your door.

This is number

5

of a series
of American songs
to supplement popular collections

Additional verses to this song
will be welcomed, as will be also
suggestions for future issues of the series

Song-sheet front and back cover, "Down in the Valley," 1936. "Powder Mill Jail" refers to a set of protest lyrics sung by striking mill workers. *Library of Congress, Music Division, Sidney Robertson Cowell Collection.*

The
DODGER

Song-sheet cover, "The Dodger," 1936. *Library of Congress, Music Division, Sidney Robertson Cowell Collection.*

WAYFARING STRANGER

1. I'm just a poor wayfaring stranger, a-travelling thru this world of woe;
2. I'm just a poor wayfaring stranger, a-travelling thru this world of woe;

But there's no sickness, toil nor danger in that bright world to which I go.
But there's no sickness, toil nor danger in that bright world to which I go.

I'm going there to see my father, I'm going there no more to roam,
I'm going there to see my mother, I'm going there no more to roam,

I'm just a—going over Jordan, I'm just a-going over home.
I'm just a—going over Jordan, I'm just a-going over home.

L. L. McDowell, of Smithville, Tennessee, says that this is the tune and verse sung by the old settlers of DeKalb County, Tennessee. Additional stanzas were made by changing the words "father" and "mother" to "brother", "sister", etc.

The following modern verses from Virginia and Florida respectively have been received:

Our fathers dear fought for our liberty,
Across the ocean they did roam,
They suffered pain and many hardships,
For in this land to build a home.

We've lived here many generations,
And many dear ones here have died,
But still our lives are filled with trouble,
In vain a helping hand we've cried.

I'm just a poor and lonesome traveller,
Behind a mule that's powerful slow,
A-creaking on to debt and worry,
The only place that I can go.

My father lived and died a farmer,
A-reaping less than he did sow;
And now I travel in his footsteps,
A-knowing less than he did know.

Song-sheet interior pages, "Wayfaring Stranger," 1936. The first two stanzas of the addition verses were written by Charles Seeger, the third and fourth stanzas by Margaret Valiant. *Library Congress, Music Division, Sidney Robertson Cowell Collection.*

deep in the mountains," Nelle said later in an interview. "I can still hear those haunting melodies drifting out over the ball park."

Presiding over it all was Lunsford, dressed in his signature linen suit and tie, his shoes polished, his receding salt-and-pepper hair neatly brushed back. He was "a very good showman," Pete said later, recounting the scene onstage in detail: As one band performed under a spotlight stage right, Lunsford would quickly bring in the next band to gather around a mic on the darkened stage left. When the performing band finished, he would reenter the spotlight and lead the audience in applause with an announcement like, "Give a hand to the Coon Creek Boys, and aren't they wonderful?" Then he would walk the thirty feet to the opposite side of the stage, the spotlight following him, and introduce the next band, so the show would move seamlessly between acts, from one side of the stage to the other. Among the featured performers that first night was Aunt Samantha Bumgarner, a well-known musician from the Tennessee mountains who appeared at the festival every year. For Pete, Bumgarner's performance on the five-string banjo was a revelation, opening his eyes (and soul) to a new musical world. And the festival was a conversion experience: "I discovered there was some good music in my country which I never heard on the radio," he said later. "I liked the strident vocal tone of the singers, the vigorous dancing. The words of the songs had all the meat of life in them."

But for Sidney, the main event didn't happen in Lunsford's spotlight onstage. Instead, she was transfixed by Walter C. Garwick, the man who had designed the Music Unit's recording equipment, who sat behind his machine connected to a dedicated microphone onstage, recording the entire festival for the Columbia University Library. As she and Charlie sat next to him and watched him work, she was pleased when he "very amiably taught us what he could as he went along," concluding "he is by far the most skillful collector I have observed." Unlike young Pete, Sidney seemed somewhat less moved by the music than she was by this technology, cataloguing it in a matter-of-fact way in her report: "We saw 3 dance teams, 2 old-time fiddlers, 2 good banjo pickers, some rather bad children's singing and a good deal of sentimental singing by 2, 3 and 4 people, accompanying themselves on fiddle, banjo and guitar."

Festival events began each evening "long about sundown," as Lunsford liked to put it, a relaxed schedule that gave Sidney a much-needed break after her adventures with Lomax and Brown. In her report of that week's activities, she typed simply, "Friday Morning: 7/24/36. S L E E P !" That evening showcased five more dance teams and string bands in the competition, including the previous year's champions: the Limestone Dance Team from just south of Asheville and the Smoky Mountain String Band. Sidney could feel the energy building over the course of the festival, noting on the second night "a little more gayety and tension, and livelier participation by the crowd, which was larger than the night before, filling the bleachers and crowding around back of the platform."

Though she called Saturday night the "last and climactic evening" of the festival, by that final evening Sidney's attention seemed to have turned more toward her colleagues, who so rarely had a chance to be in the same place at once. With uncharacteristic brevity, she left no descriptions of the final night of music and dancing onstage or the revelry in the crowd. Instead, she wrote, "Much interesting talk afterwards with the Special Skillets gathered from the seven corners of the mountains," coining the collective nickname for her colleagues that she would continue to use in her correspondence. Their time together ended on Sunday afternoon, gathered in a cabin Charlie had found outside of town that had served as their home base during the festival. Margaret gave a reading of her play, *New Wine*, "reducing us all to tears," Sidney wrote. "I feel it cannot be said often enough how lucky Special Skills is to have her."

On Sunday night, the Special Skillets returned to their respective corners of the mountains. Sidney joined Margaret and a few others on a train back to Washington. Pete rode in the back seat of Charlie and Ruth's car, next to his first five-string banjo—lent to him by Lunsford, who had also given him a few lessons during daytime breaks in the festivities. Kirk headed on his own back to Cumberland Homesteads, the only one of the Music

Unit's original representatives who would continue to be based in one RA community.

Hampton drove due north, from the Blue Ridge Mountains to West Virginia's Allegheny Plateau, where he would begin a very different assignment. Up until that point, he had been the Music Unit's main song hunter. Based in Tennessee to capitalize on his contacts from the Highlander School, his main task had been to find union protest songs and other material suitable for the unit's song-sheet project, notating the melodies and taking down the words as they were sung, as well as identifying any promising musicians that music staffers should record on a later visit. In June, he had traveled to Roane County, where Highlander had been helping striking workers at a hosiery mill since April. His visit happened at the same time as a police crackdown on the strike, as he described in his report to Charlie:

> Thursday I went to Rockwood and Kingston trying to gather the songs of those workers. I stopped in Kingston to visit some of the girls in the jail. The sheriff wouldn't leave me alone with them so that I could really talk to them, so I gave that up. I went to Rockwood and talked to several of the people there. They were all so busy trying to get the bonds signed so they could release the strikers in jail. Twenty-four had been arrested the first of the week. I couldn't get anyone settled enough to talk to them about their songs. I did learn that the songs they sang were songs from the song books of Brookwood Labor School, and they had made up words to suit their own situation, and sang them on the picket line. Several reported that it was their singing that was responsible for their arrest.

Given this fraught climate, Hampton found it much easier to collect folk songs unrelated to union organizing. Just outside Crossville, the closest town to Cumberland Homesteads, he visited the Hughes family, who were known for playing local dances in the area. "After a great deal of taxiing around I finally got all the family rounded up at Granddad's house," he wrote. "Granddad has been 65 years old for his last ten birthdays, according to one granddaughter." When he was eighteen, Granddad had made a left-handed five-string banjo for himself, and he later made a right-handed one for his son. Now they played together with a neighbor on fiddle and four grandchildren picking guitar and singing. Hampton arrived after dinner and stayed until 11 P.M., with "someone playing or singing all the time." He heartily recommended that Charlie add them to the list of musicians to record, along with L. L. McDowell, an older gentleman whom he found "after miles of terrible back country roads" in Smithville, about fifty miles west of Crossville. McDowell had previously worked as a county school superintendent but since retirement had turned to folk music collecting. He sang "Wayfaring Stranger" for Hampton, one of many spirituals sung by White Southerners that were learned by ear and hadn't been published in books.

It was draining work. "Have been working from early to late the last of this week," he admitted in his report, "and when I do get to a bed I'm usually ready to drop right in it." A few weeks later, he described a somewhat fruitless trip to LaFollette, a small town near the Indiana border. "I had heard a rumor of a woman there who was supposed to have some songs," he wrote. "I found her, and got one song that she was able to remember." From there he stopped in Knoxville on his way to Washington, only to encounter more frustrations. "Feel sort of low today," he admitted. "Left the only two suits I own in my car for awhile last night and when I went back they were gone. There is small hope that I might pick them up in a pawn shop tomorrow." He made sure to add, "Don't worry, I still have a pair of trousers!" It was early July, and he had been called to Washington to begin a different kind of assignment that he only vaguely understood. "Who by the way is Mr. Cooley, and where are the cooperative institutes?" he inquired.

Now, after three weeks spent in Washington and the brief staff retreat at the Asheville festival, Hampton arrived in Arthurdale with a better idea of his new assignment. J. C. Cooley, director of the Cooperative Education Unit within the RA's Education Division, would be leading a series of institutes on cooperative enterprise for homesteaders and nearby residents at the RA's homesteads across the Appalachians. Cooley had come to the RA from Indiana, where he had for many years helped run cooperative education workshops in rural areas across the state, sponsored by the Indiana Cooperative Association. The Cooperative Education Unit was, like the Music Unit, hidden within the RA—perhaps more so, given its direct connection to collectivism—and cooperation between the two units made intuitive sense, since they shared goals to unify and instill a cooperative spirit among the homesteaders.

The two men hit it off immediately, as Hampton told his friends at Highlander: "Cooley is a grand fellow," and explained, "I do the recreation, singing, folk dancing, singing games and what not." Charlie had disapproved of Cooley's earlier choices for group singing at Westmoreland, but for their first institute at Arthurdale, Hampton requested 150 copies of the Music Unit's new song-sheet, "Co-operation Is Our Aim," which perfectly suited their musical and messaging needs. After this first cooperative institute, Charlie reported back to Dornbush, "Mr. Cooley says Mr. Hampton did a 'swell job.' He is all for continuing the collaboration." They would travel together from Arthurdale to offer similar institutes at Westmoreland, Red House, Tygart Valley, and Cumberland. Noting that these communities made "a nice little circuit," Charlie proposed that this collaboration serve as a model for Hampton's continued assignment, "doing the same sort of thing he has done under Mr. Cooley's direction, but on his own, so to speak? What this would amount to," he concluded, "is KL work with a co-operative accent." (KL was the internal abbreviation used for the Special Skills Division, following the New Deal's general love for the capitalized alphabet.)

Along this new circuit, Hampton continued to collect folk songs the old-fashioned way, sending in his transcriptions of words and melodies along with his reports to Charlie. By the end of August, he wrote proudly to his friends at the Highlander school, "My collection of songs was quite a success. I fixed them up into a book when I got back to the office and my boss was quite pleased with them." Hampton's collection would become the basis for Charlie's song-sheet project, but the excitement about the songs he found went beyond the Special Skills Division. "Since I have been out of Washington someone took them to Tugwell," he wrote with pride, "and the report is that he is very much thrilled about them." With approval of their collecting activities coming from the very top, it seemed time to send the recording machine out into the field.

Margaret left very little record of her activities once she returned to Washington that summer. Sidney provided a hint in one of her signature gossipy letters—not to her mother this time, but to Grete Franke, a Special Skills colleague in the weaving program who became Sidney's good friend and confidante. She began, "Do you know the classic story of the time Colonel Westbrook, who had met Margaret at Cherry Lake, telephoned her at the office in Washington?" She then described a scene that lends insight not only into Margaret's charm but also a sense of office life with Charlie:

> Margaret was out and the secty left a note on her desk asking that she call Colonel Westbrook's office. Charlie came in, saw it, hadn't met Colonel Westbrook at that time and was in general feeling that he wasn't meeting the people everybody else was. So, over Tobey's protest, he called the number and said pleasantly that this was Miss Valiant's chief and he wondered whether he could be of any assistance? The secty at the other end of the line hemmed and hawed a little, and Charlie insisted: "If I knew what colonel Westbrook wanted, perhaps I could help him?" and the secty finally blurted out: "Well, I *think* he wanted to ask her to dinner!"—which, as it turned out, he did.

Toward the end of the summer, Margaret paid quick visits to a few of the homesteads where she would now be serving as a regional representative, but she was soon on more familiar ground. At the end of August,

Charlie arranged to have the Music Unit's recording equipment shipped to Cherry Lake, so she could record—"with the assistance of Red Stevens, the redoubtable electrician"—some of the music she had found among the homesteaders. Margaret did not receive training on using the equipment herself—much later, Sidney said she thought Margaret might have been a little afraid of it. In her letter to Grete Franke, Sidney noted that with both Stevens and Steffen on hand, there was no need for Margaret to operate the equipment herself. But this perception that help was required cannot be separated from gendered assumptions about Margaret and her abilities. "Having no car," Sidney mused, "and not looking, at least, physically robust enough to struggle with those heavy cases, I don't suppose it occurred to anyone" that she would make recordings on her own. (Sidney's remarks seem to reflect a hint of rivalry that simmered below the surface in her friendship with Margaret, who here was given first access to the recording equipment despite Sidney's training.)

Over Labor Day weekend of 1936, Margaret took the familiar train ride from Washington to Madison, Florida, deeper into the summer heat. It must have been a bittersweet reunion with her friends among the staff and homesteaders; she left no letters or reports describing her visit, so the recordings and their brief track notes must speak for themselves. One track begins with the basso profundo Bill Carr singing a slow, ponderous, and astonishingly low version of the hymn "Look Down that Lonesome Road," plunging to a low-C on the penultimate note. Margaret plays a quiet and spare accompaniment, her own musical involvement perhaps one reason she chose not to operate the recording equipment herself. On another track, Stevens skillfully plays a medley of square-dance tunes on the accordion, complete with dance calls like "Swing your partner!" and "Promenade!" Two sides of another disc are filled with virtuosic fiddle tunes by Russell "Chubby" Wise, and another captures the regular Sunday night community singing organized by the homesteaders, their voices echoing through the auditorium in the angular harmonies of the shape-note southern hymn tradition. Taken together, Margaret's Cherry Lake recordings stand as a kind of greatest hits album from her time at the homestead, sonic evidence of how music may have contributed to creating capital-C Community, or at least helped lift the spirits of all involved.

Back in Washington, word of Margaret's recordings traveled across New Deal offices, piquing the interest of administration staffers intrigued by government folk music collecting and the role of music on rural resettlement projects. She held a presentation where she played examples from her recordings at a gathering that seems to have been somewhere between a business meeting and a social event. In attendance were Sidney, Charlie, Dornbush, and Steffen from Special Skills; Lawrence Westbrook and architect David Williams, whose work together creating the rural-industrial community model had brought them to the highest ranks of the WPA; Walter Packard, director of the RA's Rural Resettlement Division; John Lomax and music librarian Harold Spivacke from the Library of Congress; and several others from various departments. A few of the men in attendance brought their wives, and the syndicated journalist Dorothy Thompson, known then by her married name of Mrs. Sinclair Lewis, was also among the guests. John Lomax played a selection of his field recordings, but, Sidney reported, "Due to the particular interest in Cherry Lake which characterized the majority of the listeners, most of the time was given to the records made there." Sidney's brief report did not include her usual in-depth descriptions of the presentation or of listeners' reactions, but she did note a few details—Walter Packard asked if they could repeat the presentation for his staff in the Rural Resettlement Division, and Mrs. Lewis requested a copy of one of Bill Carr's recordings—indicating that the music and Margaret's explanations of her work had a powerful effect.

Meanwhile, Sidney was beginning to despair of ever getting the chance to take a collecting trip of her own. Just two weeks after returning from Asheville, she confessed to her mother that she already found the "office routine very dull and discouraging," and her activity reports from her time in the office seem to chart a growing boredom:

Thursday, August 6: Routine correspondence, etc. . . .

Wednesday, August 12: Work on Mr. Seeger's and my files, routine letters . . .

Friday, September 4: Reports. . . .

Saturday, September 5: Reports. . . .

Monday, September 14: Routine work. . . .

Friday, September 18: Routine office detail. . . .

Saturday, September 19: [ditto marks]

Of course, working in the Special Skills office wasn't all drudgery. But it was nothing like the freedom she had felt out on the road.

CHAPTER 9

GOVERNMENT SONG WOMAN

S teffen couldn't understand what Sidney was up to. She had parked just outside the Special Skills office and rushed in to their first-floor painting workshop asking for assistance. He and a few other artists followed her upstairs to the Music Unit's office. They helped her carry all the recording equipment down the stairs and out to the sidewalk—the two so-called portable cases, together weighing about two hundred pounds, plus the microphone stand and a box of extra records. After rearranging the gear like puzzle pieces to fit snugly in the trunk of the car, she closed the trunk and locked it. But just as Steffen and his colleagues turned to go inside, she called them back, asking them to take everything out of the trunk and back to where it had been upstairs. Once it was unloaded, she sped off, leaving her colleagues dumbfounded, the equipment on the sidewalk. "We never could figure it out," he said.

"I bought a car," she wrote to her mother that night. "1931 model A Ford convertible, 41,000 miles, probably a mistake." At the used car dealership, she had convinced the salesman to let her take the car for an extended test drive to the Special Skills office so that she could make sure the trunk could accommodate the recording equipment. She had sold her previous car before she left New York for Washington back in April, when she had planned to take a steamer ship back to San Francisco. Now it was mid-September, and she (and the recording equipment) had both been part of the Music Unit for four months. Even as Charlie kept finding more and more tasks for Sidney to do in the office, if the time ever came for her to finally have her turn with the recording equipment, she wanted to be ready.

But Charlie's enthusiasm about sending Sidney out on an extended recording trip seemed to have waned as time went on. At the end of August, just before he shipped the machine to Cherry Lake for Margaret's Labor Day recording sessions, he wrote a memorandum to Dornbush that amounted to a list of excuses why he and his unit hadn't made more use of their hard-won recording equipment. He appeared to have had a change of heart about the importance of RA field recordings, as he now claimed, "The Garwick Electrograph was purchased primarily as a copying (transfer) instrument." He went on to explain, "Enough good material exists in the Library of Congress and in the hands of private collectors and other institutions to last us for many years and to serve most of our purposes. Secondarily, the instrument can be used in case we find need of material that is unavailable in these sources."

In September, when he drafted an extensive report outlining his plans for the Music Unit through the end of the year, Charlie made no mention of possible travel costs of a collecting trip for Sidney. In fact, her presence in the office had become so valuable that he made sure to note, "We cannot spare Mrs. Robertson at headquarters unless we get a substitute." After Margaret's successful recordings at Cherry Lake—and their positive reception from administrators in Washington a few weeks later—Charlie proposed that any new recordings follow that model, being made by field representatives as they led musical activities at RA homesteads.

Though she had hoped to be sent on the road, Sidney managed to enjoy aspects of office life. She liked spending time with her coworkers—the "Special Skillets," as she liked to call them—based in the workshops on M Street, including painters, ceramicists, furniture designers, weavers, landscape designers, and architects. She described her colleagues to a friend as being mostly artists, "all of them vital and interesting people." Once, while copying records at the Special Skills furniture warehouse on

L Street where the recording machine was kept, she had a surprise visitor: "The evening guard at the door was so intrigued with Mr. Seeger's record of square dancing at Arthurdale that he came jigging down the room, and told me he'd square danced every Saturday night of his life, out at Anderson's Corners, Md., until he came into Washington eight months ago!" Perhaps inspired by this encounter, or simply deciding that she would bring the joys of the road to the office if she wasn't allowed to experience them otherwise, Sidney took action. A few weeks later, she organized a square-dancing class for the entire Special Skills Division with an "old time caller" from the Virginia mountains. She wrote happily to her mother, "28 people came and *clamored* to repeat—such fun! The head of the division & the messenger boys & stenogs had an equally fine time."

Charlie's altered vision for the recording equipment consigned both Sidney and the Garwick machine to office work, despite their readiness for the adventure of recording. He sent her across town to the Archive of American Folk Song in the Library of Congress's Music Division, where her first task was "sorting out all the records made by white people in the collection at the Library, as that is our first interest"—as always, proscribed by the musical color line that defined their work on the RA's segregated homesteads. By the middle of October, she had identified 132 such records that would be available for copying. But by then, Charlie had another drastic change of heart about Sidney's assignment.

In a memorandum to Dornbush titled "Field work for Mrs. Robertson," Charlie wrote, "I would like to suggest she be sent to California, where there appears to be a chance for a music worker to do some good work." By this, he meant the government camps for migrant farm workers streaming into California from the Dust Bowl, spartan but clean facilities built by FERA and now taken over by the RA. "There is some very good material there, necessary for successful work in California, as yet uncollected, so far as I know." A few weeks later, he outlined an even more expansive scope for her assignment: "There are a number of recording jobs along the 'Broadway of America,' leading through Tennessee, Arkansas, etc. that have been waiting for some time," he wrote. "If she went by car she could do these."

Here was an epic recording adventure beyond what Sidney had thought possible, well outside the boundaries of the Music Unit's work at RA homesteads in the southeast. But it needed to happen right away so Sidney could arrive at the California camps by Christmas, with several stops to collect music on the way, and then lead music programs during the migrant workers' "slack time" in January and February. She was thrilled, as she wrote in a brief postcard to her mother, "I'm really crazy about my job! I never thought to be so eager over Arkansas & Missouri! I'm also going through western N. Carolina again, hooray!"

Sidney immediately began making preparations. First, she met with an engineer in the Sound Preservation Division of the National Archives to discuss some of the technical aspects of the Garwick machine. Among other details, he told her the current must be alternating with a 60-cycle frequency, and that the best way to determine what current is used in a new town is to call up the local electric company and ask. He showed her many of the finer points of running the machine—how to tell when the pulley wheel needs to be adjusted, to tighten the screw on the control switch, and to use Vaseline if the turntable needed greasing. She got in touch with Hampton and a few other RA contacts to get names of people she should visit, and then sent letters to arrange meetings and recording sessions until she had mapped an itinerary of musicians and folklorists as far as Missouri.

By early November, everything was set—until it wasn't. "The day before I was to leave," she later recounted, "Charlie got cold feet, told Adrian and me, too, that I could not possibly do it, and he called the trip off." In the end, regardless of all the preparations and planning, Sidney's technical training on the machine, and her own readiness to get on the road, Charlie decided he needed her help in the office too much to let her go.

But Dornbush had had enough. It had been nearly six months since the equipment had arrived, and he felt that too little had been done under Charlie's supervision to justify the expense and trouble it had taken to procure it. As Sidney remembered it later, Dornbush took her aside, saying, "You know, it took a special request to the president of the United States to get that recording machine," and someday, he said, the president is going to wonder, "Wait, what did anybody *do* with that recording machine?" Dornbush told her, "I'm taking you out from under Charlie Seeger, although he's not to know this." She should continue to keep Charlie informed but send her official reports directly to Dornbush. She should "disregard Charlie's inevitable orders to come back," instead following her own judgment and taking directions only from Dornbush. As she later explained, "I was not to return to Washington until I had something to show the president when he got around to remembering that recording machine—as, being FDR, he surely would."

As reluctant as Charlie might have been to let her go, the advice he gave her before this trip had a deep influence—both for her collecting and for the field at large. She later described it:

> "Record EVERYthing!" he said as emphatically as he could. "Don't select, don't omit, don't concentrate on any single style. We know so little! Record everything!" What he was trying to do was to inoculate me against contagion from the local collectors I was to meet, for each of them as a matter of course picked and chose items for his collection according to some personal standard of authenticity, or taste, or esthetic quality, or topical interest. Charlie knew it was important to disabuse me of any notion I might have that any particular part of the tradition was more important than any other. Nothing should be omitted!

Such an open approach was unheard of in folklore collecting at the time, and it matched Sidney's own conclusions about how a collector should behave. "And except for the fact that no three lives would suffice to get all this done," she said, "he was perfectly right."

On November 7, 1936, Sidney pulled her Ford convertible away from the Special Skills office on M Street, the recording equipment again packed securely in the trunk, and headed northwest toward Westmoreland Homesteads in Pennsylvania. It was the beginning of her second cross-country road trip, more than a year after she had driven from California to New York City in the summer of 1935—but this time, it would have a soundtrack.

⟨⟩

Sidney couldn't believe she had no way to reach anyone. Out here, far from the city, it just wasn't possible to call or send a wire on a Sunday, so she couldn't explain what had happened. After just a short time on the road, she had discovered that her car—her "elderly Ford," a discontinued model from five years earlier—had a burnt-out ammeter that shorted out the ignition, leaving her to spend most of her first day searching for a garage that could fix it. She arrived at Westmoreland too late for the recording session she had arranged for that afternoon, but luckily the musicians—members of a local string band led by a well-known fiddler in the area named Tink Queer—agreed to come the following day. On Monday, she made her way to the Elks Club hall in Ligonier, Pennsylvania, about thirty miles from Westmoreland, to meet Tink and his band for the moment she had been waiting for—her first solo recording session. But as she reported to Dornbush, "When I set up the machine there was a microphonic howl such as you've never heard—nor had I!" After Sidney had managed to turn off the machine and they had recovered from the jolt, one of the musicians found a young radio man in the town to come take a look at the recorder. He diagnosed the problem as defective tubes, which she would need to go to a larger town to get replaced. Sidney apologetically made yet another appointment with the band for the following night and spent the next day getting the recorder repaired at Supreme Radio Service, a dingy but helpful radio shop in nearby Greensburg.

Now it was Tuesday evening; the banjo player wasn't available, one of the guitarists couldn't meet until 9 P.M., and another said the Elks Hall was too cold and asked to meet at his house instead. So at the appointed time, Sidney unpacked the microphone and the recording machine in the tiny living room of the guitarist's modest home, with the musicians gathered around awkwardly. She set the machine to record, the stylus cutting its groove into the rotating aluminum disc, and signaled to the musicians to play. They launched into "Down Yonder," a tune made famous by a hit recording by the Skillet Lickers a few years earlier. But when they listened to the recording, it was a noisy mess, with the levels too high and the guitars drowning out the fiddle. After she asked the guitarists to move farther away and play more quietly, they played the same tune twice more until they were happier with the sound.

Here, finally, was the music she had imagined encountering—joyous old-time fiddle tunes, complete with stomping and dance calls, that she described as "fine dancey music, rather smoother fiddling than most country fiddlers." (One of the fiddle tunes they recorded, "Sharon," had also been played by Chubby Wise for Margaret's recording session at Cherry Lake, creating a satisfying connection from one RA homestead to another.) She set up the next disc and prepared for a late night, since the musicians had named at least fifteen more songs that they could play. But unforeseen technical difficulties continued to plague Sidney and Tink Queer's band in Ligonier:

> A little before eleven a bakery nearby started up its electrical dough mixers, and the intermittent disturbance made recording impossible, to the great disgust of the band, who were rather inclined to feel that I was inventing an excuse for not bothering with them because they weren't good enough! I don't know whether or not I succeeded in dispelling this feeling; but I promised to return, and I think it would be well worth the trip.

The next day, she headed south to West Virginia, hoping to leave her technical and mechanical woes behind her. In Morgantown, she met with Hampton, who served as her primary informant about music in and around the RA's Appalachian homesteads. It was Hampton who had suggested she record Tink Queer and his band, having heard them play at square dances at Westmoreland Homestead. He told her that he had sent word to his Tennessee contacts—the Hughes family and the folk collector L. L. McDowell—to expect her arrival the following week.

Hampton took her on a tour of Arthurdale, where he was based at the time. "Then," she reported, "I went on to Elkins for the night and fell asleep fully clothed and dinnerless at 8:30!" Sidney had not recorded any music at Arthurdale, nor did she stop at Tygart Valley Homesteads near Elkins. Instead, she continued south toward Virginia, where the focus of her trip would shift away from Hampton's orbit, as she planned to explore the heart of the Appalachian folk festival circuit on her own.

First was Marion, Virginia, home of the White Top Folk Festival, which Eleanor Roosevelt had famously visited in 1933. Sidney had been warned to give festival founder Annabel Buchanan "a wide berth" since she was a bit territorial about her folk sources and wouldn't allow them to be recorded by an outsider. So Sidney tried out her own unique approach to finding out about real musicians admired by locals. "My system took about half an hour," she reported. She began driving to gas stations in the area, buying two gallons at a time and inquiring about local accommodations off the tourist track. At the third station, she was pleased to report, "I found a local country boy who directed me to the Mill Stream Tourist Inn, where he said 'they wasn't so stylist as to be high costly!' Just good old Virginia folks. Result: I now have the names of a dulcimer maker, 2 fiddlers, 2 banjo pickers and a singer!" Having driven more than 250 mountainous miles in the rain from Elkins, she was grateful for a bed and even found herself a bit homesick for life at the Special Skills office. "I miss 2216 M very much," she confided in her report to Dornbush that night. "It seems so strange to be a free floating agent suddenly."

The proprietor of the inn suggested Sidney first visit the Russell family, a household that included three generations of musicians—eighty-one-year-old grandfather S. F. Russell on dulcimer; his son Joe on fiddle and banjo; and Joe's three teenaged children, one on guitar, and the other two joining in the singing. Sidney spent two days with the Russells, recording nine discs in all and making special note of the older man's beautiful singing and skill playing a dulcimer he had made himself.

In Marion, Sidney's on-the-job equipment training continued with yet another small-town radio man she sought out when the machine developed a persistent hum. This real-world education session focused on grounding equipment as sensitive as the Garwick machine, or as she called it, "'When is a ground not aground'—or something." She learned she couldn't attach her ground wire to a painted radiator, but needed to use the radiator pipe or, even better, a water pipe. The lesson proved extremely valuable when she brought her machine to the Russells' house and followed instructions to use a pipe stuck into the ground outside when no other metal was available. "It worked beautifully for a while, then unaccountably the loud hum began again. The only thing that had changed, that I could think of, was that the sun had come out, so I asked Mr. Russell if he thought the ground could have dried out around the pipe." She continued triumphantly, "He looked doubtful but went and emptied the pan full of dirty dishwater that was sitting on the back stoop around the pipe and lo! The hum stopped."

Sidney clearly found deep satisfaction in all of her technical discoveries. "One just goes on learning about a machine like this indefinitely," she wrote separately to Charlie. She also expressed appreciation for the helpful technicians she met on her travels: "I do like radio men, like good mechanics in garages. They form a devoted sort of brotherhood, like a religious order, with special insights into magic, and distinctly special skills."

Sidney's second stop on her tour of the Appalachian folk festival circuit brought her back to Asheville, a visit that inspired an epic report, even by Sidney's standards, of eight single-spaced pages. "Because it shows clearly a number of interesting aspects of recording problems," she explained, "and also because I can't bear to be having all this fun all by myself, I want to report very fully on the work I did in Asheville." She began by describing trying to get directions to Lunsford's house outside of Leicester. "I kept getting directions like this: 'Wal, you go on out this road a good piece, and time you come to the most likely-lookin' road, that'll be it.'"

When she finally found Lunsford, he suggested they drive out to see Nate Marlor, a singer in his eighties who lived in Boyd's Cove, about twelve miles away. It was bitterly cold, and over the last two miles the mountain road "degenerated into a sort of cowpath full of sharp rocks and clay mudholes," but her elderly Ford somehow managed the terrain.

Marlor and his wife welcomed them to come in by the fire. "After a few polite disclaimers about his singin'—'I kain't sing, I kin jest holler a little some'—the old lady said sharply: 'Well, what makes ye so slow?' so her husband started in suddenly and nearly made me jump out of my chair with the volume of his voice. Such joyous hollerin' you never did hear!" He hollered a steady stream of well-known Child ballads like "The House Carpenter" and "Barbara Allen," plus a few folk songs and hymns Sidney had never heard before. Sidney later remembered Mrs. Marlor coming in with more wood for the fire,

> followed indoors by a very fat pink pig who made room for himself as a dog might, between us in front of the fire. "That's my leetle pig, he's very friendly," Mr. Marlor explained unnecessarily as the three hundred pounds of winter meat anchored me to the ground by lying on my feet the whole time Mr. Marlor sang, leaning comfortably against my knee.

Sidney and Lunsford were both eager to record Marlor's singing, but since no one in Boyd's Cove had electricity, they decided to return a few days later and bring him back to Leicester with them, the old man settled in the passenger seat and Lunsford behind him in the rumble seat. "I wish I could re-produce our conversation as we went along, it was marvelous," Sidney wrote to Dornbush. She shared her favorite story in a letter home: "We came through a gap to a panorama of mts. in which two inhabited cabins were visible. He looked at them disapprovingly and said, with a wave of the arm, 'These mountains is gettin' moughty crowded!'"

They arranged to record at the house of Lunsford's friend, appropriately named Mrs. Current, who served as Leicester's postmistress and lived right behind the post office in the center of town, where they felt the electricity would be most reliable. As Sidney described,

> Once at Mrs. Current's house, [Marlor] could hardly wait to get started, and once we had set up an irrigation system for his

continual spitting (audible between verses of the songs on some of the records!) he was perfectly happy. He sang twelve songs for us—5 records—which at 81 is perfectly extraordinary. All the words are clear, and his voice firm and strong.

The recordings reveal the fun they had during the session, with Sidney following her own rules about collecting being a social event and making sure the musicians enjoyed themselves. Their recording of the Child ballad "Little Silver Cup" begins with Sidney saying gently, "All right," as she started up the equipment and ends with Marlor belting a high, trilling yodel, then asking, "That do?" He ends another track laughing at himself after dropping dramatically to the low octave at the end of "Baptist, Baptist Is My Name," and after singing the hymn "Mourn, Jerusalem, Mourn" toward the end of the session says, "Ah, that's enough of that, I seem like I'm right hoarse. That's a good'n, no?"

Lunsford got involved in the recordings by making spoken announcements between songs, which Sidney found to be "one of the funniest things that happened all day." She asked him to give the name of the piece along with Mr. Marlor's name, age, and place of residence, but Lunsford couldn't resist adding a plug for himself, his festival, and the region in general. After they had driven Marlor back to Boyd's Cove, Sidney found Lunsford "was dying to record something himself and try his voice and banjo," so they returned to the Currents' house for a few more hours of recording. Sidney enjoyed spending time with Lunsford, making a similar assessment as Charlie had when she wrote, "He really is an extraordinary person."

Sidney seemed to come into her own as a collector in this stretch of her trip. Conquering technical difficulties gave her confidence with the equipment, but it went beyond that—her friendly curiosity and ease with people, her reportorial instinct, and her independent streak all seemed perfectly suited for her new role of "government song woman," as she later referred to it. She left both Marion and Leicester already itching to return. "Marion is after all very near Washington," she had written. "I could spend a month there without running out of material." From Asheville, she reflected, "To dig in really thoroughly anywhere is not as simple as Mr. Seeger and I supposed when we discussed the desirability of recording *all* the music some of these people know." But for now, she stuck to her scheduled itinerary and continued west into Tennessee.

After the steep mountain roads of the Appalachians to the east, the Cumberland Plateau seems to stretch to the horizon forever, recently described jokingly by one longtime resident as "pretty dang flat for a mountain." Sidney sent a cheerful dispatch to the Special Skills office soon after she arrived in Crossville, just north of Cumberland Homesteads, referring to her car by its nickname and including the kind of details she loved about small towns: "My 4x4x4 home and castle, Leander by name, now boasts a banjo for which I paid $5.75. . . . Tomorrow morning a gentleman by the name of Winkie Walker, brother of the town cobbler ('Shew Renewry' says the sign) is going to do some chording with me."

In Tennessee, Sidney would largely be tracing the path laid out by Hampton in his summer collecting. She drove to Smithville to record the singing of the folk collector L. L. McDowell and his wife, Hampton having written to them ahead of time to inform them of her plans. This session would follow a similar pattern as her time with Lunsford in North Carolina, both in terms of the location (at the postmaster's home at the center of town, which had the strongest electricity) and because the recording served the collector's interests as well as the RA's (for McDowell, helping to publicize his collection of old hymns, *Songs of the Old Camp Ground*, soon to be published by the Tennessee Folklore Society). Over the course of two days, Sidney recorded McDowell and a small group he had assembled singing fourteen hymns from his book, and Mrs. McDowell sang seventeen songs, mostly traditional ballads with British roots. Despite Sidney's primary focus on music in current use, it seemed she couldn't help but fall into the typical folklorist's habit of prizing old British songs, especially when she was working with collectors like Lunsford and McDowell. She acknowledged later on her trip that she had "retreated to the 17th century" during her time in the Appalachians, and joked to Charlie, "Don't feel I'm going antiquarian on you entirely!" Recording members of the musical

Hughes family at a Crossville church the next day, she was disappointed their grandfather hadn't been invited despite her expressing interest in his banjo playing. The Hughes children were well-known musicians in the community, but Sidney was not particularly impressed, calling their singing "attractive and sweet, but full of dead and dying mothers and lugubrious valleys." Nevertheless, she stuck to Charlie's instructions and recorded everything she encountered.

Sidney would soon come out of her antiquarian stupor in pursuit of a distinctly modern form of music-making. When planning her trip, she had declared to Hampton, "Of course the thing I am most anxious to get, on the whole trip, are contemporary workers' songs." Her first exposure to these sorts of protest songs had been at the Henry Street Settlement House, where she led singing with the interracial Council of the Unemployed, which met weekly in one of the settlement's rooms. At the RA, she became more curious about labor unions' strategic use of music in protest, especially given Hampton's experience and Charlie's interest in harnessing those songs on the RA homesteads.

Her interests seemed to fit in well with the administration's strong support for labor unions. The Wagner Act, passed in July 1935, guaranteed workers' right to form a union and required employers to bargain with union representatives, which legal scholar Ahmed White has called "the strongest expression of government support for labor rights in American history," demonstrating that labor rights were not only critical to rebuilding the post-Depression economy but could "perhaps reorder society in a more just way."

Just before Sidney left on her collecting trip that fall, she drove to New York City to consult with labor organizers at Henry Street's Workers Education Center, who in turn suggested she talk to Mark Starr, the education director of the International Ladies' Garment Workers Union, in his office in the Flatiron district. "When he had recovered from the unfortunate effect of my fur coat," she wrote to Charlie in a confidential memorandum, "he was very cordial." She learned that the union's educational staff made simple recordings of union songs and played them on portable victrolas to get people to sing at union events. "Here is music as a social tool being consciously used with a very clear aim in view," she observed, concluding, "This technique struck me as something well worth KL consideration."

She hoped to follow up on Hampton's attempt to collect protest songs from the striking workers in Rockwood, but she was nervous. "Could I possibly manage the Rockwood workers without you, and on short notice?" she asked, noting, "It takes time to win confidence of labor groups, as I know from long experience." There was a further complication: in Rockwood, she also hoped to find Becky Tarwater's grandmother to hear her versions of the old ballads like "Barbara Allen" that Becky had sung for them at Charlie's first recording session in June. But, she wrote, "I understand—maybe you told us—that the Tarwater contingent is the owner group whom the strikers have been fighting." Indeed, in an earlier visit to Rockwood in support of the striking hosiery mill workers, a state union leader had specifically called out the family for their repeated anti-union activities. "The Tarwaters owned the mines in Rockwood when the state mine inspector was refused because they didn't want him to see the conditions," he declared. "The Tarwaters own the Harriman mills, where Fred Held was kidnapped. They have an interest in the Rockwood mill," where the current strike was taking place amid violent arrests and another kidnapping. Sidney made sure to clarify her pro-union stance to Hampton: "I don't care what the Tarwaters think; but I'd hate to have the strikers made suspicious if I go from them to the Tarwaters." Hamp responded simply, "As to Rockwood and the workers I would say no. They are all scattered now, and would be more waste of time than the results would warrant."

Sidney thus made her way to North Kingston Avenue in Rockwood, lined with stately homes inhabited by the town's wealthiest and most powerful families, to seek more ancient Appalachian ballads—this time sung in a formal parlor room rather than a modest mountain shack. "I went out to Lockwood today to see Nippy Tarwater, Becky's sister," she reported back to Dornbush. "I had written ahead mentioning I had hoped to record her grandmother's singing. Today she told me her grandmother had died in 1931!" Apparently, no one at that first recording session in June had thought to ask whether she was still alive. Penelope and her mother found this misunderstanding endlessly amusing, and although it left Sidney empty-handed, she spent a pleasant afternoon with the Tarwater women. It seems somewhat surprising that Sidney failed to comment on any disparity between the grand Tarwater home and others she had visited, but perhaps her own wealthy background made this setting on some level more comfortable and less noteworthy than the rest of her trip.

Instead of recording the Rockwood strikers, Hampton suggested that Sidney find a homesteader named Hershel Phillips, who had been a student at Highlander Folk School. Phillips had written protest songs for a 1934 strike at Harriman Mill, with lyrics that were then included in Highlander's collection of songs taught to students and sung at strikes. Sidney asked Kirk to help her find Phillips, and the two of them drove three miles along Deep Draw Road, the main dirt road leading from the administrative offices. The Phillips family lived on Open Range Road, a circular track where the homestead's original houses were built, all made from local Crab Orchard stone mottled with varying shades of brown and tan, their interiors paneled with deep brown native pine. Phillips seemed pleased to hear that his songs were considered worthy of recording, and they made a plan for Kirk to bring him and a banjo player he knew to the Crossville church to record.

The next day, after hurrying back to Crossville from that day's recording session with the Hughes family, she waited for several hours at the church before Kirk came in to say that Phillips was nowhere to be found. But Kirk had found a musical family among the homesteaders willing to record—Henry and Ida Garrett and their fifteen-year-old son Carl—all of whom played guitar and sang, often providing entertainment at homestead dances. Sidney's official report of her session with the Garretts includes none of her usual lively descriptions or really any information beyond the musicians' names and the songs they recorded. It even seems to express some of her disappointment about the session, with one song noted by a parenthetical aside almost lamenting, "probably learned on the radio," and another note that two guitars and a mouth-harp "records surprisingly well, but their playing wasn't so much."

"I never did discover what happened to Phillips," Sidney wrote to Dornbush. "He may have got cold feet, but neither Kirk nor I felt that was likely. He was perfectly open about the songs." Still, the timing of Sidney's visit made recording union songs on the homestead especially fraught, as recent events had highlighted the fact that homestead managers did not share the Roosevelt administration's pro-union stance. Just when she arrived, underlying tensions between pro- and anti-union factions on the homestead had erupted into a public fight, as homesteaders who had formed a union pushed back against a proposed cut in back pay and accused management of intimidation tactics. "The management has sent a man to join the union as a spy," a union committee declared in a statement released to the press. "The project is honeycombed with spies." The same day, Tugwell issued a notice posted at the Cumberland Homesteads main office stating the official RA policy as "non-interference and complete recognition of the rights of collective bargaining." Given the Music Unit's general propensity for secrecy, Sidney already understood she would need to be especially discreet about her interest in union strike songs at Cumberland, since they not only would serve as ready ammunition for the RA's critics but could also fuel the growing controversy on the homestead.

This explains why no protest songs appeared in her official report of her session with the Garretts, and likely why the report was so perfunctory—since it was essentially functioning as a cover. It turned out that Henry Garrett, described by Sidney as "an old miner from Kentucky full of tales of hard strike periods there," knew several of Hershel Phillips's songs and was more than willing to sing them for her. One of them, "Roane County (Strike at Harriman, Tennessee)," was exactly the kind of protest song they had expected to find in the region, with new protest lyrics set to the melody from a traditional prison ballad called "The Hills of Roane County." Another of his songs, "The Chiseler's Sorrow," borrowed its melody from the popular country song "Twenty-One Years," demonstrating the fundamental flexibility of the protest genre in using whatever well-known musical material was readily available.

She described all the hidden details of the session in a separate, confidential memorandum to Dornbush. "I won't again try to combine recording of labor and more orthodox songs in the same locality, it is too difficult to manage," she began, but added, "I think my tracks were kept fairly clear, and the songs are good." Given all the strife over union activity at Cumberland, Sidney worried these recordings of strike songs might be interpreted by homestead management "as a sort of encouragement to the enemy's camp," so she did everything she could to keep them hidden—but record them she did. To distance the recordings from the DC office, she told the Garretts that "labor songs were just my own little hobby I was covering on the side, as I felt they were part of the contemporary picture and scholars would someday be glad they were recorded." (Certainly, at least one scholar is glad.)

CHAPTER 10

WE AIN'T DOWN YET

The uncertainty crept in early in Sidney's trip in November 1936. "There's a hitch in the California arrangements," Charlie wrote less than a week after she had left. He expressed confidence that it would be cleared up, but Sidney did not seem so sure. She went from making concrete plans to stop in Tulsa on her way west to casually hedging her bets in a letter to a friend, "There is some talk of sending me out to work with the camps for migratory workers in California . . . but I don't know—I may go back to Washington." Then, the day before she arrived at Cumberland Homesteads, a bombshell announcement blanketed front pages across the country: Rex Tugwell Resigns (or, as the newspaper in nearby Knoxville made sure to note, "Handsome Tugwell Resigns").

In the run-up to the election that November, Tugwell served as an ever-reliable target for Republicans, who could not afford to attack the popular president directly. They painted Tugwell as the leader of a nefarious group of intellectuals who had taken control of government policy away from the public's beloved president. At the same time, the RA was under increasing attack not only for what conservatives saw as its dangerous socialistic tendencies, but also for its size (with a workforce of over thirteen thousand employees and a budget of $46 million) and a lack of congressional oversight that gave Tugwell too much power. One Republican group warned voters that "the present administration is honeycombed with extremists," focusing their fearmongering on the twin threats of Tugwell and the RA. "Resettlement Rex is a very honest man; he makes no bones about what he wishes to do in this country, about these openly avowed plans of Rex the Red," they declared. "The voters are entitled to know: If the American people re-elect you, Mr. Roosevelt, will Rex re-settle the country?"

FDR won his election in a landslide, and Democrats in Congress gained enough seats to hold a stunning three-fourths majority. Yet the political landscape for the RA was more complicated than it might appear. A conservative coalition began to emerge, uniting Southern and rural Democrats with Republicans in opposing progressive New Deal initiatives like the RA, which they felt deviated too far from capitalism, business interests, and the traditional American ethos of individualism. Tugwell had no interest in moderating his approach or appeasing his opponents. Given the constant criticism from his enemies in the press and on Capitol Hill, he felt he had become too great a political liability, and that the RA would stand a better chance without him. "I am afraid that I was more to blame for everybody's difficulties in Resettlement than anybody else," he said in an interview later. "I thought the program would go on better if I left." Although Tugwell's well-regarded deputy, Will Alexander, was appointed to serve as RA director beginning in January, it was unclear what the agency's post-Rex future would look like.

Neither this larger question about the future of the RA nor any snag in her California plans seemed to bother Sidney. Perhaps her response to the uncertainty about her trip applied to the big-picture question as well. "Things like that never worry me," she had written back to Charlie. "If I never go to California there'll still be something else that's nice to do." She left Cumberland Homesteads a few days before Thanksgiving, heading east toward Little Rock and set to begin a new phase of her trip, leaving the constraints of the RA and its homesteads behind.

In Little Rock, she met up with Laurence Powell, who had been hired as a music representative that June but seemed somewhat detached from the rest of the unit at his distant outpost in Little Rock. A classically trained composer from England, Powell continued to serve on the faculty of the University of Arkansas and directed the city's fledgling orchestra. He fit Charlie's original vision for his field representatives' work in musical engineering, often incorporating folk songs that he collected from the region into his compositions and arrangements. He had originally been hired to lead music activities at Dyess Colony, but despite reports that music was "the outstanding cultural interest of the colonists," he found that the huge farming homestead was far too spread out to sustain a cohesive program.

In recent years, Powell had become well-known among folk collectors for notating some of the melodies sung by Emma Dusenbury. A blind woman in her seventies living in a remote cabin outside Mena, Arkansas, Mrs. Dusenbury's astonishing memory for old ballads and folk songs had been discovered by teachers and students at nearby Commonwealth College, a training school for labor activists similar to Highlander. In August 1936, Powell accompanied John Lomax to record her singing—a trying experience that he and Sidney bonded over. "It's a long time since I had anything to do with so overbearing a bald-head," Powell had written her. A slight man about Sidney's age with dark hair and glasses, quirky and witty in a distinctively British way, Powell and Sidney got along well. They (and Charlie) shared a similar background in classical music combined with a newfound interest in folk music. How could she not enjoy the company of someone who signed off his letter to her, "It's time I practiced the mixolydian mode on the guitar now so I'll quit this and send it on."

Powell had several ideas for Sidney's collecting in Arkansas. Much to Sidney's delight, he told her it would be worthwhile for them to visit the legendary Emma Dusenbury, who it turned out had not sung her entire repertoire of songs for Lomax. She wrote to Charlie with excitement, "It seems that Mrs. Dusenbury knows still more songs! Some of which she avoided offering to [Lomax] whom she didn't like; others he waved aside and refused to record or, sometime, to hear!" But unfortunately, that week's incessant rain made the trip impossible, as the overrun creeks would completely wash out the dirt road to the remote shack where the singer lived.

Instead, Powell suggested they go to Red River, a small community built by a group of Black families who left North Carolina seeking greater opportunities in the late 1890s. It was one of a handful of Black towns across the state, part of what one historian dubbed "the Other Great Migration," when many African Americans from the southeast moved west between the end of the Civil War and World War I, with the highest numbers settling in Arkansas. Powell and Sidney were both interested in the folk music traditions that had migrated along with the families in this community, and he arranged for Sidney to record several older singers in neighboring Clinton. Sidney described their drive in Powell's car:

> We were engaged in a lively discussion of the merits of Sibelius as a composer when the car ceased to respond to its driver's urging. "Well," said L. P. parenthetically, "the car seems to be stopping doesn't it! In Sibelius' Fourth symphony . . . etc." and he continued placidly with what he had to say for a full two minutes before condescending to investigate the trouble.

They pushed the car into Clinton with help from a passing truck (luckily it was downhill into town), where they discovered that the gas gauge was broken and they had run out. "But," Sidney wrote, "nothing ever delighted me more than our sitting calmly in a stalled car on the top of an Ozark, miles from anywhere, engrossed in the mysteries of Sibelius' orchestration, and refusing to be interrupted by any mere hazard of the road."

Hauling the recording equipment into the Clinton general store while Powell attended to the car, Sidney discovered that the singers they had arranged to meet had gone home, despairing of the two collectors ever arriving in the rain. Unfazed, Sidney began chatting with a Black family in the store—Estelle McNeeley, her teenage daughter Hazel, and her son-in-law Will Wright—and asked them if they would like to sing any songs for her to record. She discovered that the family was "continually making up songs," as Estelle and Hazel sang several original songs and duets, and they also joined with two other men in the store to sing a few spirituals in quartet style. But it was an original blues song sung by Will Wright, a young man who worked as a highway laborer for the Public Works Administration, that most captivated Sidney. She began her report to Dornbush by noting, "I think Will Wright's blues entitled 'Mister Roosevelt' should certainly be passed on to the Roosevelt family." Wright begins with a quick introduction that is almost sung, followed immediately by the first line in a blues cadence sung in a mid-tenor range: "I thank Mister Roosevelt for the good that he has done." Sidney made note of the rare experience of integration in the Clinton general store—quite a contrast from the Whites-only homesteads and sundown towns like Crossville where she had stopped thus far. "This seemed a particularly free and independent group—on fairly equal terms with the white people who run the store," she wrote. "And we all sat around the stove and ate sandwiches and drank Coca Cola together at noon."

Sidney's recording session in Clinton was the first documented moment in which the Music Unit broke free from the segregation of the southern homesteads where they worked. Earlier that fall, Charlie had hoped to hire a Black choral conductor named Nell Hunter to serve as a music representative at Newport News, one of the only RA communities created by and for African Americans, but her appointment was never approved. Charlie had also tried to hire Lawrence Gellert to collect protest songs among Black workers, but the idea proved unworkable given Gellert's need to protect his sources. "Too hot," Charlie summarized in a confidential memorandum to Dornbush.

Sidney later recalled how she needed to be careful about trying to record Black musicians, having been warned "not to risk running afoul of local ordinances forbidding association between blacks and whites." However, her next stop, in St. Louis, would involve risking this and more in pursuit of the kind of music she wanted to record most.

Sidney's idea of including St. Louis on her trip had been planted earlier that fall when the artist Joe Jones visited his friend Dornbush at the Special Skills office in Washington. Jones, a self-taught painter from a working-class family in St. Louis, had joined the Communist Party and dedicated himself to making protest art and propaganda, becoming part of a network of left-wing activists, both Black and White, protesting for the rights of workers and the unemployed. When Jones heard about the Music Unit's work and their interest in protest songs, he told them about an all-night singing protest that had been staged in St. Louis the previous spring by an integrated group of unemployed from the American Workers' Union, as a response to cuts in the city's relief rolls. The group took over the Board of Aldermen's chamber in City Hall and pledged not to leave until more money was made available for relief—a sit-in that one newspaper called "a new form of demonstration which has been showing up all over the country." Reports at the time made note of the protestors' unique use of music, with one describing them as "a singing, noisy crowd" and another taking particular note of a song that called out Mayor Barney Dickmann by name: "Most often repeated of the songs they sang was a mournful refrain, somewhat after the fashion of a Negro spiritual, which ran: 'Dickmann, oh Dickmann, what shall we eat?'" When Jones described this protest and mentioned "that there was an active group there composing protest songs that were sung widely by large groups and had been adopted in other cities," Sidney wrote, "I somehow had a very strong hunch that this was something worth doing."

Sidney knew she needed to keep especially quiet about this portion of her trip in her official reports. "I don't know *what* to say about St. Louis," she confided to Charlie, "so shall say nothing except that I went there—no, I guess I won't even do that." But, being Sidney, she couldn't keep the experience entirely to herself. In a characteristically chatty letter to Tobey, she wrote,

> I've written Adrian a long funny letter about what I did in St. Louis, and sent it in your care because I don't know his personal address and it is far too full of Communist organizers to go through the office. Joe Jones was such a skeleton in the closet I didn't dare suggest to Adrian that he show the letter to you and Charlie, but he may anyway. If not I'll show you my

copy when I come! It's too long, but it's a good letter, she said complacently. (I had good material!)

The letter to Dornbush includes Sidney's vivid description of her stay at a cheap hotel around the corner from Jones's studio in an abandoned warehouse on the riverfront, where she was "awakened at 3 a.m. by the staccato conversation of a 'lady of the streets' who had brought her quarry, a mild and timid-sounding youth, into the next room." It then details how her recording session in Jones's studio the next day was presided over by the painter's large framed portrait of a sex worker suffering from syphilis, which Sidney assessed as "too strong a statement to be sentimental; but also too compassionate to be shocking, and I really liked it," before adding, "However, far be it from me to deny that the lady does rather jump out at you at first!" She described the scene, after waiting for several hours for word of their session to travel among Jones's contacts:

A steady stream of people, sent in by the grapevine operating among the comrades, their friends and relations, came wandering in either to sing or to listen until 7 pm. We drank beer and chatted between whiles, and enough reminiscing about the origins of the songs went on so that I was able to be sure that I was actually getting songs that had been sung over a considerable period of time, and by large groups of people. . . . Everyone was tremendously enthusiastic (the machine is highly flattering to untrained voices); Joe got so excited he could hardly talk; and of course I was interested and entertained clear to my boots.

Sidney noted that those in attendance were an interracial group made up of "all kinds of people": the head of a local labor school, Communist Party organizers and "rank-and-filers," steel workers, and union organizers.

Early on, she recorded the "Dickmann Song," which the newspaper article had mentioned, making special note that "this is the one
that was sung so much during the demonstration at the City Hall,
the sound rolling out into the neighboring streets hour after hour."
A group of three Black teenaged sisters named Gladys, Juanita, and
Mattie—members of the Young Communist League—told Sidney
they had spent most of a recent jail sentence composing the songs they
sang for her, their close harmony evoking vocal groups like the Boswell
Sisters, who were popular at the time.

Sidney included the full lyrics to "a song that's popular among the girls in
the garment workers' union and other central trades (very non-Communist)
groups" sung to the tune of "Rock-a-bye Baby":

> *Rock-a-bye baby, on the tree top*
> *when you grow up, you'll work in a shop.*
> *When you get married, your wife will work too,*
> *so that the rich will have nothing to do.*
> *Rock-a-bye baby, on the tree top,*
> *when you grow old, your wages will stop;*
> *When you have spent the little you save,*
> *first to the poor-house, then to the grave.*

Below these lyrics, she urged, "Sing it over once to that naive lilting tune
and see if you don't think that's a beauty! The girls adore, and are perfectly
aware of the light irony, in the contrast between the bitter words and the
childlike tune."

The session helped Sidney understand which songs work best to mobi-
lize a group, causing her to reconsider her bias against using well-known
melodies:

> All but four of the songs were set to familiar tunes. I used to
> be rather scornful of the tendency of radical groups to adapt a
> familiar song instead of writing their own; but since I've begun

to learn how many of the songs we think of as folksongs have been built up in just this way, I see these songs in a new light.

In her role as collector for the Music Unit, Sidney was in a position of listening rather than creating. She was learning the difference between the power of protest songs emerging from within a group and the kind of "respectable propaganda" at the root of other facets of the Music Unit's work.

Back in Washington, Charlie was engaged in a different lesson on the use of traditional tunes as he assembled his next round of song-sheets. The songs he selected continued to be guided by Hampton's collecting and past experience with group singing at the Highlander School, representing a mix of songs with words intended to foster the cooperative spirit and rural-themed folk tunes, some with an added connection to union activism. The cover for "We Ain't Down Yet" features a serious-looking farmer sitting on a rock next to what may be a broken-down wagon pulled by a pair of skinny mules (perhaps the same wagon from the first song-sheet, "The Farmer"). Since "cooperate" does not appear in the title, Pollock's illustration features the word prominently on a road sign above the farmer's hat. The song's lyrics list a litany of farmers' troubles with crops, livestock, operating costs, and a broken wagon, concluding the first verse, "get up dobbin we'll CO-OPERATE," and repeating that spirit of togetherness in the final refrain, "CO-OPERATE dobbin! We'll all pull through."

The text on the back cover explains that the words come from the Farmers' Union Cooperative Education Service and identifies the tune "as the familiar 'Turkey in the Straw,' one of the most widely known fiddle tunes, also called 'Zip Coon.'" This explanation points to the ugly tangle at the root of American vernacular music—as a fiddle tune, "Turkey in the Straw" existed as an early nineteenth-century adaptation of a traditional British song, "The Old Rose Tree," but it became universally known only after being used in the pervasive popular music form of the late nineteenth century—blackface minstrelsy. Zip Coon was a racist blackface stereotype meant to serve as an urban counterpart to the rural caricature of Jim Crow, its presence here serving as yet another example of minstrelsy's inescapable reach in American culture.

Another song-sheet released that fall, "Down in the Valley," appears to be a simple, gentle love song with a lilting melody, and its cover depicts a picturesque rural scene: a man sitting on a worn porch with a banjo, looking out over a farmhouse set between gentle slopes of two tree-covered mountains. The lyrics say nothing of economic hardship or the need to cooperate, instead ending with a familiar, earnest pronouncement of affection, "Roses love sunshine, violets love dew; angels in heaven know I love you." However, a tiny detail in the text on the back cover may have served as a subtle signal to labor activists now living on the homesteads. In describing alternate lyrics, the text explains, "This song is also widely known as 'Birmingham Jail'; but the names of other cities are found in its stead. 'Barbourville Jail,' in Kentucky; 'Powder Mill Jail,' in Tennessee, etc." Birmingham and Barbourville are towns, but Powder Mill is not—those lyrics were created and sung by striking aluminum workers on the picket line to taunt the scabs who were locked in the factory, which they called a "Powder Mill 'jail.'" With "Powder Mill" casually included in this list of towns, the song-sheet contained a message that could be decoded only by those who understood its past connection to protest—what social scientist James C. Scott has called a "hidden transcript" that could slip by those in power but reach its intended audience. This "Powder Mill" message was likely subtle enough to avoid detection, but there was no guarantee that the Music Unit's work could stay hidden forever.

Sidney could not have anticipated that she would run into trouble in Springfield. After the clandestine adventure of collecting in St. Louis, her southwest route to the Missouri side of the Ozarks brought her back to the familiar collecting practices that she had followed in Marion, Asheville, and Crossville: befriend a regional folk expert, who would record their own songs and identify the best local musicians to record. In Springfield, this was May Kennedy McCord, known as the "Queen of the Hillbillies." Lunsford had worked with McCord to mount a regional folk festival in Springfield a few years earlier, and he had recommended that Sidney seek her out when she got to town. In fact, McCord had missed that year's Asheville festival and was said to be dangerously ill, so Lunsford was eager to know if she had recovered. Sidney found McCord "very much alive," an energetic woman in her fifties who seemed to know every folk musician in the Ozarks, who was "the kindest, most enthusiastic soul in the world."

But Sidney also expressed a note of caution: "I rather have some reservations about her—she's a terrific talker and struggles in vain to keep to the point, and I found her rather overwhelming today." One imagines it would take quite a bit of talking to overwhelm Sidney, who was herself an avid talker and had calmly handled other highly stressful situations throughout her journeys. McCord also told Sidney that she was "a known Republican," which may have been part of the problem—and also may explain the unfortunate situation that arose for Sidney the next day. "What Mr. Lunsford had neglected to mention," she recalled much later, "was that she was a feature writer for the local Republican newspaper."

McCord's "Hill-Billy Heartbeats" column had run regularly in the Springfield *News-Leader* since 1933, and the day after Sidney's arrival, the paper published the kind of coverage the Music Unit had worked so hard to avoid. With the headline "Old Ballads Resettled," the article named names, identifying Dornbush, "one-time art teacher" in Springfield, as the director of the RA Special Skills Division and "Mrs. Sidney Hawkins Robertson" as the government staffer "making records of old ballads." It also subtly questioned the Music Unit's purpose within the RA and exposed its secretive impulses: "Asked what relation there is between resettlement and collecting old ballads, Mrs. Robertson said she 'wouldn't dream' of explaining it; explained she is definitely instructed not to discuss the program." Not only were her words taken out of context, but as feared, the article used the RA's music work to make politically motivated insinuations about the RA's priorities. "I was of course alarmed and distressed," Sidney said later, "as we all knew without being told of the dangers of getting involved with the newspapers." But luckily, the Springfield paper had a limited circulation, and the story wasn't picked up elsewhere; perhaps Tugwell had been right that the target on the RA would fade with his resignation.

Sidney's stop in Springfield was noteworthy even without the unwanted press exposure, as she wrote proudly, "I've done the first recording of traditional material that has been done in Missouri, apparently—and, except for Lomax's foray to Mena, anywhere in the Ozarks." McCord invited local musicians who had participated in the regional folk festival to come to her comfortable house on North Jefferson, where Sidney had set up the recording equipment. Over the course of three days, thirteen local folk musicians came through the makeshift recording studio in McCord's living room: the guitarist Slim Wilson and three of his six sisters; the Denoon family band, with Ray R. Denoon on fiddle and his two sons Jim (on guitar) and Roy (on mandolin); father-son ballad singers Ben Rice and David Rice; Frank Hendrick, a popular square dance fiddler; and, of course, May Kennedy McCord herself, who sang twenty of the seventy-four songs that Sidney recorded. In addition to the traditional folk ballads and fiddle tunes that she had come to expect, this session included several songs that she thought might be unique to the Ozarks, such as Ray Denoon's comic nonsense song "Risselty, Rosselty" and spelling songs "from the Old Blueback Speller" sung by Ben Rice.

But unlike all her previous recording sessions, Sidney's time in Springfield has no accompanying report filled with the kind of details she loved. Her attention likely shifted away from reporting after her second day in Springfield, when she received a telegram from the Special Skills office informing her she needed to return to Washington immediately, picking up Kirk in Crossville on her way, for a staff conference. In a letter to Tobey, Sidney used a string of symbols to succinctly express her shock and disappointment about receiving the wire ("??!!?"), lamenting, "I hate like everything to come home now." She planned to finish her collecting in Springfield by Thursday, then spend the weekend recording Mrs. Dusenbury in Mena before driving east. "I shall be sort of glad to see you again," Sidney joked, "but I'm a little mad at spending Xmas dashing madly across Tennessee, or wherever!" She planned to be back in the office by December 28, and she mockingly warned, "If I've not been hauled back for something *good*, why heaven help you!"

Sidney was determined to record Mrs. Dusenbury before she left, but her attempts seemed to be cursed, first thwarted in Little Rock by washed-out roads and now, in Springfield, by a flu that kept her in her hotel bed through the weekend. So she made a decision, sending a telegram to the Special Skills office: "Attack of flu necessitates cancel schedule," it began. "Will not leave here without finishing Dusenbury. If my return urgent any particular date wire me immediately."

When she finally navigated the eight miles of dirt roads deep into the woods outside Mena, she found Mrs. Dusenbury and her "sickly, frail" middle-aged daughter Ora living at a level of poverty Sidney hadn't experienced up close before. Their home was an abandoned shack with only a partial roof, where Mrs. Dusenbury slept in the bed with no blankets and Ora was left to sleep "scrunched up in a box set on two chairs in the corner with some misfit coats, contributed last year by the relief, over her."

Emma Dusenbury had made a deep impression on the men who had made the trek to see her. The poet John Gould Fletcher wrote that ever since he had first heard an old ballad "sung in a leaky-roofed, decaying cabin by an old, blind, and illiterate woman, dressed in flour-sack clothes, . . . I too have regarded the Ozarks as a magic land." John Lomax described her as having "the serene face one finds in the pictures of saints and martyrs." But perhaps not surprisingly, for Sidney, Emma Dusenbury became something closer to a friend whom she wanted to help:

> The only time I ever paid a singer was when I was bringing Mrs. Dusenbury from her mountain shack daily into Mena, Arkansas, for electric current for the machine. She expected to sing, she said, from "kin to kain't"—e.g., from "kin see" to "kain't see," dawn to dusk, and she mentioned that a day's wages in those parts were $1 a day. She and her daughter were living on her $12-a-month Civil War widow's pension (she had married a

Confederate drummer boy when he was 15). I gladly paid her wages but found it difficult to avoid a ten-hour day. She was blind but loved the car and the ride across two streams at shallow rocky fords: "Make us splash, Sinny!" she always told me happily.

During the one-day break between their two recording sessions, Sidney did what she could for them, helping Ora buy supplies in Mena and delivering them afterward. Seeing their plight gave her new insight into the limitations of the RA to serve people as hard-hit as the Dusenbury's, realizing who their program was leaving behind. In a memo that she wrote to raise money for them among her RA colleagues, she noted, "There is no way for Resettlement to help them because obviously they can never qualify for rehabilitation."

The recordings from these sessions reflect the warmth Sidney cultivated in all of her collecting as well as the fondness that seemed to have emerged between the two women. Bursts of laughter and conversation punctuate the songs, such as when Mrs. Dusenbury finished singing "Bought Me a Cat" and cracked, "That's the end of that fool song." Another track, which Sidney labeled "Personal Interlude," captures the singer taking a break: "All right," she says. "Let me get my breath a little bit. I guess I ate too much dinner. Just filled up my guts! It makes my—ah, this rubber's much too tight around my waist." Sidney says something inaudible in the background, and they break into laughter. They recorded forty-two songs together, several of which Mrs. Dusenbury hadn't sung for John Lomax. For example, in the track list for the English ballad "Gilderoy," Sidney noted that "Mrs D. considered this not a song to be sung before men!"

Pleased that she had been able to squeeze extra time out of her epic recording trip, Sidney returned to Springfield and prepared for the long drive back to the Special Skills office. She calculated that by the time she got back to Washington, she would have driven between 4,600 and 4,700 miles. Instead of expressing disappointment in not making it to California, she framed it as a positive, reasoning that if the West Coast assignment were to come up again the following year, it would mean she could go back to the Ozarks and continue her recording work on the way. But it must have been at least a little disheartening to face a return to the office after Charlie explained one reason why he had called her back to Washington: "You are needed here like the dickens. There is just too much for one person to do. Lunsford and Kirk are both here and need attention," he wrote. Copies needed to be made of Lunsford's seventy-nine records. More song-sheets. A "stack of literary work to do."

Sidney would also return to a general sense of unease about the future of Special Skills after Tugwell's departure from the RA. There was talk of the agency being folded into the Department of Agriculture, a move Tugwell thought would provide it with more permanence. Yet the Special Skills Division was his brainchild, and it was unclear whether other agriculture officials would share his commitment to incorporating the arts into resettlement work. Plus, as an emergency agency, the RA's budget did not require Congressional approval, but this level of protection would vanish once it became part of the Department of Agriculture. "We expect to go under Agriculture in a very short time," Charlie wrote to Sidney at the end of December. He then added casually, "Chances of surviving are much discussed."

CHAPTER 11

WAYFARING STRANGER

When Margaret first heard the news of Tugwell's resignation in November 1936, she had just arrived at Skyline Farms in northeastern Alabama, recently renamed from "Cumberland Mountain Farms" to avoid confusion with Cumberland Homesteads in Tennessee. Here, Margaret was tasked with replicating in a matter of weeks what she had accomplished at Cherry Lake in six months. Both communities had been among the first to be built by FERA in 1934, and, like Cherry Lake, Skyline Farms made a rather dismal first impression on Margaret, who described it "with houses and barracks seemingly without design as they were without paint." But that might be where the similarities between them ended, seeming otherwise opposite in geography and culture. Skyline was carved out of the forest on the southern portion of the Cumberland Plateau that stretched south into Alabama. Residents were chosen from among poor White sharecroppers, tenant farmers, and farm laborers on relief. Families were large, with an average of five children, and more than three-quarters of adults could not read or write. Coming from isolated areas with no social activities outside of church, Skyline's residents also shared what historian Wayne Flynt calls a "cultural pattern of fierce individualism, pride, and general cantankerousness." Margaret

encountered this last quality early on, as she described in a brief vignette
included in her report:

> KL Representative (eagerly, to local woman): "Good morning!
> My business here is music and my name is _____ _____."
> Local woman (spitting across road): "Who said 'tweren't?"

Skyline was also plagued by class conflicts between the homesteaders and
the salaried RA staff who lived among them. Kirk and Hampton had come
up against this division in September, when they were sent to Skyline to
help stage one of the minstrel shows that had insidiously become a regular
part of the Music Unit's work. Kirk reported that people automatically
introduced themselves as either "salaried" or "settler," and that salaried staff
tried to take all the stage roles. Hampton said this was the only community
where he had ever seen such a "quite definite class division." In fact, Flynt
argues that the condescension and "cultural paternalism" shown by Margaret and other Washington staffers toward the entire Skyline community
was just as much of a problem as their internal class conflicts. Racism also
seemed especially virulent at Skyline, located in an all-White county made
infamous just five years earlier by the trial of nine Black youth wrongfully
convicted of rape in nearby Scottsboro. Staying within the stark boundaries
of Jim Crow, the RA had established two separate communities for Black
families in Alabama: Gee's Bend in Wilcox County and Prairie Farms in
Macon County, both more than two hundred miles to the south.

Within a few weeks of her arrival at Skyline, Margaret was able to find
her entry point to this fractious community. Learning that they had no
community celebration planned for Christmas, she quickly wrote a play and
received approval from the community manager to produce it (apparently
with the comment, "That's dad-blamed good stuff."). But she soon found
several roadblocks to mounting the production:

> The weather on the mountain is sometimes an animate perverse
> enemy. The cold, rain, and fog of December made the roads

impassable, particularly at night when the absence of electricity presented an additional handicap. There was the problem of making acquaintances under these conditions, finding talented or interested persons for the cast, and arranging rehearsals. And in addition, plodding through the mud in high boots twice a day to the school to teach the children their first Christmas carols. Also, there was the problem of food and lodging for the KL representative. Not only was there no place in the inn, there was no inn. . . .

The KL representative finally persuaded a lady to rent a room—totally without heating facilities, where it was necessary to rise and make the bed by lamplight, and trudge half a mile by flashlight to 6 am breakfast. The only way this differed from the rest of the life on the mountain was that most people got up earlier, had more pre-breakfast work, and had fewer suitable warm clothes.

Still, Margaret was able to find a cast of seven willing participants, four of whom were homesteaders rather than employees, which, she noted, "in itself was new prominence."

Margaret based her play, *A Christmas Masque*, on the old legend that animals can talk to each other on Christmas eve—eschewing traditional religious figures to tell a universal story, as she had done with Cherry Lake's Easter pageant. Another practical advantage of this framing was that it called for a very simple set of animal stalls as well as minimal costumes, augmented by animal masks created by Special Skills artist Olle Nordmark and shipped to Skyline from Washington. The play, set in "a new barn on Cumberland Mountain on Christmas eve," features a conversation between a cow, a pig, a horse, a donkey, a blind dog, a cat, and a goat, joking with each other and discussing how their lives have changed (mostly for the better) since they've moved to the homestead, with a few allusions to their ancestors in that long-ago Bethlehem manger. In the last scene, the animals go silent as a young couple stumbles into the barn, seeking shelter from the cold. When they're discovered by the angry farmer, the young man pleads, "We come up here 'cause we heard a fellow was willing to work could get a chance to make a living and a home for his family." In a speech borrowing a theme Margaret had introduced in her Cherry Lake play *New Wine*, the farmer relents and extolls the virtues of community: "Stranger, you done right. A bunch of us come up here a while back mighty near beat. We kinda got a break and we helped each other keep our eyes lookin' up and our stomachs held down." The play ends with the farmer calling, "Merry Christmas to all you critters!" as the animals "bray, neigh, moo, etc.," followed by a children's chorus singing Christmas carols. Margaret deemed this first play "a big success, due to the familiarity of the materials drawing on their actual experiences, the fun of hearing barnyard animals talk, and the fine performances of the cast."

Margaret had also discovered that without any help from the Music Unit, a group of young men from among Skyline's residents had already organized themselves into an excellent string band. They had two fiddlers, two guitarists, a virtuoso mandolin player, and a singer named Chester Allen whose flexibility astonished Margaret, ranging from hymns, ballads, and dance tunes to imitations of hog-calling and cackling hens. She reported back approvingly, "To these natural musicians one could only hope to offer additions to their repertory and to their opportunities." Charlie knew just the person for the job: Bascom Lamar Lunsford, whom he had finally convinced to join the Music Unit staff in December 1936. After spending almost a month in Washington—during which Charlie nearly gushed to Sidney, "Having Lunsford here is everything I had hoped"—Lunsford was sent to Alabama to see what he could do.

Lunsford was not the only new hire Charlie was able to make that winter. Since the fall, he had been pushing Dornbush to bring on a dedicated staffer in drama, building on Margaret's work at Cherry Lake and pushing beyond the increasing demand for minstrel plays across the homesteads. "We must have more than amateurs in drama on our staff," he wrote urgently to Dornbush. "We must have professional standards as in our other activities." Charlie mentioned "having his eye on" Nicholas Ray, an activist actor and

stage manager from the Federal Theatre Project who had recently joined
the faculty at Brookwood Labor College. "We might still get him," Charlie
wrote in October, and by January his prediction proved to be correct. After
a brief training in Washington, Ray's first assignment brought him to
Westmoreland to help the newly formed Co-op Players write and produce
a play on cooperative themes. He followed the basic model Margaret had
set, as his biographer later described: "He would go to the place, listen to
the people, get them to talk about their lives, write a play based on their
material, and stage the play with the people who had lived it in reality."
Ray asked Charlie to set a few of his lines to music:

> Look, here we have our hands
> Our hands don't bring us much
> But with our hearts and with our hands
> We'll make this world our own, our own
> We'll make this world our own.

With Sidney's help, Charlie made recordings of three musical settings
for Ray to choose from, with gentle lilting melodies and regular rhythmic
patterns that were all very different from his earlier atonal compositions.

A few weeks earlier, Charlie had briefly revisited that previous musical
world. In mid-January, the Music Unit contributed a set of three acetate
records to a scrapbook assembled by the Special Skills Division as a farewell
gift for Tugwell. Sidney made a compilation of her favorite recordings from
her trip, but Charlie decided to compose an ode to their former director by
writing new lyrics to his 1934 Composers' Collective composition, "Pioneer
Song: Who's That Guy?" After he and Sidney set up the recording equipment in the after-hours quiet of the press shop next door, Charlie sang
(and whistled!) the song's angular melody punctuated by rhythmic chord
clusters on the guitar. The new lyrics sing Tugwell's praises and include a
playful pun on his middle name (Guy): "Tugwell! Who's that Guy? He's
the man who showed them why, the crops all wither and capital die, and
farms go up in the dusty sky."

WAYFARING STRANGER

As a B-side of Charlie's new composition, he and Sidney recorded the Music Unit's unique take on the Southern hymn "Wayfaring Stranger." The Music Unit had issued a song-sheet of this hymn a few months earlier and included a set of alternate lyrics introduced with an expert use of the passive voice to avoid specificity: "The following modern verses from Virginia and Florida respectively have been received." In fact, Charlie had written the first set of lyrics, conveniently referencing his home address just across the DC border to evoke countrified Virginia; and Margaret wrote the others "from Florida," even though she was no longer living at Cherry Lake. For Tugwell's gift, they used the recording Sidney had made in Tennessee of L. L. McDowell for the first verse but recorded themselves singing the Music Unit's new second and third verses—both clearly enjoying the opportunity to perform. Charlie sang his own verse (which Sidney later criticized as displaying "a surprising and ludicrous lack of feeling for the nature of such a text"), and Sidney sang Margaret's lyrics, which seem both more at home with the simple melody and tied in with many homesteaders' experiences, as in her first stanza:

> I'm just a poor and lonesome traveller, behind a mule that's powerful slow.
> A-creaking on to debt and worry, the only place that I can go.
> My father lived and died a farmer, a-reaping less than he did sow;
> And now I travel in his footsteps, a-knowing less than he did know.

Dornbush had shared Margaret's "Wayfaring Stranger" verse with Tugwell back in November, asking him for comments and suggestions before noting, "The manuscript of this song was sent to your office some time ago, in the hope that several verses of your own might be forthcoming to add to this edition." One might imagine that the director of as vast and complex an agency as the RA would not have time to write song lyrics, but Dornbush's note indicates that Tugwell may have wished to stay deeply involved in the Music Unit's activities.

Tugwell's departure put the Special Skills Division in a precarious position. Becoming part of the Department of Agriculture may have given the RA more stability than a freestanding agency, but it made budget cuts all but inevitable now that they were dependent on Congressional approval. And while incoming RA director Will Alexander had been Tugwell's staunch progressive ally throughout his time in government, it remained to be seen whether he shared his predecessor's commitment to incorporating the arts into their work. In an oral history interview years later, Alexander called the Special Skills Division "very controversial" and seemed to find it quite mysterious: "It was always kept under Grace [Falke] . . . It was the most precious of them all, and she wouldn't let anybody else get close to it. Much of it was between her and Rex." Historian Sidney Baldwin notes that Alexander "found it particularly difficult to support what he believed were the esoteric projects of the Special Skills Division."

For Charlie, the first sign of trouble arrived early: a terse memo from the Business Management Division, dated January 4, informing him that the RA would no longer print the Music Unit's song-sheets. Losing support for this project, which Dornbush had called Charlie's "most important job," was certainly a blow. At that point, they had released just nine of the fifty-two songs Charlie had planned for the series, with two more waiting to be printed—the gold-rush ballad "Sweet Betsy from Pike" and the labor anthem "Solidarity" featuring cooperative-friendly lyrics. And the song-sheets they had produced appeared to be working as intended on the homesteads. "The songs were very well received at last night's meeting," Hampton reported from Tygart Valley that November. "The homesteaders seem to treasure them a great deal."

The RA's decision to discontinue the song-sheet program may have been more a result of large-scale cuts to the printing budget than a move specifically targeting the Music Unit. The agency's overall printing expenses had become an embarrassing source of criticism after the release of its annual report on Christmas Day. The report itself was slammed as a "luxurious" symbol of overspending—a doorstop of a publication at nearly two hundred pages, printed on slick paper and bound in cardboard with a six-color slipcover. But after further examining the report's contents, the *New York Herald* disclosed that the RA had printed or mimeographed a whopping 319,778,902 pages of material, to which the reporter added sardonically, "No figures were given on the number of reams of paper used, or how many times it would girdle the globe if it had been used for globe girdling instead of for resettlement's purposes."

In addition to the RA's overall printing woes, it appears that the song-sheets had created their own quiet controversy. Dornbush sent a lengthy memo to Martin G. White, the Department of Agriculture's solicitor, that began, "We have been informed of your interest in the song-sheet series of traditional American music which the Special Skills Division of Resettlement Administration is issuing." It seems likely that Mr. White's interest was not simply spurred by casual curiosity or a personal affinity for folk music, given the solicitor's role representing the department at congressional committee hearings, as well as the fact that Dornbush's memo reads as a vigorous defense explaining the program's rationale and success. A month later, Falke wrote to RA director Will Alexander with a description that seems to exaggerate both the grassroots nature and the cost-saving benefits of the project. She explained that the song-sheets were "distributed at the request of the people occupying our communities. Music and words were furnished by them. The series consists of nine traditional American folk songs which people in these communities use in their gatherings and form an integral part of their daily lives." It was only after determining that published song books could not be acquired for less than $5 a copy, she continued, that they "decided upon the present method of distributing song-sheets sent in by community members with an exchange between communities in various sections of the country." (Of course, the only song-sheet lyrics that were credited as having "been received from Virginia and Florida" were in fact generated by Music Unit staffers.)

Falke's letter offers a clue about the newfound interest in song-sheets from the solicitor's office when she mentions the low costs of a particular song-sheet that had been issued that fall: "'The Dodger' is one of a series of nine song-sheets published by the Resettlement Administration, each publication consisting of approximately 1,000 copies at a cost of slightly less than half a cent each. The cost of publishing 'The Dodger' was five dollars; the total cost of the series was approximately $45.00."

"The Dodger" comes from Emma Dusenbury, likely transcribed by Laurence Powell after his visit accompanying John Lomax. (Sidney also recorded "The Dodger," but not until after this song-sheet was published in the fall of 1936.) While all the other song-sheet covers depict people in realistic scenes directly related to each song's lyrics, the cover for "The Dodger" is more symbolic, showing the rear view of a jackrabbit as it jumps over a log and away from the viewer deeper into the forest. The jaunty dotted rhythm and quick tempo match the biting humor of the lyrics, which begin by repeating that "the candidate's a dodger" and explaining why: "He'll meet you and treat you and ask you for your vote, but look out, boys, he's a-dodging for a note!" Subsequent verses give similar treatment to other roles (lawyer, doctor, preacher, merchant), and more generous words for a farmer ("He'll make a living just as sure as you're born!"), all followed by the short refrain admitting that everyone participates in the dodging game.

In an interview years later, Charlie recalled that the Music Unit's trouble began when a congressman somehow discovered "The Dodger" and found its skewering of politicians offensive, calling the office and threatening to cut the RA's budget for publishing a song he described as "an insult not only to the elected officials in the United States, but to the American government as a whole and the American people thereby." Charlie remembered that the congressman, "a staunch Democrat," was placated by an explanation that it originated as a Democratic campaign song from 1884. (Writer and folklorist Stephen Winnick has called this history into question, positing that Charlie was "a magnificent dodger himself" for coming up with the story.) But regardless of how the trouble was resolved, "The Dodger" clearly created a headache for the entire Special Skills Division, despite the innocuous rabbit on its cover.

Away from this tumult in Washington, Margaret's work in the field remained largely unchanged. In March, she returned to Skyline Farms to help produce an Easter pageant, with the suggestion that she simply adapt her Cherry Lake Easter play "to the Skyline situation." This was her children's pageant, *Easter: Its Origins and Celebration in Many Lands*—the one that began with a pagan sacrificial dance set to Stravinsky's *The Rite of Spring*. Learning of this plan, Sidney drafted a quick letter to Margaret: "I was so incensed to hear a letter being dictated to you saying please go and do what you did last year—with no provision for supplying you with material, that I went down and squandered $13 on you!" Sidney sent sheet music for three Easter carols and a few records she had found, including several Margaret had used at Cherry Lake. "I am not sure you can do anything at all with this," she admitted, "but it just might be interesting to try it on Alabama!" Administrators at Skyline felt otherwise, however, and strenuously objected to such a nontraditional Easter program for their devout Christian community. Margaret pledged to take a more conservative approach, promising, "It will be such as I experienced, at the age of eight, in the Bible Belt of Mississippi." Instead of pagan rituals and folk dancing, there was a cross filled with flowers, with Easter lilies on the piano and children singing familiar hymns. "Everyone seemed satisfied," she reported and then acknowledged, "The mountain knows what it wants."

While Margaret adapted her program to suit its audience, Sidney had no such inclination, despite increased criticism and scrutiny of the Music Unit's work. In March 1937, a delegation from the Southern Tenant Farmers Union (STFU)—an integrated group of Black and White share-croppers, tenant farmers, and farm laborers—came to Washington to seek financial and political support. Founded in Arkansas in 1934 with support from Socialists and Black church leaders, by 1937 the STFU had grown to represent tens of thousands of farm workers across six Southern states. As Sidney later recounted,

> The man who had brought them [to Washington] knew about our program and called up to say that they had made up some songs and didn't we want to record them? Charlie was not in the office, so I dashed, asked them to meet me at the warehouse where the equipment was at the moment, went over there and

met them, and they sang some wonderful songs; one of them
had made up a lot of songs.

This was John Handcox, a young Black sharecropper from Arkansas
known as the "sharecropper's troubadour" or "poet laureate of the STFU"
for his songs and poetry dedicated to the union's cause. Sidney recorded
Handcox reciting two poems (one called "Landlord, What in the Heaven
Is the Matter With You?") and singing six of his songs that drew from
Black musical traditions such as spirituals, blues, and work songs. In
compositions like "Raggedy, Raggedy Are We" and "There Is Mean
Things Happening in This Land," Handcox's songs lament the treatment of farmworkers and trumpet the union's power. Of course, the New
Deal had long offered support to labor unions, but spending government
dollars to record their protest songs would likely not be high on a list of
essential RA activities. As Charlie realized that the RA was now "a much
more conservative set-up than under Tugwell," he became worried about
the Music Unit's "side-collection" of labor songs. He alerted Sidney, "The
collections are off my desk! It would be best not to refer to them or to any
new material in official letters."

The same week as the John Handcox recording session, Sidney confided
to her mother, "Drastic cuts have been made everywhere in the RA, some
divisions having been cut as much as 50 percent. Our division, being a
small, skeletal affair anyway, is only being cut one-third, but even that
is a lot." In the first rounds of cuts, the Music Unit lost Tobey, Kirk, and
Lunsford—a decision, based on his recent date of hire, that Sidney called
"a great shame." Although painful, this move by the RA's new administration to cut payroll costs was somewhat predictable, given the constant
stream of criticism over the RA's oversized staff and bloated administrative
costs. Even having survived thus far, Sidney admitted that "everything
is very uncertain, and for temperaments more inclined to worry than
mine, very nerve-wracking. We have no real assurance that our whole
division will not be disbanded, of course, as its activities are not exactly
agricultural in nature!"

Unfortunately, Sidney felt that the stress of this job insecurity brought out the worst in her boss. She understood why Charlie might be particularly worried about finding another job, given his age (fifty-five) and his growing family (with two young children and a third on the way), but she still took offense at his actions: "He considers that his best bet is to take all the credit for all the work I've done and keep me out of the public eye as much as possible." Much later, Sidney remembered Dornbush calling her into his office that winter, informing her "with some impatience that one didn't just ignore invitations to the White House; one accepted, and went, or if absolutely impossible an explanation and apology was in order. I knew of no such invitation and said so." It turned out that Dornbush had gone to some trouble to arrange an invitation to the White House so they could share Sidney's recording of Will Wright's "Mister Roosevelt" with the president and First Lady, but Charlie had neglected to inform Sidney. In her absence, Charlie had played the recordings "rather awkwardly since he was unused to the equipment," Sidney recalled. "He could not answer questions about the circumstances, which were naturally of interest, and Adrian was provoked with me. I had to say that this was the first I had heard of any such invitation, Charlie had simply kept the center of the stage to himself by leaving me out." It was a pattern she would see again and again. "He never did seem to realize that there was any difference between thinking up the idea of recording, and doing the actual work."

CHAPTER 12

LET THE PEOPLE THEMSELVES MAKE THE MUSIC THEY NEED

t was just a few days before the Ides of March when Sidney received the news. She wrote to her mother later that night:

> Tonight I was sitting chatting with Mr. Seeger and Miss Franke, a swell old gal who is in charge of the field work, and the big boss, Adrian Dornbush, came a-riding by on his highest and largest horse, quite paralyzing the conversation. I was thankful to be small and unimportant and out of harm's way—I thought!—when bang, he dissolved into smiles most cordially and said: 'Tomorrow we must talk about your next job: I'm going to send you to Region 2 (Wisconsin, Minnesota, and Michigan) as Regional Representative for all Special Skills activities—how would you like that?' (This to me.) . . . As I had not been feeling at all sure that I wouldn't get notice of the termination of my job next Monday, the 15th, I was quite astounded.

A few weeks later, Sidney was back on the road—heading northwest instead of south, the trunk of her car seeming much too big without the recording equipment. "My goodness but it was a long way up here!" she wrote to Charlie when she arrived in Milwaukee, realizing she had driven almost a thousand miles. She also suffered from culture shock: "People up here are so damned rude—on the streets, in shops and hotel, I mean—that I was in a temper the entire time for the first couple of days. It's just the contrast with the South, I suppose; they can't all be as ill-tempered as they sound." At first, she worked out of the regional office in the city, helping to coordinate a furniture exhibit at Duluth Homesteads and sending materials about cooperatives out to the homesteads. She also took charge of personnel activities among the regional office staffers, who had already begun planning a fundraiser for the employees' emergency fund. It was to be yet another RA-affiliated minstrel show, proving the racist form was by no means limited to the Jim Crow South. Sidney reported nothing about the details of her role in mounting the show, saying only, "I found I had to tread very delicately to avoid a reputation as another of those Meddlesome Managing Women!"

After a few weeks getting acclimated, she left the office for her first homestead assignment of her RA tenure at Austin Acres, about one hundred miles south of Minneapolis. "I do like it here, the town, the people," Sidney wrote to Charlie in early May, before commenting on weather that was surely difficult for a Californian to understand: "The countryside is at last turning green, I thought spring would NEVER come! The sun has shone for three days now and it is almost warm." Since nearly all Austin Acres' residents were low-income workers already employed at the nearby Hormel factory (which hadn't closed down, given the steady demand for cheap canned meat), she had been told they would have little time for or interest in community activities. Still, Sidney found enough enthusiasm for recreation to keep herself busy, with a garden club, 4-H club, baseball team, and efforts to open a library and bring playground equipment to the homestead. Interest in any music activities remained minimal, much to the frustration of the community manager, who unleashed an exasperated tirade after their half-hearted response to group singing at a homesteaders' meeting: "He told them in no uncertain tones that the federal government wanted them to sing, Mrs. Robertson was here to make them sing, and by God they were going to do it!"

Sidney focused most of her musical energies off the homestead, eager to get back to recording. She arranged for Charlie to send the recording machine to the regional office in Milwaukee, and at the end of May, she drove with it packed carefully in her trunk to the fourth National Folk Festival in Chicago. Compared to the narrow focus on Anglo-American folk traditions presented by Southern festivals like White Top and Asheville, the national festival offered a much broader definition of what constituted American folk culture, drawing on a variety of regional traditions far beyond the Appalachians. In addition to the familiar performances from Lunsford and his usual group of top-notch string players, ballad singers, and square dancers from the South, Sidney recorded Indigenous musicians and dancers from the local Winnebago tribe, clogging and yodeling lumberjacks from Wisconsin, and a combined gospel choir of more than two hundred voices from several Black churches in Chicago. She found songs and instruments she had never heard before from nearby enclaves of recent European immigrants—the dulcimer-like *psalmodikon* played by a group of Norwegian women from Wisconsin, the zither-like *kankles* featured in a Lithuanian band from Chicago, traditional Finnish singers from Minnesota performing ballads with ancient texts. When she left Chicago, Sidney resolved to hold on to the recording equipment and use her spare time to collect more of these musical treasures hiding in the rural enclaves of the Upper Midwest.

Back at Austin, she received a letter from Nicholas Ray, whom she had befriended in their brief time together in Washington. He wrote from Penderlea Homesteads in North Carolina, where he had been sent to help Margaret stage a pageant, calling the experience "occasionally trying. I dislike all the pretense being pushed into this affair and it dulls enthusiasm. Mine, at any rate." Ray did seem to be alone in his lack of enthusiasm. The Penderlea pageant was the highest-profile event that the Special Skills Division had ever mounted, planned as part of the Strawberry Festival in nearby Wallace, North Carolina, at the beginning of June. Eleanor Roosevelt had promised to attend.

Penderlea Homesteads sat about forty miles inland on the Coastal Plains of North Carolina, its residents having been selected from White farm families on relief across North Carolina. Margaret seemed charmed by it, as she described her first experience there, playing for a square dance in February 1937: "The piano was surrounded by an eager friendly crowd unused to seeing a woman performing in an orchestra (?) of men (one guitar, one banjo and one fiddle). In the midst of the gaiety, suddenly a man shouted, 'Say, lady, you want to get married?'" Of course, this incident says as much about Margaret's effect on people as it does about Penderlea, but Margaret sensed a feeling of openness that seemed very different from Skyline: "Penderlea was ready to welcome everything. From the start the community had got the breaks. Planned—as the first farm city—by a group experienced in community planning, farm economics, and folk culture, the homestead and the homesteaders gave immediate evidence of wise choosing and rosy possibilities." Arriving soon after Skyline's Easter pageant, Margaret consulted with the homestead's six original families and soon developed the idea to contrast their pioneering experience with that of the area's eighteenth-century settlers, generating a preliminary title that stuck: *From Settlement to Resettlement.*

Likely because it was known that the First Lady would be in attendance, this pageant proved to have the largest cast of homesteaders of any of her productions, with eighteen speaking parts; seventy singers in three separate choruses of women, men, and boys; a "kitchen orchestra" of twelve women playing pots and pans; and the homestead's three-man string band. Community workers built an outdoor stage with five hundred seats, Ray served as director, and sets were created with supervision from Olle Nordmark—the same Special Skills artist who had created the animal masks for Skyline's Christmas play.

The pageant opened with a women's chorus singing a "Song of Welcome," for which a homesteader had written the words. In her report, Margaret described how the chorus had come together in just a few months:

The chorus was at first just a group of women: some came for the ride (the KL representative usually had to fetch and carry them from their widely separated homes); some to get acquainted or swap gossip and recipes. But they all enjoyed singing of one kind or another and they—and all others interested—were encouraged to use songs, especially those wherein progressive and cooperative ideas meet, as a social medium rather than as music for music's sake. Of necessity there were different women present each Monday, some being kept home by one duty or another. The quality of the music . . . suffered therefrom, but the larger social purpose was well served. We met, sang, fed babies, darned socks, shelled peas, and sang.

Margaret created a theme song for the pageant from a "Sharecropper's Lament" that had been sent to the Music Unit office by the RA's regional office in California. The lyrics originally came from the Arvin migrant camp community manager Tom Collins (who would later serve as the basis for the character of Jim Rawley in John Steinbeck's *Grapes of Wrath*). In his weekly report, Collins noted that this song "brought encore after encore" at a community sing at Arvin, but since he was only able to transcribe the lyrics (not the melody), the region's information chief sent the words to Charlie, asking if anyone could provide the tune. Not only did Margaret know the melody, but the song's arrival inspired her to incorporate it into the Penderlea pageant, sung by a men's chorus in a scene set during the early days of the Depression, with the first line, "Seven cent cotton and forty cent meat, how in the world can a poor man eat?"

In the final scene celebrating the creation of Penderlea Homesteads, the entire cast sang the pageant theme song with new lyrics (presumably written by Margaret), which were printed in the program in case the audience wanted to join in:

> *We'll raise our cotton, we'll raise our meat;*
> *We'll raise everything we eat.*
> *We'll raise our chickens, pigs and corn;*
> *We'll make a living just as sho' as you're born.*

These lyrics follow the themes established by the discontinued song-sheet program—in fact, the fourth line, extolling farmers' resilience, is a direct quote from "The Dodger" song-sheet—serving as just one small example of how Margaret was able to continue the more contentious aspects of the Music Unit's work under the radar.

Likely aware of the First Lady's penchant for joining in square dancing whenever it presented itself, Margaret wrote a passage in the pageant manuscript where the announcer tells the string band, "You've got some pretty good musicians up there. Why don't some of them strike up a tune?" The next line includes a stage direction guessing what would happen next: "after Mrs. Roosevelt is seated." This prediction proved correct: in the pageant performance, someone onstage called out, "We want Mrs. Roosevelt!" during the dancing, and the First Lady sprang out of her seat and onto the stage. At the end of the pageant, she addressed the homesteaders with admiration: "The eyes of the nation are on you, who are building not only a new economic mode of living, but a mode of living more happily." In her address to a large crowd representing people from across the state—White and Black, rural and urban, children and adults—she voiced the community-oriented goals of the RA in simple terms, urging them to "cooperate with each other and to search with each other for what is best for the whole of your community."

The Penderlea pageant was deemed an overwhelming success, with glowing newspaper stories featuring photos of the First Lady dancing with the homesteaders. The event later came to hold such significance for the community, Margaret reported, that "subsequent conversation at Penderlea usually includes, 'Was it before or after the Pageant?' as scholars might say 'B.C.' or 'A.D.'" Regional director George S. Mitchell wrote to Will Alexander in Washington alerting him of "the remarkable performance of the Penderlea homesteaders under the direction of Miss Valiant and Mr. Ray," and offering his thanks to them for "their very large share in the ease, happiness, and sincerity with which the occasion went off." Charlie was pleased in his understated way: "There were no hitches," he wrote to Sidney. "Perhaps that is enough to show competent direction. The people became much attached to Margaret and Nick. Both were asked to return at a later date." In fact, Penderlea's community manager sent in an urgent request for Margaret to be assigned to their homestead permanently.

This public triumph must have added to a growing hope among Special Skills staffers that the new administration would recognize the value of their work and spare them from further cuts. A week after the pageant, in mid-June, Charlie wrote to Sidney, "We are gradually getting used to thinking we shall go on as usual." By July 10, 1937, Margaret had returned to Penderlea to help the 4-H club produce their first play. Nick Ray, back at Westmoreland to work with the Co-op Players, became increasingly interested in folk music, attending all-night music sessions at the home of Tink Queer, the fiddler who had played in Sidney's first RA recording session. Hampton continued his circuit as a traveling music representative among the Appalachian homesteads, but he had for the past few months spent most of his time at Arthurdale, where he had met and fallen in love with a homesteader. (The couple married on July 3, 1937.) Although Lunsford was no longer on the RA's payroll, he secured a position with the WPA that allowed him to continue his work at Skyline Farms, where he had put together a precision square dancing team to join the homestead's talented string band and invited both to perform at the Asheville festival in August.

Outside of her official RA duties in Region 2, Sidney stayed busy laying the groundwork for a recording trip in the Upper Midwest, following up on contacts she had made at the folk festival in Chicago. When she was sent by the regional office to visit several homesteads just north of the Wisconsin border, she decided to take advantage of her time in the field. "I have really unearthed some excellent material here," she wrote to Charlie. "Without asking anybody's permission in detail, I am going to travel furiously in Wisconsin recording whatever I can." She decided to tell her colleagues in the regional office "that I plan to spend the rest of July winding up some technical matters for KL," and assured Charlie,

"They won't mind, though they would think it was crazy if I told 'em in detail what I was doing."

But when she returned to her temporary office in Duluth after this first foray into the field, a stack of mail awaited her that would put all of her plans into question. First was a handwritten letter from Dornbush, who took a somewhat breezy tone: "Things here have as you may have guessed been somewhat jittery. However, we have survived—even though there'll be some unwelcome envelopes sent to quite a number of the division. But there are some slim new prospects on the horizon that keep up our hopes." It is unclear whether Dornbush didn't yet know who would be receiving those unwelcome envelopes, or if he simply didn't want to break the news, but Sidney's mail held one of those dreaded letters of termination. In a handwritten note sent a few days later, Grete Franke sadly explained, "We have fought and struggled to keep you on but we are being cut down to almost nothing. . . . There is nothing more to say than just we are sorry it had to be." A few days later, Charlie wrote with a few more details: "Suffice to say that the '50%' cut was a euphemism for the fairly quick elimination of KL." Margaret and Nick were being transferred to the Department of Agriculture's Education Division, and Charlie had received word of his termination as of October 31. Only Dornbush and a handful of artists from the furniture department would remain.

Sidney seemed to accept this news in her usual unruffled way, but she was determined to hold on to the one thing she still had some control over: the recording machine. She ignored increasingly insistent requests from Dornbush and Charlie that she ship the equipment back to Washington, deciding it was more important to continue her collecting than for the recorder to be repurposed as a copying instrument at the Library of Congress. In her remaining months, she fit in her collecting on the side as she traveled between RA homesteads in her work as a regional representative. By September, she had collected thirty-six discs worth of music—ballads and work songs sung by lumberjacks in Crandon, Wisconsin; Balkan dance musicians playing the *tamburitza* in Eveleth, Michigan; epic ballads and a thirty-two-string *kantele* performed by Finnish immigrants in the Minnesota towns of Cloquet, Virginia, Ely, Winton, and Mountain Iron; an Irish fiddler from the Isle of Lewis who lived in Duluth; a French-Canadian fiddler in Rhinelander, Wisconsin; and music from a one-of-a-kind handmade dulcimer in Ortonville, Iowa. With these recordings, Sidney went far beyond the boundaries of the Music Unit's work on the homesteads, and she was among the first collectors to include the music of ethnic immigrants in a broader collection of American folk music.

At the beginning of October, she packed up the recorder and discs and shipped them all back to Washington, using the RA's just-announced new name on the address label: the Farm Security Administration (FSA). A week later, she began the drive back to California, taking a northern route to complete a circuitous round trip that she had started when she left Carmel two years earlier. She summed up her time with the RA in a letter to her ex-husband Kenneth, "I've been seeing the world, on the North American continent, in a big way the past year, and have driven almost 25,000 miles for the government."

∝≫⌐

In Washington, Charlie hoped to finish a few projects that would show what the Music Unit had accomplished and leave a record of what they had learned for any future government music workers. With fewer than ten representatives working in six communities, his unit's quantitative achievements on the homesteads would not appear particularly impressive as presented in a typical government report. The recordings (658 tracks from thirteen states, almost all collected by Sidney) seemed a remarkable accomplishment, but their direct connection to the RA's mission was difficult to explain, not to mention that the labor protest songs needed to stay hidden. So instead, Charlie took a qualitative approach. Since Margaret's program at Cherry Lake had been by far the most successful, he repurposed a condensed version of her field reports—which Sidney had originally created for training purposes—to now serve as the unit's final report. The field representative is referred to as "Margaret Doe." This may have been an attempt to augment the universality of the report, or as a form of protection from critics, but it also left the real Margaret uncredited for her work. To this compilation, now titled "Journal of a Field Representative," Charlie added a foreword that explained the larger issues at play: "The main question should be not, 'Is it good music?' but, 'What is the music good for?'"

Charlie expanded on these ideas in a much longer document, simply called "Music Manual," which he hoped would allow the Music Unit's approach to inform any of the government's future music-related endeavors. He worked on the manual for months, spending afternoons writing in the quiet of the wood-paneled Music Division at the Library of Congress. The manual begins with a dense twenty-page review of the three branches of American music (traditional, popular, and academic) and their history—typical of Charlie's style but likely skipped by all but the most academically inclined government worker. The next section presents a set of "guiding principles for group-work in music," a helpful distillation of lessons learned from the Music Unit's experiment, many of them gleaned from Margaret's success:

1. Take people as they are.
2. The essential thing in music is the making of it.
3. Quantity should be the immediate, quality an ultimate objective.
4. Let the people themselves make the music they need.
5. Develop local leadership.
6. Consolidate the existing musical background.
7. Group activity is more to be emphasized than individual accomplishment.
8. The basis of musical activity in America is the employment of the traditional idiom.

9.   There is no valid ground for conflict between traditional, popular and academic music.
10.   Music should be cultivated not so much as an end in itself [but] as a means of achieving large social ends. . . .*
12.   He who would teach the people must first learn from them.

In his final months, Charlie oversaw the Department of Agriculture's amateur music program for its employees, which included a chorus and a full orchestra. As his final task in November 1937, he put together a concert as part of an Exhibition of Rural Arts celebrating the department's seventy-fifth anniversary. For the concert's first half, Charlie composed three symphonic arrangements of folk songs—finally getting a chance to do the kind of musical engineering he had first envisioned—played by the orchestra with Margaret as the vocalist. After the intermission, the Resettlement Folk Singers took the stage, a group of about a dozen men and women, most of them current and former government staffers and their families, among them Dornbush, Grete Franke, and Ruth, led by Charlie and Margaret on guitars. They sang the folk song "Careless Love" in simple harmony together, then broke into solos on the jaunty verses of "Cindy," most of them with a distinctly northern lack of twang, such as Dornbush rolling the r's in his verse to comic effect. Their performance was followed by community singing by the audience, which could have been an excellent use for the Music Unit's leftover song-sheets, had they not become such a source of controversy. Charlie had alerted Sidney a few months earlier to "keep the song-sheets all under lock and key, except for very confidential use. Do not give

---

* Principle no. 11 should probably have been omitted from the report and published in an academic journal, since Charlie's six-page discussion does little to explain how it would apply to a government music worker's activities. It reads: "Music serves a number of functions simultaneously, but it is always, and above all, a discipline—or a dissipation."

any away, officially. They are under ban—pictures highly disapproved of. Some words also."

The Resettlement Folk Singers performance was a public version of musical gatherings that had been taking place among Special Skills staffers at parties and informal get-togethers since the division's inception. It was also a kind of reenactment of Tom Benton's jam sessions, perhaps serving as a satisfying final bookend to Charlie's first visit to that Greenwich Village apartment, where he had first learned folk songs like "Cindy," and where the Music Unit was born. But for Margaret, these bookends held little significance. She had discovered folk music long before those Greenwich Village music sessions, and the work she began with the Music Unit would continue long after this concert.

CHAPTER 13

NEW GROUND

A t the end of August 1938, Tugwell's name once again splashed across newspapers nationwide. Among the first to break the story, the *Chattanooga News* headline inquired, "Has Tugwell's Daughter Found Romance at Crossville?" On July 30, 1938, according to the Cumberland County Court clerk's office, a marriage license had been issued to Tannis Tugwell (age twenty-one) and Sevier Watley (age twenty-two), the son of a former miner who was one of the original settlers at Cumberland Homesteads. The *Chattanooga News* reported that Tannis had been at the homestead helping to produce a pageant, that she was now back in Washington, and that she denied the romance and had no plans to marry the miner's son.

As the news spread, other articles followed. Some swooned that Sevier "resembles Don Ameche of the movies" or called him "a husky mountaineer" with the tough-sounding nickname of Stub. According to a front page story in the *Nashville Tennessean*, Sevier's father, Lon Watley, had persuaded his son that he was not ready for married life, since he was only twenty (not twenty-two, as he had claimed on the marriage license) and still had high school courses to finish. But the romance had been real, as other homesteaders confirmed that they knew about the couple's marriage plans. "They tore their license in two," Lon shared with reporters, "my son keeping one half, and Miss Tugwell the other." Still, Tannis kept to her story, telling reporters that "somebody else" must have taken out the license, despite all evidence to the contrary. The *Knoxville News-Sentinel* cast Tugwell in the familiar role of villain and whipping boy—not only was he blamed for breaking up the lovebirds by insisting Tannis return to Washington, but it occurred in the same week his wife, Florence, had filed for divorce, as the headline blared: "Tugwell Loses Wife As He Keeps Girl Single."

Margaret played a small role in this drama as Tannis's supervisor at Cumberland Homesteads and the one who brought her back to Washington a few weeks afterward. Margaret had even joked about the possible marriage when she wrote to Tugwell on July 16 encouraging him to attend the pageant. "You'd love the drive down, and the Cumberland Mountains are glorious now. And we've erected a charming amphitheater, and a fairly entertaining pageant will be presented. And you should see the homes and the people. *To say nothing of what may turn out to be your future son-in-law.*"

Although many articles reported that Tannis had only been at Cumberland Homesteads for the summer, she had in fact first come the previous September, when it was said that she "promptly fell in love with a Homesteader's son." A few weeks earlier, Tugwell had asked FSA administrator C. B. Baldwin to arrange a job for his daughter as Margaret's assistant. According to Sidney, Tugwell "thought Margaret would do Tanis [*sic*] good. . . . Tanis wanted to see life, or something, and her father was trying to direct her toward social problems instead of society." When Margaret was informed of this arrangement, she wrote to Baldwin from Crossville: "I can't imagine what she will do around our office—if that is the plan—until my return. Therefore I suggest she join me at Cumberland Homesteads—where I will be for approximately a month. I can meet her somewhere and would enjoy doing it." Following the Music Unit's instinct for confidentiality, she sent this as a handwritten note, explaining, "Inasmuch as I could not reach you by telephone I'm writing in this way, not knowing how much concerning her is a matter of office knowledge."

By this time, Margaret had acquired "a little second-hand car" after growing tired of relying on trains to get from one homestead to another and asking for rides to travel across the communities. At Cumberland, her first task was to meet with homesteaders and those living in surrounding communities, collecting songs they knew and stories about their own backgrounds and the history of the area to serve as the basis of the pageant. Homestead staffer Leta Smith, who was asked to show Margaret around the area, later described her as "a brilliant girl who carried her old guitar with her everywhere she went." She still remembered one of the visits they took, "to an elderly man that I knew to be an interesting character and a teller of tall tales." As she described,

> As I arrived with Margaret and her guitar, he moved his rocking chair to the other end of the porch as if to say he would have nothing to do with New York or Washington. When I came out of the house after a short visit with his wife, he had pulled his rocking chair up near to Margaret and was slapping her on the knees and telling her a big tale. I don't know to this day how she broke the ice with him.

In November 1937, Margaret and Tannis left Cumberland for Washington to help Charlie with the Department of Agriculture concert. Tannis had a lovely singing voice, and in addition to joining in with the Resettlement Folk Singers on the group songs (and singing a solo verse on "Cindy"), she and Margaret performed duets of "Cotton-Eyed Joe" and "I'm Just Here To Get My Baby Out of Jail," which they had heard a woman at Cumberland Homesteads sing as lullabies to her son.

Tannis continued to act as Margaret's sidekick in her music work, and the two spent most of the winter and spring of 1938 preparing for the pageant at Cumberland, planned to commemorate the opening of the new school building in July. In April, the WPA's Federal Theatre Project sent Drama Supervisor Sande Jaffray, a director from New York City, to help lead the production. Jaffray worked with Margaret on the script, blocking the material into scenes and rewriting her dialogue for "dramatic effectiveness," co-directed the play, and oversaw the construction of an amphitheater with room for 3,500 spectators, set into a nearby hollow by homesteaders and a crew from the Civilian Conservation Corps (CCC).

Margaret sent a handwritten report describing her progress at Cumberland to John O. Walker, the director of the FSA's Resettlement Division, who now served as her supervisor. She found that the "settlement to resettlement" arc of her Penderlea pageant could be readily adapted to her new surroundings on the Cumberland Plateau. The pageant would be called *New Ground* and would "trace the struggle of the 'Cumberland' family in their pursuit of life, liberty, and happiness from their first settlement in 1838 on a land grant from the government (which, in turn, the government obtained from the Cherokees) until the present time." Unlike at Penderlea, where Margaret found almost unanimous interest in the pageant among the homesteaders, at Cumberland, the research, planning, and much of the cast came largely from Crossville town residents and those in nearby communities. Jaffray found the homesteaders "for the most part either indifferent or hostile to the whole enterprise."

Eleanor Roosevelt wasn't able to attend; neither was Tugwell, nor US Secretary of State Cordell Hull, a longtime Tennessee politician who was the event's honoree. But on July 28, 1938, an estimated five thousand people from across the region came to the homestead to celebrate the dedication of its handsome school buildings: a high school and elementary school set across from each other, both within view of the imposing water tower atop the administration office—the tallest building for miles. The dedication ceremony was followed by lunch and a tour of the homesteads, after which participants followed a path that bent around the cannery building and down the hollow to the new amphitheater.

This pageant involved a larger proportion of the community off the homestead than any of Margaret's previous productions, with only a small troupe of actors from among the homesteaders (Sevier Watley among them). The first scene of Act Two featured actors from the nearby town of Linary, the second scene citizens from Crossville—including Congressman J. Ridley Mitchell playing the part of the railroad baron Jere Baxter. Chorus members came from several church choirs in Crossville and smaller singing groups in Big Lick, Grassy Cove, and Vandever; the Crossville Band and Dorton String Band provided accompaniment; and young men from the nearby CCC camp were recruited to play soldiers and members of a Cherokee tribe. Longtime residents from throughout the area loaned their keepsakes dating back one hundred years or more to be used as props and costumes for the early historical scenes: saddle bags, churns, rifles, shawls and dresses, and an early-nineteenth-century iron pot from a family in nearby Sparta. The happy ending followed a familiar formula for Margaret's pageants, with a "Homesteader" arriving to lead the poor family to salvation from the Great Depression—a welcome contrast to the earlier scenes of devastating work at the mill and the mines that had left the audience in tears—and a celebration to the tune of "Happy Days Are Here Again."

Cumberland's pageant was deemed a success, so much so that there were calls to make it an annual event. Of course, Margaret did not have much time to bask in her achievement, since Tannis and Sevier applied for their marriage license on July 30, just two days after the pageant. On August 4, Margaret sent Major Walker a terse telegram from Crossville: "Leaving today for Washington. Please authorize 2 weeks leave beginning August 8." According to Sidney, "Margaret disliked the job of cicerone, and after the Cumberland Homesteads incident she gave it up firmly, Tannis having I judged proven too much responsibility for anyone outside her own family."

By then, word of Margaret's achievements had spread to other corners of the FSA. Jonathan Garst, the director of Region 9 based in San Francisco, made arrangements with Major Walker to have her come to California. "I have heard of her work, and am sure she would find many opportunities in our projects and camps toward lifting these people out of their rut," Garst told Walker. "Greatly appreciate your offer to lend her to us." In California, Margaret would be taking on the music job in the FSA's migrant camps that had first been proposed for Sidney when she left on her collecting trip in November 1936. Now, nearly two years later, Margaret had the chance to take her own solo road trip, farther into the western United States than she had ever been before.

On her way to California, Margaret stopped for a three-week assignment at Fairfield Bench Farms in Teton County, Montana, on the eastern slope of the Rockies. In her report to Major Walker, she marveled at her new surroundings and how different they were in every way from her previous assignments: "The change from hill and valley to prairie and butte; from 40 acres and a mule to 80 acres and a tractor; from 'wet farming' to 'dry farming'; from [last names of] Smith and Johnson to Schmidt, Jonson, Jansen, Hanse, and Hanz; from 100 in the shade to 50 below in the sun." The community was largely made up of German-Russian immigrants who had been relocated from submarginal farmland in the eastern Montana plains to establish a denser settlement of irrigated farms drawing from newly built canals. Historian Brian Q. Cannon notes that many of these families especially appreciated the project's social activities, their enthusiasm for social functions inspiring the community manager to playfully refer to them as "dancing fools."

As Margaret explained in a handwritten report, "I can't send you the pageant I wrote about the west for the simple reason that I didn't write it. It was already written (grace à Dieu) when I arrived by the Community Manager. And when a Community Manager writes a play, that's news. A good job too." The cast had already been chosen by a well-organized Pageant Committee, and nearly one hundred participants made time for rehearsals despite the busy harvesting season. The production, she reported, was staged "with whole-hearted cooperation and with a minimum of disappointments," drawing the largest crowd in the area's history. In her report, she reflected on her time at Fairfield Bench, and in the west more generally: "The westerners are naturally cooperative (cooperative in the real sense of 'neighborly'). Of their own initiative they got up a farewell party for me the night before I left (every woman brought pumpkin pie with whipped cream, and the office furnished coffee). This never happened to me before." The landscape on her drive west from Montana was equally new and astonishing to her, as she wrote, "One of the most impressive moments was coming through a straight lane of virgin white pine that rose straight as lodge poles for 300 feet. The landscape gardeners who planned Versailles and the Pitti

gardens would have felt sick with envy. And I came through Idaho! It had
never seemed possible before to think of Idaho as a state. (It was either a
place in Nevada or a song by Cab Calloway.) And the Lookout Pass! I was
so scared I could hardly drive!"

Margaret did not send this handwritten report to the FSA office; she
sent it to Tugwell, with the informal greeting of "Dear Rex," rather than
the typical header of an official memorandum. Her letter serves as concrete evidence that since resigning nearly two years earlier, the former RA
director had remained personally involved with his beloved Special Skills;
in the division's final days, Dornbush had called him "still as much as ever
our patron saint." When he left his government post, Tugwell had briefly
served as vice president of his friend (and former Brain Truster) Charles
Taussig's molasses company, but by 1938 he had returned to the public
sector, appointed as the first director of the New York City Planning Commission. This still left him well outside the governance of the FSA, but in
an interview years later Margaret said she had been "sent to the migrant
camps by Rex Tugwell."

Once on the West Coast, Margaret's first stop was the FSA's regional
office in San Francisco, located in a stately building downtown that had
once held the California Supreme Court. Dornbush had known the
regional director, Jonathan Garst, from the early days of the RA, when
they sat at desks across from each other in the Planning Division. He
called him "a fine chap," remembering that "he was always very much
interested in my work." Roy Stryker, the longtime director of the RA/
FSA photography program, described Garst as "quite something—bull
voice, burly guy, trained in geography in Scotland, very likable guy who I
had warm feelings for." But Margaret approached her meeting with some
trepidation, having been told that Garst "didn't like women in positions of
government." (When Sidney had called Garst about a job soon after she
returned to San Francisco, he told her "that the only jobs open to women
were as nurses and public health instructors.")

Margaret later remembered sitting in the waiting room: "I was outside
the glass door, before reaching the august presence of Jonathan Garst, and I

heard this roaring out, over the transom, 'Tell him to go to hell! Tell him I'll see him when I wish to see him. And that may be never.' And then, I am summoned." For anyone familiar with Margaret's superpower-level charisma, the outcome of this meeting should come as no surprise. "Soon, we got to be really good friends," she said. Garst wrote to Tugwell a few days later, seeming to renounce his earlier scorn for women in government: "I think Miss Valiant is going to make a big contribution to our projects out here."

In Region 9, much of the FSA's work focused on improving living conditions for the growing numbers of poor White migrant farm workers from Oklahoma, Arkansas, Missouri, and Texas—all derisively known as "Okies"—who had fled drought, failing crops, and the crushing effects of the Depression to seek a new life in California. Back in 1934, when Falke visited California's Imperial Valley in her travels with Lorena Hickok, she had been horrified at the living conditions of the farm laborers, writing, "I can truthfully say that I have never before seen such abject poverty. They have absolutely no sanitary facilities and they drink the water from the ditches." The RA built migrant camps to provide a more humane life for these migrants, work that continued under the FSA. Historian James Gregory has explained that 95 percent of these southern migrants were White, as Black farmers from the South were more likely to migrate to northern cities during this period. This Whiteness—what Gregory called "the empathetic value of white skin"—contributed to the use of these so-called Dust Bowl migrants as poster children for the New Deal's efforts to help the poor. At the same time, the Associated Farmers—a powerful network of growers and agricultural business leaders—and the conservative press worked hard to sway public opinion in their favor, smearing the Okies as unworthy of sympathy.

After spending Thanksgiving with her long-lost aunt Eugenia, who had fled Mississippi to San Francisco decades earlier, Margaret made her way to Los Angeles. Christmas was only a month away, and she wanted to create something beyond a local pageant—a Christmas special for radio broadcast that would both boost morale on the FSA's migrant camps and raise public awareness about the migrants' plight. Garst thought she could get support from Hollywood, and on November 21, he wired Tugwell asking him to help her set up a meeting with the director King Vidor, who had shown himself to be an ally of the RA. Vidor had made his 1934 film *Our Daily Bread* specifically "in accord with the President's plan of subsistence homesteads" and had also provided critical support to Pare Lorentz in the making of two documentaries produced for the RA and FSA: *The Plow that Broke the Plains* (1936) and *The River* (1938). Tugwell immediately sent Vidor a letter asking him to meet with Margaret ("a most delightful and entertaining person, rich in experience and with a point of view which you will appreciate") and wired Garst joking that they should "keep her away from Hollywood or we will lose her altogether."

Tugwell may have acted quickly because he knew he would soon be unavailable. The next day, after presiding over a three-minute planning commission meeting that the *New York Times* quipped "set a record for brevity," he and Falke were married by Mayor LaGuardia at City Hall, then left for a brief vacation to celebrate. The archives provide few clues about their romance. Even Sidney's gossipy letters failed to mention the possibility—in fact, Sidney had it wrong, writing just a few days before the wedding that she suspected that Tugwell "would like to marry Margaret eventually."

Back in Los Angeles, Tugwell's pre-wedding letter to King Vidor seemed to have done the trick. A week later, Margaret wrote to thank him: "Bless you. I saw Vidor yesterday. He was swell. So has everyone been. . . . I am snowed under by the Alice-in-Wonderland growth of this project." Margaret's idea for a radio broadcast had converged with plans for a Christmas party for the children at the FSA camps by the John Steinbeck Committee to Aid Agricultural Organization, led by the Hollywood couple Helen Gahagan and Melvyn Douglas. The committee named the event "Christmas for One-Third of the Nation," after Roosevelt's description of "one-third of the nation ill clothed, ill housed and ill fed." The party would take place at the Shafter camp, just north of Bakersfield, and the FSA would pay for transportation for migrants from three other camps—Arvin just thirty miles away; Brawley in Imperial County; and Indio in Riverside

County. The committee had been busy soliciting donations: seven thousand toys, five thousand gingerbread Santa Clauses, hundreds of pounds of candy, two truckloads of oranges, and enough ice cream for seven thousand children. NBC promised a one-hour national radio broadcast, which would be split between the party at Shafter and performances at a Hollywood studio by big-name stars who couldn't make the two-hour trip to Kern County.

Shafter was the largest of the FSA's migrant camps, with space for 240 families, their tents set in a neat grid of roads surrounding a central community building. On December 24, two enormous circus tents rose from an adjacent field. Cars began to arrive at 9 A.M., though the party would not begin for hours, and by the afternoon parked cars lined roadsides for a mile in each direction. At 1 P.M., the standing-room crowd of nearly eight thousand gathered in the main tent, entertained by the Clam-Bake Cats swing trio from Hollywood, as well as by what the *Fresno Bee* called "home talent"—people from among the migrants living at the camps, including string bands, solo fiddle players, singers, and poets. FSA camp managers like Tom Collins had encouraged musical activities since the early days of the program, with weekly community sings becoming "so popular that there was no room for visitors" and weekend dances accompanied by string bands attracting hundreds of guests. In the weeks leading up to the party, Margaret said she had "combed the migrant camps for the best talent, performers and works to perform." Among them was a poem called "The Migrant," written by a Shafter resident for the event, which Margaret remembers creating a particularly poignant moment: "As it was recited by the writer's lovely daughter in the old-fashioned 'Night Before Christmas' sing-song, it was too much even for calloused ears." The poem's last lines give a sense of its effect:

> *As we traveled tonight in the cold and the rain*
> *Our minds wandered back down memories' lane.*
> *To a once happy home and a fireside bright*
> *Where we all used to gather on Christmas Eve night.*

The kiddies would talk of what Santy would bring
They knew there'd be lots of very nice things.
But those are fond memories, for tonight we must spend
In a cold ragged tent, where the trail will end.

Amid the Hollywood whirlwind that had taken over the event, Margaret's public role shrank to a brief appearance, scheduled to coincide with the beginning of the radio broadcast. At the appointed time, she led a group of singers from among the migrant workers in a spirited rendition of "Goin' Down the Road Feeling Bad," a song that had become a mainstay at community sings on the camps. She later wrote that many people called it "the song of the 'Okies,' but it is sung in some variation by nearly everyone." While the singers received vigorous applause from the audience at Shafter, radio listeners heard only the end of the song's last verse as the broadcast cut in a bit behind schedule, almost as if they had walked into the party by mistake and interrupted the festivities. As emcee, Melvyn Douglas sounded a bit flustered, thanking the singers before explaining, "Ladies and gentlemen, in the excitement of getting on the air, I haven't yet said hello and good afternoon properly, nor explained the why's and wherefores of this program." Confidence returned to his voice as he continued:

> This is meant to be a Christmas greeting to the nation, represented here by the thousands of men, women, and children gathered in this migratory camp at Shafter, a city of tents established by the United States department of agriculture to provide homes for the workers who must follow the shifting harvests up and down the thousands of miles of California's agricultural valleys. . . . The government has made a start toward helping these homeless people, people for whom jobs are few and far between. And now, on Christmas Eve, those of us from Hollywood can't help but remember those youngsters and grown-ups, too, whose Christmas might not be as bright as our own.

Helen Gahagan then sang two folk-inspired Christmas carols, followed by a short radio play titled "Tomorrow's My Birthday" enacted by the small troupe of actors who had made the trip to Shafter. After this, Douglas called out, "Hollywood, it's yours!," and the radio audience was transported to a boisterous party of movie stars including Joe Penner, Bob Hope, Dick Powell, Anne Shirley, and Virginia Bruce. The comic sketches and monologues that followed took on a distinctly different tone, a stark reminder of the luxury that existed beyond the camps. In his monologue, Bob Hope told jokes about Christmas shopping that seemed especially jarring, with lines like, "That store was so big you have to hitchhike!" and "I love to ride on those escalators."

Gahagan later wrote that she and Douglas often felt dismayed at the lack of compassion shown toward the migrants by their Hollywood peers, lamenting that "there was an entrenched aversion to recognizing that a problem existed." Such a disconnect seemed very much on display during the next segment of the broadcast, in which Dick Powell and the actress Virginia Bruce asked to talk to some of the people in Shafter over the radio. Bruce spoke with a young man named Lorenzo Wheeler, the breeziness of her questions highlighting the difference in mood between the two Christmas parties, and she seemed taken off guard by the seriousness of his responses:

Bruce: What would you like most if you could have a gift this Christmas?

Wheeler: Well, I'd like best to have a little home, back on the farm, and a chance to live.

Bruce: Oh, I don't blame you. How did you come to California in the first place, Mr. Wheeler?

Wheeler: Well, the drought took me out at home, and I come out here lured out here by the promise of high wages and lots of work.

Bruce: Oh, I see.

Dick Powell had a similar experience trying to make small talk with Joe Carter, who said he was from Elk City, Oklahoma:

Powell: Do you like it up there in the valley?

Carter: Not too good, no sir.

Powell: You don't like it up there, huh?

Carter: No, sir.

Of course, none of this mattered to the children at the Shafter Christmas party, who had lost interest in the radio broadcast as they lined up in the tent next door for food, candy, and oranges, then received gifts delivered by Santa and watched screenings of Disney shorts. "If several thousand wild-eyed kids are any criterion," one event committee member wrote to Garst's office, "it was a howling success. And there were many swell people on hand who could not have missed the social significance of it all. . . . The radio program was accepted locally as 'weak' in spots but enjoyable and probably served its purpose generally." Garst, predictably, had a blunter assessment: the party, he reported to Tugwell, had "toys, sandwiches, oranges—entertainment for the whole lot without a hitch—a miracle. The broadcast was rotten. Margaret let Hollywood do it. Their hearts were right but they are terrible on 'documentary broadcasting.'"

For Margaret, the Christmas party was just the beginning. She began the new year on assignment at Casa Grande Farms in Arizona, about halfway between Phoenix and Tucson, where the desert landscape felt like a different planet but the community structure was quite familiar. Unlike the FSA's temporary migrant camps, Casa Grande was an experimental cooperative farm set up as a permanent place for migrants to live. In less than a month, Margaret somehow launched a rather robust music program, drawing on all her experience in RA communities. She helped create a youth group and hosted music-themed youth activities, recruited music leaders for weekly community sings, rehearsed and produced a one-act play, and transcribed the songs that people liked to sing, handing out simple song-sheets for future use.

In February, she wrote to Alan Lomax, who had taken over from his father at the Archive of American Folk Song, announcing cheerfully, "The FSA has sent me a recording machine!" Made by Radioscriptions, the machine was smaller than the Garwick and thus more portable, but it lacked some of its bells and whistles, like its high-end thorn needle for playback or its copying ability. It is unclear what inspired this purchase, but it may have been that hearing the Shafter camp musicians at the Christmas party had piqued FSA officials' interest. Whatever the reason, Margaret wasted no time in putting the recorder to use, following her own interests when she was away from the FSA projects. She made a special effort to record the Mexican American musicians she encountered while traveling through Arizona in Phoenix, Tempe, and Tucson. In Phoenix, she was also invited to what she called simply "the Indian School" to record children singing traditional music from their own tribes. Her recordings include boys and girls variously singing a Hopi butterfly dance, Pima circle dance, Apache sunrise dance, and Mojave bird song. "I was the first person to record in an 'Indian school' in Arizona," she told an interviewer, the memory still vivid nearly forty years later. "They sang me this beautiful little butterfly song."

Margaret also made extensive use of the recording equipment in her work on the FSA projects. She explained her first attempt at Casa Grande Farms: "Recordings from other parts of the country were played to this fascinated audience after which old-timers and young-timers were encouraged to perform their traditional or contemporary songs, some of which were recorded, to the delight and pride of all." Margaret's use of the recording equipment connected with the goals she had always set for her government music work—to restore dignity and hope among people who had lost everything. She later explained that the purpose was "to say, look friends, be proud of what you know. Be proud of what you have learned. Be proud of whatever you have around you to be proud of, and take pride in yourself."

After finding such success at Casa Grande, Margaret brought the recorder on a tour of FSA camps and surrounding areas running through central California: Calapatria, Indio, Brawley, Arvin, Shafter, and Visalia. At each, she would hold an event that was a cross between a talent show and a recording session, where she would play recordings she had already made and invite anyone to come up and perform whatever music they wanted—whatever kept them going. Margaret cultivated a personal connection with the musicians she recorded, drawing on her own background as a performer to put them at ease, as she described later, "I began to learn the trick of getting people to sing, because I would take my guitar, and I would strum a little, . . . that breaks down the reserves, and they would see that I was modest about it, and honest about it. And then, well, [they would say], 'Oh, my granddaddy used to sing such-and-such,' and 'Well, I made up a song the other day.'" Old folk songs, popular songs from the radio and movies, original compositions, hymns, poems, skits, tap dances—all were welcome. Some songs evoked home and the sadness of leaving or the trials they faced as they migrated, but others were funny, and overall the recordings reveal a joyful party atmosphere—perhaps giving a hint of the magic that Margaret had brought to her work, beginning at Cherry Lake. Unfortunately, as had been true at Cherry Lake and elsewhere, following the participants' musical choices meant the inclusion of a few songs with racist lyrics from blackface minstrelsy and the "coon song" music genre from earlier in the twentieth century.

As she traveled to the different migrant camps, she recorded several renditions of groups singing "Goin' Down the Road Feeling Bad," including one that ended with a rousing pro-union verse of "O come and join the C.I.O!" A teenager named Curley Reeves sang a yodeling blues song, and twelve-year-old Zanadia McCrea from Oklahoma performed a tap dance. Performers included traveling musicians like the King Family string band, or just families who sang together, as Margaret described in notes accompanying a song called "Old Blue":

Four members of the Franklin family—papa, mama and 2 daughters—at the government camp at Indio, California. At first, the Franklins said they couldn't sing this song because the son, who imitated the dog, was at school (the remainder of the family was illiterate). At a request for a volunteer to fill in, many were eliminated before the Franklins—and the crowd—were satisfied with the proper dog sounds.

Somehow, as the last woman standing from the RA's Music Unit, Margaret managed to fulfill the program's original goals of using music to improve morale and unite a community while simultaneously breaking from many of its established conventions. In the RA's Music Unit, recordings had a long-term goal of folk song preservation and were mostly kept separate from the field representative's work on the homesteads, with a never-realized plan to bring the polished records to the communities. But in just a few months with the machine, Margaret had shown what was possible if the two were integrated. The people on the projects found joy in making their own records and listening to those of others, the kind of joy in sharing a part of themselves that could help build community and improve morale. She discovered that songs didn't need to be provided by a folklorist or an expert performer, and didn't really need to be a particular *kind* of music to serve this purpose. Music was music.

At the same time, Margaret made a decisive break from the Music Unit's past secretiveness, and in fact had the opposite impulse, wanting nothing more than to make her recordings public. She hoped to create a compilation of her favorite songs that could be used as a sort of aural accompaniment to the FSA Information Division's photographs. She thought music and the people's own voices would be a powerful way to highlight the humanity of the migrant workers, supporting the Information Division's efforts to build public support for the FSA's work and to combat anti-migrant messages in the press.

In March 1939, she held a press conference in Los Angeles where she played a sample of her recordings and gave an impassioned speech:

So long as our least-privileged citizens have the right of self-expression, can laugh when hungry and go around throwing

tunes instead of bombs, we need not fear for American democracy. . . . In Tempe, Ariz., a young Spanish-speaking boy—who
had never traveled farther than 10 miles and was as American
as you or I even though his ancestors came over the Mexican
border—sang one of the most beautiful Spanish songs I've heard
in all my travels. . . . After hearing the King family ('Reckon
we're the only family ever did come *clean* from Arkansas') play
together, right down to little Billy who played a bull-fiddle as
big as he was, it is impossible to think of these folks as people
without wit or culture.

When Margaret's western assignment ended the next month, she still
hoped to convince the FSA's Information Division to share her recordings
with the public. Back in Washington, she worked with an engineer to make a
master set of her favorite recordings and began to compile the song lyrics and
stories behind the recordings to accompany them. "The value of documentary
photographs to illustrate the reforms which our country needs has now been
demonstrated and accepted," she wrote in a draft introduction to her lyric
sheet. "Wherever these photographs are used—for exhibits, lectures, or other
educational purposes—documentary recordings can intensify their effect."

Eleanor Roosevelt, who had become a friend since they had met at the
Penderlea pageant a few years earlier, was much impressed when Margaret
had a chance to share the recordings with her. "Miss Margaret Valiant,
who has been making a study of cultural backgrounds in various parts of
the country," the First Lady wrote in her daily newspaper column, "came
in at tea time and brought some records she has made of songs heard in
the migratory workers camps of the Southwest and Western Coast. Some
of them are really extraordinarily interesting and show great talent, which
is remarkable to find under such strained economic conditions."

Writing to Mrs. Roosevelt that summer, Margaret shared her continued
hopes for the recordings: "I have tried to interest Farm Security in devel-
oping this [recording] activity along with their photographs as documentary
sources. It is my feeling that the voices of our disinherited people, together

with their faces, can do more to persuade outsiders of their vitality and worth than anything our information or education divisions can write."

With the usual bureaucratic delay, Margaret had to wait several months for the FSA Information Division to make a few copies of her compilation available for distribution. On September 15, 1939, President Roosevelt sent a letter to Secretary of Agriculture Henry Wallace:

> My Dear Mr. Secretary,
> I just want to tell you how pleased and interested I was to see that set of recordings and transcript of the words of that fine collection of songs, which you were good enough to send me. Mrs. Roosevelt joins in sending sincere thanks for your kind thought. Please convey to Miss Valiant an expression of our appreciation.

In her written introduction to the song lyrics accompanying the records, Margaret articulated the role, so often hidden, that music plays in sustaining us through the hardest of times:

> Here are the voices of families, like the Franklins and the Kings, who stick together in spite of hell and high water, and move on, singing together. Old songs that frequently constitute all that remains of the possessions they set out with, and new songs they have improved out of a new situation. Here are the voices of their children . . . singing the current tunes with all the romantic hope of youth. Here too are the voices and characteristic rhythms of our Spanish-speaking natives, to remind us that the "Round Up" began with them.
> And, finally, here are the voices of individuals and groups from all parts of our land who use such tunes as they know or can invent, with such words as they command, with such courage as they can summon, to express their suffering, their protest, and their simple love of life.

EPILOGUE

I t was January 1965, and Richard Doud had set up his tape recorder in the sunny Santa Barbara home of the Honorable Rexford G. Tugwell—esteemed political science scholar and former governor of Puerto Rico. Doud had spent the past few years conducting oral history interviews for the Smithsonian Archives of American Art, trying to uncover the lost history of the documentary photographs made by the RA and FSA. Roy Stryker, who directed the photographers in the Information Division, had told him several things about the RA that needed clarifying.

Doud was likely puzzled that Mr. Tugwell invited his wife Grace to join their interview—and that she was doing so much of the talking—until Tugwell said about the documentary program, "Grace had charge of all that. I really didn't." Doud turned to her. "You were secretary to Mr. Tugwell?" he asked. "No," she replied. "I was executive assistant in charge of [several] divisions, you see. Labor was one of them; Special Skills, Information." Doud may have thought this was a technicality; "executive assistant" certainly sounded like a fancier word for secretary. Doud continued, "Roy mentioned one time that there were some very good disc recordings made . . . Do either of you know anything about those?" Mr. Tugwell responded, "Would this be the folk songs? We had a whole division for that. . . . Margaret Valiant was the one who did most of the folk music." Mrs. Tugwell added, "The folk music was under Adrian Dornbush."

Doud hadn't known anything about the Special Skills Division, but it seemed an important part of the story. Six months later, on a humid June morning just before a rainstorm, Doud tracked down Dornbush in his modest home surrounded by the El Yunque Mountain rainforest, about thirty miles east of San Juan, Puerto Rico—about as far removed from the bureaucratic halls of Washington as he could imagine. When Dornbush left the FSA back in 1938, he quickly transferred to the WPA, where he was put in charge of "the applied arts," since the WPA already had established programs in the fine arts. Charlie and many of the other Special Skillets also landed at the WPA, where, with Eleanor Roosevelt's support, they helped organize folk music concerts at the White House. In May of 1938, they arranged for Lunsford to bring twenty-eight musicians from Skyline Farms as the entertainment at a monthly tea the First Lady held for women administrators across the government. Their highest-profile event took place in June 1939, when FDR "insisted that a program of American folk music be given" for King George VI and Queen Elizabeth, who were the first British monarchs to visit the United States. Performers included the North Carolina Spiritual Singers, directed by Nell Hunter (the choral director who Charlie had once hoped to hire as a field representative), the Coon Creek Girls from Kentucky, and Lunsford's champion Soco Gap Square-Dance Team. In the first years of the 1940s, Dornbush had become good friends with the First Lady and was her frequent companion at the symphony in Washington, but by 1942, he had retreated to Puerto Rico, where Tugwell had been appointed governor. The reasons for such a dramatic life change—from a director-level government administrator to managing a small handicraft business in a remote part of Puerto Rico—remain uncertain, but it might not be coincidental that the timing just preceded the beginning of the Lavender Scare, an anti-gay crusade that forced many gays and lesbians from public service in Washington.

Speaking with Doud in the summer of 1965, Dornbush tried to explain just what they had been up to in Special Skills, perhaps wanting to avoid setting off any alarms amid the anti-Communist fervor of the Cold War. "What we did do and did very effectively was our community programs," he said, describing how on the RA homesteads, "there was no social-cultural unity to bind [the homesteaders] together. . . . It was their own participation and activity, and that's how we got started on folk music activity." He added that the Music Unit's collecting activity "is the one tangible thing that we did in the Special Skills which has really lasted and boomed. . . . I think it was the starting point of the current interest in folk music."

The hidden life of the Music Unit serves as a kind of prequel to the origin story for the folk revival, its fingerprints everywhere once you start to look for them. All kinds of songs—from Sidney's and Margaret's collecting, the song-sheet project, and even the lyrics that Margaret wrote to "Seven-Cent Cotton and Forty-Cent Meat" for the Penderlea pageant—would go on to feed the revival. The songs show up in printed folk music compilations with attributions that show a direct link to their roots in the RA, and these collections then served as sources for recordings that circulated the songs further. As Mike Seeger's biographer later summarized, "Without realizing it, [Charles] Seeger and his RA colleagues were helping to build the sound track for the emerging folk music revival."

Sidney, in one of several reminiscences she wrote and recorded in her later years, reflected on the Music Unit's collecting work and the song-sheet project: "It never occurred to us that song-sheets, however attractive, play no role in oral tradition, nor that it was unnecessary to search for clients' community traditions in the places they had left. The fact is, their traditions travelled with them right in their own heads. Nonetheless, our ignorance led to a lot of musically valuable work." The Music Unit had launched Sidney into a new life as a song collector. After returning to San Francisco from the Midwest in 1937, she created and directed the California Folk Music Project, under the auspices of the WPA, to conduct a broad survey of musical traditions in Northern California. Continuing the approach she began in the Upper Midwest, she cast a wide net to record music from ethnic European immigrants, recording thirty-five hours of music in twelve languages from throughout the region, much of which had never before been documented. Alan Lomax's organization, the Association for Cultural Equity, has acknowledged that "it was probably more through Sidney Cowell than anyone that Lomax first became familiar with the musics of the diverse ethnic enclaves of the United States."

In 1941, Sidney surprised many when she married the avant-garde composer Henry Cowell, the friend she and Charlie had found they had in common. Cowell had recently been paroled from San Quentin prison after serving time for breaking California's morals code (he was bisexual and had been arrested for having sex with an underage man), and Sidney had been one of many allies who worked to get him released and, later, pardoned. This marriage gave Sidney financial and social stability and the associated benefits of joining her life with a celebrated figure in the art-music world. During and after the war, Sidney accompanied Henry on music-collecting trips sponsored by the US State Department and the Rockefeller Foundation, and in the 1950s released three commercial recordings of music she had collected in Nova Scotia, Wisconsin, and Ireland. But by 1964, she had stopped collecting, and after Henry Cowell's death in 1965, Sidney dedicated her remaining years to promoting his work and protecting his legacy.

Sadly, Charlie found himself in a similar position, becoming a champion of Ruth's compositions after she died from cancer in 1953. He wrote to Margaret in 1973, having been out of touch for decades, and asked, "Have you seen any of the recent reviews of the *Quartet 1931* that [Ruth] brought back on the ship that you both came back from Europe on?" Charlie was by then an eminent scholar of ethnomusicology, an area of study often defined as "the study of music in culture," which he had helped to establish as a recognized academic field in the United States in the early 1950s. After holding a research appointment at the Institute for Ethnomusicology at UCLA, he retired to an eighteenth-century farmhouse in Bridgeport, Connecticut, which had been in his family for generations, having by then attained what his biographer called "a perfect balance" of academic writing and lecturing, travel, and family. In his letter to Margaret, he acknowledged the impact of her RA work on his thinking: "I've told the story of your stay at Cherry

Lake all over the country. It's the best answer I've ever found for the question, so often asked: 'What is the use of music?'"

Charlie's letter describing how he publicly praised her achievements without crediting her by name—just as he had done with the "Journal of a Field Representative"—may have served as the inspiration for a manifesto of sorts that Margaret penned around this time, reflecting on her experience with the Music Unit. In looping cursive, she wrote in an abandoned elementary school notebook that she had repurposed as a makeshift diary:

> I have always lived in a man's world, or rarely dared to challenge that fact—until now, at 75.
>
> Men have always been gallant to me. None has ever abused me, in any way.
>
> But it was made clear to me, when I was invited, by a man, to join the government (in 1935) in its effort to rejuvenate hope and effort in our people, nation-wide, that I got minimum pay for maximum effort, and he got maximum pay, plus credit title!
>
> What I have accomplished is this: I have survived! I have survived the *vanitas vanitatum* of the guys who took credit and pay for my achievements. I have survived by acquiring friends rather than money; experience rather than spoils.

When Margaret left the FSA in the summer of 1939, she—like Sidney—took on a leadership role in another New Deal agency. National Youth Administration (NYA) director Aubrey Williams hired Margaret to serve as director of music programs, working alongside Grace Tugwell, who directed the agency's Arts and Crafts program. Margaret collaborated with the conductor Leopold Stokowski to create youth orchestras across the country and recorded African American youth singing groups at NYA training centers. When the NYA shut down three years later, she tried to launch an independent career writing plays and staging pageants. She moved to New York, accepting Sidney's offer to sublet her and Henry's Greenwich Village apartment when they moved full-time to their country house in Shady, New York. After a brief stint writing plays for Pearl S. Buck's East and West Association, she took on freelance scriptwriting jobs but struggled without the stability she had found in her government work. In 1950, she moved back to Tennessee to care for her ailing father when no one else would. She cut ties with her friends in New York and Washington almost completely and started over in Memphis, working as a secretary at the Memphis Academy of Art and becoming deeply involved in activism around civil rights and reproductive freedom.

Despite leaving Washington behind, echoes of Margaret's time as a New Dealer reverberated through her new life in Memphis. She lived at Lauderdale Courts, one of the first public housing projects in the country to be built by the Public Works Administration in 1936. She scraped by on social security (another New Deal invention), with a small amount of financial help from friends she had first met in Washington, including the Southern Tenant Farmers Union leader H. L. Mitchell and the widow of Aubrey Williams. She kept a signed, framed photograph of Eleanor Roosevelt prominently displayed in her small third-floor apartment. The former First Lady had written about Margaret in her "My Day" column in 1955, after a brief reunion during a layover at the Memphis airport: "Miss Margaret Valient [sic] also came to the airport to see me. Those who worked in Washington with the arts and crafts projects during the Depression will remember her and her talents. . . . I was indeed glad to see her again, for she is the kind of warm person you never forget when once you know her."

Unlike Sidney's RA recordings, Margaret's collection of songs from the migrant camps did not feed directly into the folk revival. Although FDR and the First Lady had expressed their approval of her compilation, other obstacles kept them from being released to the public. One was skepticism from the person ultimately responsible for distributing the recordings—Fred Soule, the information officer for Region 9, a cynical former newspaperman described as "looking like Abraham Lincoln's ghost." As he wrote to John Fischer, the Information Division director in the FSA's Washington office, about Margaret's recordings:

I have no doubt that she turned in some good migrant music. They sing swell and it is a joy to hear them. It is a marvel to me how they can sing at all under the conditions. Such courage is admirable and no doubt music keeps up their morale, but their songs aren't going to soften up the hate that is being poured upon them by the Associated Farmers and the Hearst and Chandler press in California. It may be that there is too much migrant and too little artist in me, but I can't help feeling a bit dubious about the results.

Still, Fischer and Margaret's direct supervisor, Major Walker, pushed for having a set of master discs created, responding to interest in using the recordings from Hollywood and elsewhere. But by the fall of 1939, Margaret had some misgivings about making all the recordings public; perhaps concerned about the pro-union songs, or the bawdy and racist songs that some migrant workers had chosen to sing, she wrote a note of warning to Fischer: "May I call your particular attention to the several unexpurgated ditties (to put it mildly) and beg you to play them only where they will do none of us harm?"

Technical issues with the recordings served as another barrier to making them public. Margaret had never received training on her Radioscriptions equipment, which already tended to produce lower-quality recordings than the Presto machines that had by then become the standard. As a result, many of her recordings are distorted or cut off mid-song. Unlike any of the other folk song collectors of the time, for Margaret, the recording itself was not the primary goal of her sessions, which she arranged more to meet the community's needs than to optimize sound quality. This may all explain why Alan Lomax, who knew about Margaret's recordings, nevertheless arranged for the Library of Congress to support a 1940 recording expedition to the migrant camps by two young male graduate students from New York, one of whom had been at the camps in 1939 and heard some of Margaret's sessions (though he made no mention of her in reporting his "discoveries" to Lomax). The resulting recordings, known as the Todd/

Sonkin Collection, have served as the primary source for Depression-era migrant songs, both in folk song anthologies and for scholars. One history of the Dust Bowl migration that highlights the Todd/Sonkin collection mentions Margaret only in a footnote, erroneously calling her "an amateur folklorist" when collecting was, in fact, part of her job. Since then, Margaret's groundbreaking collection—and the fact that the FSA was involved in collecting folk music at all—has remained virtually unknown.

In her recordings, Margaret seemed to have a special knack for finding talented musicians who would go on to become famous. In California, this was the King family, who were subsequently cast as the band in the iconic dance scene of the 1940 *Grapes of Wrath* film. In Arizona, her recordings of Mexican American musicians included the guitar quartet Los Carlistas featuring a young Lalo Guerrero, who would later be lauded as the Father of Chicano Music. And at Cherry Lake, she recorded the ace fiddler Russell "Chubby" Wise, who would go on to join Bill Monroe's Blue Grass Boys and be inducted in the Bluegrass Music Hall of Fame.

Cherry Lake Farms, where Margaret's program had been praised as a model for the Music Unit's work, was unfortunately later framed as a different kind of model, exemplifying all the reasons that the RA had failed: its soil was sandy, submarginal, and could not be improved; the predicted market did not materialize for specialized crops like scuppernong grapes or for attempted ventures such as a handicraft factory or an exotic bird enterprise; its cooperative factories were not sustainable; acreage allotted for farming, poultry, and dairy enterprises was not sufficient for success. By the early 1940s, many homesteaders had begun to leave, most returning to Florida's cities. In 1943, the co-op store building and its entire stock were destroyed by fire, and the community center that Margaret's *New Wine* play had celebrated met a similar fate in 1969. By then, only eleven of the homesteader families had put down roots and stayed. According to original homesteader June Frazier Johnston, by the beginning of the twenty-first century, "a small number of the families, or their children, who came there in the beginning are still there. Some of the original houses remain, some were moved away, and some were left to disintegrate and fall to the ground." This narrative of failure aligns with many historians' characterizations of the RA overall: Sidney Baldwin called it "little more than an esoteric experiment"; Paul Conkin described it as "a fascinating adventure in idealism and disillusionment."

And yet. June Johnston, who had grown up at Cherry Lake as one of the original homestead families, expressed deep fondness for it. "I suppose you always hold dear to your heart the place where you felt the happiest and secure," she said, and described a reunion of former homesteaders where she found people unanimous in the belief that "the Cherry Lake experiment was a time of optimism, enthusiasm and hope." She acknowledged, "The Cherry Lake Project fell far short of what the government planned but at the same time was a great success for the people who came there." This echoes almost precisely what Eleanor Roosevelt biographer Blanche Wiesen Cook wrote about Arthurdale: "For sixty years, pundits and politicians judged Arthurdale a failure. But . . . for the people, Arthurdale was marvelous, and they called it 'utopia.'" Many of these homesteads—including Cumberland, Arthurdale, and Penderlea—have active historical societies and museums that continue to celebrate their New Deal roots. To honor Eleanor Roosevelt's championing of their communities, Red House renamed itself "Eleanor" and Westmoreland became "Norvelt" when the homesteads incorporated as towns.

It is worth noting that the more recent inhabitants of Norvelt—66 percent of whom voted for Donald Trump in the 2016 election—may not relish their New Deal history. This also speaks to a larger truth about the RA and its legacy, as its failure to refute Jim Crow perpetuated housing segregation in some communities for generations. At the same time, several RA communities that were open to Black Americans now show what was possible and what might have been, providing stability for the families who lived there and going on to play important roles in American culture. Newport News, renamed Aberdeen Gardens, was the middle-class neighborhood of the NASA mathematicians made famous in *Hidden Figures*, and the Gee's Bend homestead in Georgia became known for the resplendent quilts crafted by several generations of women in the community.

The flaws and missteps of the Music Unit and the RA as a whole reflect the messy, painful struggles of American life that persist today: structural racism, sexism, and other social divisions that feel unbridgeable and ever-widening: rural versus urban, wealthy versus poor, red state versus blue, ideologies of individual rights versus collective responsibility, views of government as a help versus a hindrance, debates about whether music and politics can ever mix. But at its core, the story of the Music Unit and the legacy of its recordings demonstrate the important role of music—in all its forms—in providing hope, affirming community, and communicating resilience and resistance, even in the darkest of times.

ACKNOWLEDGMENTS

This book was made possible by fellowships and research grants from the Library of Congress (Kluge Fellowship), National Endowment for the Humanities (Public Scholars Fellowship), Franklin & Eleanor Roosevelt Institute (Beeke-Levy Research Fellowship), Music Library Association (Dena Epstein Award), Society for American Music (Judith McCulloh Fellowship), Association for Recorded Sound Collections (Research Grant), American Musicological Society (Janet Levy Award for Independent Scholars), and the Southern Association for Women Historians (Anne Firor Scott Mid-Career Fellowship).

Many thanks to all my amazing Patreon newsletter subscribers who helped power me through my final year of research and writing. Special acknowledgment for patrons in the Grace Falke and Eleanor Roosevelt tiers: Lauren Antonoff; Becca Burrington; Kenneth Connor; Krista Enos, Laura Smith, and Cooper Enos-Smith; Sue Gale; David Kaskowitz and Susan Kahn; Catherine Hiebert Kerst; Lexy Mayers; Shira and Bill Shore; Zed Starkovich; and several other patrons who wish to remain anonymous. And thanks to my Patreon supporters at every level: Eric Anderson, Jill Auckenthaler, Ryan Bañagale, Sofia Becerra-Licha, Andrea Bohlman, Eric Breit, Avital Chatto, Elizabeth Craft, Alfred Cramer, Louis K. Epstein, Rebekah Gardner, Marc Gidal, Glenda Goodman, Lisl Hampton, Rita Hao, Todd Harvey, Joan Heller, Louis Kaskowitz, Robin Meyer, Seth

Petchers, Alexander Rabb, Ellen Rose, Marilyn Rose, Vanessa Ryan, Jessica Seidel, Rebecca Shaykin, Joanna Silver, Anna Solomon, Sara Webb-Schmitz, and Martine Zilversmit.

I owe so much to the staff at libraries and archives who helped me with my research. At the Library of Congress, huge thanks to Nancy Groce, Todd Harvey, Ann Hoog, Nicki Saylor, Judith Gray, John Fenn, and Stephen Winnick in the American Folklife Center; Travis Hensley in the Kluge Center; Robin Rausch, Bob Lipartito, and Paul Allen Sommerfeld in the Music Division; David Sager and Harrison Behl in the Recorded Sound Resource Center; Barbara Orbach Natanson in Prints & Photographs; and Thomas Beheler in Reference. Thanks to staff at the four branches of the National Archives and Records Administration where I conducted research: Joseph Schwartz, Cathleen Brennan, and Amy Reytar in College Park; Aaron Seltzer in San Francisco; Maureen Hill in Atlanta; Eric Kilgore, Holly Rivet, Sarah Rigdon, and Dean Gall in St. Louis; and Virginia Lewick, Matthew Hanson, Kirsten Carter, and Patrick Fahy in the Franklin D. Roosevelt Presidential Library. Thanks also to Jessica Perkins Smith and Jennifer McGillan at Mississippi State University Library, Anne Jordan at the Roosevelt-Vanderbilt National Historic Site, Cecilia Peterson at the Smithsonian Institution's Center for Folklife and Cultural Heritage, Susan Krueger at the Wisconsin Historical Society, Katelyn Herring at the State Archives of Florida, Manuel Erviti at the UC Berkeley Hargrove Music Library, and Antonia White at The Rhodes Trust, Oxford, UK. Special thanks to student research assistants Libby Walkup at the University of Iowa and Marian Masson at Purdue University Fort Wayne, as well as to Prof. Ann Livschiz at Purdue. Finally, a heartfelt thanks to the staff of the public libraries in Berkeley, Oakland, and San Francisco, and those in the LINK+ consortium.

From my trip to Crossville, Tennessee, thanks to Bob Fulcher at the Cumberland Trail State Scenic Trail; Brian Hall, Christine Josy, and Sue Vandever at Cumberland Homesteads Tower and House Museums; and Joyce Rorabaugh at the Cumberland County Archives.

Many others have provided help with my research along the way, including Catherine Hiebert Kerst, Cheryl Thurber, Jon Findley, Judith

Tick, Carol Oja, Ellie Hisama, Glenda Goodman, and Kiri Miller. Thanks to Anne Trubek and Margaret Balch-Gonzalez for writing help, to my amazing coach Jodie Mader (and to Katherine Lee for connecting us), and to Kathryn Tomaeno, Abel Bumgarner, and Frances Wocicki.

Huge thanks to my agent, Laurie Abkemeier of DeFiore and Company, for believing in this project, and to the team at Pegasus for making it happen: my editor Jessica Case, Maria Fernandez (production), Nicole Maher (publicity), Victoria Rose (copyediting), and Stephanie Marshall Ward (proofreading). Thanks also to Molly von Borstel at Faceout Studios for the cover design and to the talented and infinitely patient Shira Bezalel for my author photo.

I'm so grateful to all my friends and family for cheering me on in various ways during the seven (!) years since I first started my research—too many to name, but thanks to Norah Shaykin for your generosity and support; Robin Mayer for hosting me in Washington; Joanna Silver and Lisl Hampton for coming to my first presentation at the Library of Congress; Anne Lessy and Emily Straus for talking US history with me; and the women of Solstice for truly providing a chance to harmonize: Becca Burrington, Christina Bogiages, Emily Bender, Kim Warsaw, Krista Enos, and Sara Webb-Schmitz.

Special thanks to all my parents—Shira and Bill Shore, David Kaskowitz, and Susan Kahn—for your love, generosity, and everything else you've done to help make this book happen, from child care to research assistance. Thanks to my amazing boys, Ezra and Elliott, for tolerating my research trips and writing retreats, and for never giving up on me—regularly asking when, exactly, my book was going to be done.

And to Ben: I never could have written this book without your belief in me and your willingness to support this project in so many ways for so many years. I'll paraphrase Christopher Robin: This book is a book because of what someone did, and we all know who it was, and it's his book, because of what he did, and I've got a present for him. And here it is.

NOTES

ABBREVIATIONS

SRC: Sidney Robertson Cowell (used as author for materials after 1941)

Archival Collections
FDRL: Franklin D. Roosevelt Presidential Library, Hyde Park, NY
   RGT: Rexford G. Tugwell Collection
LOC: Library of Congress, Washington, DC
   AFC: American Folklife Center
   CSFSA: Charles Seeger Farm Security Administration microfilm, Music Division
   KKP: Katharine Amend Kellock Papers, Manuscript Division
   LFC: LaFollette Family Collection, Manuscript Division
   RSRC: Recorded Sound Research Center, Music Division
   SRC: Sidney Robertson Cowell Collection, Music Division
MSU: Mississippi State University Library Special Collections, Starkville, MS
   AEC: Allen Eugene Cox Papers
   MV: Margaret Valiant Collection
NARA-ATL: Records of the Farmers Home Administration, Record Group 96, National Archives at Atlanta, Morrow, GA
NARA-CP: Records of the Farmers Home Administration, Record Group 96, National Archives at College Park, College Park, MD
NARA-SF: Records of the Farmers Home Administration, Record Group 96, Region 9, Office of the Director, National Archives at San Francisco, San Bruno, CA
NARA-STL: Personnel Files, 1932–1951, Department of Agriculture, Farm Security Administration, Record Group 146, National Archives and Records Administration, St. Louis, MO
NPS-JWF: Jannelle Warren-Findley Papers, Home of Franklin D. Roosevelt National Historic Site, National Park Service, Hyde Park, NY
NYPL: New York Public Library for the Performing Arts, New York, NY
UI-CBBC: C. B. Baldwin Papers, University of Iowa Special Collections, Iowa City, IA
UM-HSS: Henry Street Settlement Collection, Social Welfare History Archives, University of Minnesota, Minneapolis, MN
WHS-HREC: Highlander Research and Education Center Records, 1917-2017, Mss 265, Wisconsin Historical Society, Madison, WI

Oral Histories and Interviews

SI: Smithsonian Institution, Washington, DC

   AA: Archives of American Art

   RR: Ralph Rinzler Folklife Archive and Collections

Dornbush interview: Adrian Dornbush, oral history interview by Richard K. Doud, 13 June 1965, SI-AA

SRC-Goldsmith interview: Sidney Robertson Cowell, interviewed by Peter Goldsmith, 3 January 1992, Shady, NY, Peter Goldsmith Papers, SI-RR

Tugwell interview: Rexford Tugwell and Grace Tugwell, oral history interview by Richard K. Doud, 21 January 1965, SI-AA

Valiant-AFC interview: Margaret Valiant, interviewed by Jannelle Warren-Findley and Cheryl Thurber, 1979, AFC-2019/052

Valiant-Cook interview: Margaret Valiant, interviewed by Fred Cook, 9 June 1971, MSU-MV.

Valiant-Gaume interview: Margaret Valiant, interviewed by Maude Gaume, May 29–30, 1980, LOC-RSRC.

Valiant-Rinzler interview: Margaret Valiant, interviewed by Ralph and Kate Rinzler, April 17, 1975, SI-RR

Epigraph

p. ix   "We in the United States": President Roosevelt to Paul Green, statement for National Folk Festival, March 2, 1934, PPF 1342, President's Personal Files, FDR Papers, FDRL.

Prologue: The Key West Experiment

p. xiv   Beginning in the mid-1920s: Durward Long, "Key West and the New Deal, 1934–1936," *Florida Historical Quarterly* 46, no. 3 (1967): 209–10.

p. xiv   "seemed to be living mostly": Elmer Davis, "New World Symphony," *Harper's*, May 1935, 644.

p. xv   "Your city is bankrupt": Gary Boulard, "'State of Emergency:' Key West in the Great Depression," *Florida Historical Quarterly* 67, no. 2 (1988): 172.

p. xv   At the same time, FERA's social service department: Long, "Key West," 214.

p. xv   He and his team of eleven FERA staffers: Boulard, "State of Emergency," 170, 173.

p. xv   The idea never took off: Ibid., 174; Davis, "New World Symphony," 651–52.

p. xvi   Stone turned to Edward Bruce: Dornbush interview.

p. xvi   Artists taught residents how: Federal Writers' Project, *WPA Guide to Florida* (1939; New York: Pantheon, 1984), 199.

p. xvi   forming a marimba band: Richard Rovere, "End of the Line," *New Yorker*, December 15, 1951, 84.

p. xvi   A theater group called the Key West Players: Long, "Key West," 216.

p. xvi   In October 1934, Stone: "Jules F. Stone Gives Talk at Banquet," *Key West Citizen*, October 15, 1934.

p. xvi   the professional director: Dornbush interview.

p. xvii   "a clean and shining": "Roosevelt's Aides See New Key West," *New York Times*, March 30, 1935.

p. xvii   "Greenwich Village, Montparnasse": Davis, "New World Symphony," 648.

p. xvii   At Pena's bar, regulars: Ibid., 651.

p. xvii   "an outsider who deeply resented": Rovere, "End of the Line," 81.

p. xvii   "starry eyed bastards": Dan Monroe, "Hemingway, the Left, and Key West," in *Key West Hemingway* (Gainesville: University of Florida Press, 2009), 95.

p. xvii   For many conservatives off the island: Boulard, "State of Emergency," 177–78.

p. xvii   On February 19, 1935, as the orchestra played: "'Pirates of Penzance' Staged."

p. xviii   the tenor from Miami: Dornbush interview.

p. xviii   "This program has completely changed": Boulard, "State of Emergency," 175–76.

p. xix   "Somehow you felt actually": Ibid.

p. xix   Newspapers dubbed Key West: Michael Szalay, *New Deal Modernism* (Durham, NC: Duke University Press, 2000), 149; "Former Relief Administrator Is a Freshman at Law School," *Harvard Crimson*, March 21, 1938.

p. xix   The press couldn't help: See, for example, "National Affairs: Hard, Soft & Red," *Time*, January 8, 1934; "Recent Books," *Time*, January 7, 1935; Lyle C. Wilson, "Tugwell Believes Roosevelt's Program Dodged Radical Leap," *Imperial Valley Press*, April 24, 1934.

p. xix   "a very handsome gentleman": "Tugwell Wins in Senate by 53–24 Margin," *Indianapolis Times*, June 15, 1934.

p. xix   a turning point for the New Deal: David M. Kennedy, *Freedom from Fear* (New York: Oxford University Press), 247–48.

p. xx   Tugwell first came: V. N. Namorato, ed., *The Diary of Rexford G. Tugwell* (New York: Greenwood Press, 1992), 217, 230.

p. xx   "was intensely interested": Dornbush interview.

p. xx   "must have found paradise": Christopher Hommerding, "As Gay as Any Gypsy Caravan," *Annals of Iowa*, 74 (2015): 403–404.

p. xx   "a very, very congenial": Dornbush interview.

p. xxi   budget of more than $375 million: Paul Conkin, *Tomorrow a New World* (Ithaca: Cornell University Press, 1959), 161.

p. xxi   Absorb forty-six disparate programs: Charles Roberts, *The Farm Security Administration and Rural Rehabilitation in the South* (Knoxville: University of Tennessee Press, 2015), 52.

p. xxi   "everybody else's headaches": Sidney Baldwin, *Poverty and Politics* (Chapel Hill: University of North Carolina Press, 1968), 93.

p. xxi   the DC press loved: See "Uncle Sam Takes Over Walsh Home," *Washington Star*, July 19, 1935; "Famous Mansion to House Rural Resettlement Administration," *Washington Post*, July 21, 1935.

p. xxi   "What influence do we want": Conkin, *Tomorrow* , 159.

p. xxi   Dornbush's new job title: Appointment-Oath Statement, May 1, 1935, NARA-STL-Dornbush.

p. xxii   his staff had found a job description: Tugwell interview.

p. xxii   "matters pertaining to the field of arts": Personnel Recommendation, May 20, 1935, NARA-STL-Dornbush.

p. xxii   For Tugwell, voluntary democratic cooperatives: Conkin, *Tomorrow*, 202–203.

p. xxii   "easiest, most natural thing": Ibid., 204.

p. xxii   "one of the most open breaks": Ibid., 6.

p. xxii   "We now realize as": Franklin D. Roosevelt, Inaugural Address, March 4, 1933, "The American Presidency Project," https://www.presidency.ucsb.edu /node/208712.

p. xxii   "Was he expected to make": Drew Pearson and Robert S. Allen, "Washington Merry-Go-Round" (syndicated), June 28, 1935.

p. xxii   Tugwell had said he wanted: Dornbush interview.

Chapter 1: Music as a Social Function

p. 1   When Margaret Valiant left Memphis: Valiant to Cammy Wilson, [n.d.], private collection of Margaret Valiant's papers.

p. 1   The notarized document: Oath of Office, January 8, 1936, NARA-STL-Valiant.

p. 1   "Well, our country is in trouble": Valiant-Gaume interview.

p. 2   "farming country, where we grew everything": Valiant-AFC interview.

p. 2   "smattering of this and that": Valiant-Cook interview.

p. 2   "could run like a rabbit": Valiant to Wilson, [n.d.].

p. 2   when Aunt Annie somehow found: Kay Pittman Black, "View from Housing Project Still is Rosy," *Memphis Press-Scimitar*, October 12, 1977.

p. 3   "I never thought of myself": Valiant-Gaume interview.

p. 3   "acquiring friends rather than money": Valiant, notebook of writings [n.d., c. 1976], MSU-MV.

p. 3   Margaret's reinvention began: Valiant-Rinzler interview.

p. 3   "I don't think I'd ever had $90": Valiant-AFC interview.

p. 4   Margaret had her Paris debut: *Salle des Agriculteurs* program, April 13, 1926, MSU-MV.

p. 4   A review in the *New York Herald*: Louis Schneider, "Music in Paris," *New York Herald, Paris*, April 15, 1926.

p. 4   She stayed in Europe: Arthur Moss, "Around the Riviera," *New York Herald (European ed.)*, January 1, 1927.

p. 4   "Ziggy lined us all up": Black, "View from Housing Project."

p. 5   "short and swift": Valiant to Wilson.

p. 5   "Yes. Next question.": Valiant-Cook interview.

p. 5   "was an unfortunate affair": Edwin Mims Sr. to Parker, April 2, 1936, NARA-STL-Valiant.

p. 5   "folk singing, dancing, painting": Personnel Recommendation, December 17, 1935, NARA-STL-Valiant.

p. 5   she gave concerts of lighter material: Cheryl T. Evans, "A 'Valiant' Effort," *Center for Southern Folklore Newsletter* 3, no. 1 (Winter 1980): 20.

p. 5   "all these marvelous friends ": Valiant-AFC interview.

p. 6   Born in the same year as Margaret: Judith Tick, *Ruth Crawford Seeger* (New York: Oxford University Press, 1997), 8.

p. 6   Margaret later described their arrival: Valiant-Gaume interview; Tick, *Ruth Crawford Seeger*, 179.

p. 7   "Music is propaganda": Tick, *Ruth Crawford Seeger*, 194.

p. 7   the soprano chosen for the concert: Ibid., 192–93.

p. 7   Charlie became the leader: Ann M. Pescatello, *Charles Seeger* (Pittsburg, PA: University of Pittsburg Press, 1992), 110.

p. 7   "complacent, melancholy, defeatist": Richard A. Reuss with JoAnne C. Reuss, *American Folk Music and Left-Wing Politics, 1927–1957* (Lanham, MD: Scarecrow Press, 2000), 49.

p. 7   One of Charlie's contributions: Carl Sands and H. T. Tsiang, "Pioneer Song: Who's That Guy?" in *Workers Song Book* (New York: Workers' Music League, 1934), 30–31.

p. 8   "full of geometric bitterness": Benjamin Filene, *Romancing the Folk (Chapel Hill: University of North Carolina Press, 2000)*, 70.

p. 8   Ruth introduced him: Tick, *Ruth Crawford Seeger*, 235.

p. 8   Aunt Molly Jackson came to New York: Shelly Romalis, *Pistol Packin' Mama* (Urbana: University of Illinois Press, 1999), 100–101, 161–63; Reuss and Reuss, *American Folk Music*, 52–53.

p. 8   "the people could sing her songs": Pescatello, *Charles Seeger*, 135.

p. 8   Another influence on Charlie's: Steven P. Garabedian, *A Sound History* (Amherst: University of Massachusetts Press, 2020), 30, 31, 104. Garabedian refutes an earlier claim that Gellert fabricated these songs.

p. 9   "urban hillbilly" band: Archie Green, "Tom Benton's Folk Depictions," in *Torching the Fink Books* (Chapel Hill: University of North Carolina Press, 2001), 117.

p. 10   "artists, designers and craftsmen": Ed Hadley, "Iowa in Washington," *Cedar Rapids Gazette*, March 15, 1936.

p. 10   "to establish, encourage and extend": Personnel Recommendation, August 6, 1935, NARA-STL-Dornbush.

p. 10   Her first job after high school: "Facts About Grace," [n.d.], NARA-STL-Falke.

p. 10   Falke assumed her first government job: Recommendation for Promotion, December 18, 1933, NARA-STL-Falke.

p. 10   "an attractive young woman": "Facts About Grace."

p. 11   extended trip with Lorena Hickok: Falke to Tugwell, Trip Reports 1934–35, FDRL-RTG.

p. 11   working with congressional staffers: Tugwell, December 28, 1934, *Diary of Rexford G. Tugwell*, 176.

p. 11   overseeing five of the agency's: Resettlement Administration First Annual Report, 1936, 87, LOC-LFC.

p. 11   more women held positions: Susan Ware, *Beyond Suffrage: Women in the New Deal* (Cambridge: Harvard University Press, 1981), 1, 6.

p. 11   "shifting to executive and administrative positions": Will P. Kennedy, "Capital Sidelights," *Evening Star*, November 15, 1936.

p. 11   Eleanor Roosevelt played: Frances M. Seeber, "Eleanor Roosevelt and
           Women in the New Deal: A Network of Friends," *Presidential Studies
           Quarterly* 20, no. 4 (1990): 714–15.

p. 11   "the driving force behind": Belinda Rathbone, *Walker Evans* (New York:
           Houghton Mifflin Harcourt, 2000), 104.

p. 11   "they were always having squabbles": Tugwell interview.

p. 12   The RA's Rural Resettlement Division inherited: Robert Leighninger Jr., *Long-Range
           Public Investment* (Columbia: University of South Carolina Press, 2007), 148.

p. 12   Nearly half of these projects: Ibid., 141, 149.

p. 13   "in order to bind the homesteaders": Kellock to Dornbush, October 3, 1935,
           LOC-CSFSA.

p. 13   "In every one of these colonies": Kellock to Seeger, November 15,1935,
           LOC-CSFSA.

p. 13   "Mr. Seeger's professional reputation": Kellock, Interview Report, October 11,
           1935, NARA-STL-Seeger.

p. 13   Three weeks later, Dornbush sent: Dornbush to Seeger, November 4, 1935,
           NARA-STL-Seeger.

p. 14   squeezed into the back seat: Seeger to Valiant, November 2, 1976, MSU-AEC.

p. 14   "is very eager for musical assistance": Kellock to Seeger, November 15, 1935,
           LOC-CSFSA.

p. 14   "young woman of old southern family": Seeger, Interview Report, November
           18, 1935, NARA-STL-Valiant.

p. 15   Upon arriving at their assigned: Seeger to Kellock, December 12, 1935,
           LOC-CSFSA.

p. 16   the Seegers had settled: Tick, *Ruth Crawford Seeger*, 233.

Chapter 2: In the Slough of Despond

p. 17   "This thing is fraught": Bill Abbott, "Scholtz Raps FDR Critics," *Tampa
           Sunday Tribune*, May 12, 1935.

p. 17   "second of the government's unique Florida experiments": Kenneth Ballinger,
           "City Unemployed of Florida Are Happy on Federal-Sponsored Farm
           Project," *Miami Herald*, June 9, 1935.

p. 18   including home visits, letters of reference: Roberts, *Farm Security
           Administration*, 41.

p. 18   "Although noble in conception": Wayne Flynt, *Poor But Proud* (Tuscaloosa:
           University of Alabama Press, 1989), 306.

p. 18   those admitted included office clerks: Victor Bogachoff, "Pioneers of 1935 are
           Cherry Lake Farm Homesteaders," *Tallahassee Democrat*, September 13, 1935.

p. 18   racism was baked into the New Deal: Ira Katznelson, *Fear Itself* (New York:
           Liveright, 2013), 160–64.

p. 19   the Agricultural Adjustment Administration's policy: Roberts, *Farm Security
           Administration*, 51.

p. 19   the agency evicted Black tenants: Jane Adams and D. Gorton, "This Land
           Ain't My Land," *Agricultural History* 83, no. 3 (2009): 323–351; Donald

Holley, "The Negro in the New Deal Resettlement Program," *Agricultural History* 45, no. 3 (1971): 190.

p. 19   "the one bright spot": Michael Hiltzik, *The New Deal* (New York: Free Press, 2011): 314.

p. 19   "the idea of co-operation": Conkin, *Tomorrow*, 202.

p. 19   At Cherry Lake, this meant: Ballinger, "City Unemployed."

p. 19   cooperative communities were easy targets: Baldwin, *Poverty*, 56.

p. 19   "Is this local socialism?": Bogachoff, "Pioneers of 1935."

p. 20   Cherry Lake Self-Governing Club: Ballinger, "City Unemployed."

p. 20   Boxing had become a regular pastime: Elmer C. Spear, *Cherry Lake Farms, Madison County, Florida, 1934–June 9, 1939* (self-pub., 2008), 41.

p. 20   African Americans, who made up: Andrea Lakaye Oliver, "Stony the Road We Trod" (PhD diss., Florida State University, 2010), 21–22.

p. 20   "All are cheerful and happy": Margaret E. Watkins, "As I See It," Madison *Enterprise-Recorder*, December 20, 1935.

p. 20   Architects developed six different designs: Spear, *Cherry Lake*, 81–85.

p. 20   Construction was slow: Ibid., 89, 91.

p. 21   In October, Kellock visited: Kellock to Dornbush, "Analysis of Cherry Lake Farms," October 25–27, 1935, LOC-KKP.

p. 21   source of numerous complaints: Spear, *Cherry Lake*, 53–54.

p. 21   "they don't do anything but argue": Ibid., 68.

p. 21   "rebellion and complaint": Kellock to Dornbush, "Analysis of Cherry Lake."

p. 22   "man of action, not words": Spear, *Cherry Lake*, 101–102.

p. 23   "a good supply of tact": Kellock to Dornbush, "Cherry Lake Farms (confidential)," October 25–27, 1935, LOC-KKP.

p. 23   "Mr. Loomis and all other": Kellock, "Analysis of Cherry Lake."

p. 24   "Still shivering, I left": Valiant, unpublished memoir quoted in Jannelle Warren-Findley, "Reclaiming the Red Clay Country," NPS-JWF.

p. 24   "The physical aspects": Valiant, "Journal of a Field Representative," LOC-CSFSA. (Unless otherwise noted, this is the source for all quotations from Margaret's Cherry Lake reports.) Notes are reprinted in Seeger and Valiant, "Journal of a Field Representative," *Ethnomusicology* 24, no. 2 (May 1980): 169–210.

p. 24   "You can get a bath": Valiant in Warren-Findley, "Red Clay Country."

p. 25   "proceed slowly and through the children": Valiant, "Daily Work Report" [n.d., January 1936], MSU-MV.

p. 26   In one of the shacks: All quotes in this paragraph and the following in Valiant to Dornbush, "Steps toward Organizing," January 28, 1936, MSU-MV.

p. 26   "I know this is a hard situation": Seeger to Valiant, February 3, 1936, MSU-MV.

p. 27   In addition to committee chair: Spear, *Cherry Lake*, 67, 52; Valiant, "'Music for Everyone' Program," [n.d.], MSU-MV.

p. 27   "enthusiasm kept them on": Valiant to Dornbush, "Steps toward Organizing."

p. 28   "Her personality is the kind": Frances Brophy to Fred Parker, April 15, 1936, NARA-STL-Valiant.

p. 29   "In my last report I named three 'needs'": C. B. Loomis, report, January 31, 1936, in Dornbush to Falke, February 20, 1936, NARA-CP.

p. 30   "a united effort based on local daily life": Dornbush to Division Representatives, April 3, 1936, MSU-MV.

p. 31   "an activity of masses of people": Seeger to Kellock, December 12, 1935, LOC-CSFSA.

p. 32   "It was my job to stimulate": Valiant-Cook interview.

p. 32   "Because if you take pride": Valiant, manuscript fragment, [n.d.], MSU-MV.

Chapter 3: Musical Engineering

p. 33   "He has had a rather second-rate": Seeger to Dornbush, December 10, 1935, LOC-CSFSA.

p. 34   His previous experience: Pescatello, *Charles Seeger*, 81–83.

p. 35   "Above all, he will regard": Seeger to Kellock, December 12, 1935, LOC-CSFSA.

p. 36   "very ordinary run of the mill": Seeger to Dornbush, March 17, 1936, LOC-CSFSA.

p. 36   "really good turn-out": Dornbush to Falke, March 13, 1936, NARA-CP.

p. 36   "the musical factor in cooperative education": Seeger to Dornbush, March 17, 1936.

p. 36   "eager to cast their lot": Timothy Kelly, Margaret Power, and Michael Cary, *Hope in Hard Times* (University Park: Pennsylvania State University Press, 2016), 84.

p. 37   "for the benefit of the community": Ibid., 112–113.

p. 37   "rugged individualism" against: "County Homesteaders Ask U.S. to Oust Manager," *Greensburg Daily Tribune*, June 8, 1935.

p. 37   "an active distrust of 'the foreigners'": Kellock to Dornbush, August 26, 1935, LOC-KKP.

p. 37   "I don't want statistics": Lorena Hickok, "The Unsung Heroes of the Depression," in *One Third of a Nation* (Urbana: University of Illinois Press, 1981), ix–x.

p. 37   "the worst place I had ever": Michael Golay, *America 1933* (New York: Free Press, 2013), 69–70.

p. 37   acknowledged to have been: Susan Quinn, *Eleanor and Hick* (New York: Penguin, 2016), 1–7.

p. 38   The First Lady drove: Maurine H. Beasley, *Eleanor Roosevelt* (Lawrence: University of Kansas, 2010), 131.

p. 38   "Quaker model": Kelly, Power, and Cary, *Hope*, 85.

p. 38   An agrarian at heart: Conkin, *Tomorrow*, 34–35.

p. 38   mythic proportions: Leighninger, *Long-Range Public Investment*, 137. Also see Blanche Wiesen Cook, *Eleanor Roosevelt, Vol. 2* (New York: Penguin, 1999), 133–34; Conkin, *Tomorrow*, 27–34; Joseph P. Lash, *Eleanor and Franklin* (New York: Norton, 1971), 394.

p. 38   "always did, and always would": Conkin, *Tomorrow*, 34.

p. 38   "All Eleanor's executive ability": Lash, *Eleanor and Franklin*, 398.

p. 39   "West Virginia commune": Conkin, *Tomorrow*, 118.

p. 39   "Mrs. Roosevelt took the Reedsville project": Beasley, *Eleanor Roosevelt*, 134–135.

p. 39   "electric curling irons": Kelly, Power, and Cary, *Hope*, 115.

p. 39   "according to the sociological": Conkin, *Tomorrow*, 200.

p. 39   admitted exactly one: Kelly and Power, "Norvelt: Worker's Haven and Missed Opportunity," *Pennsylvania History* 86, no. 3 (2019): 343-44.

p. 40   of the more than: Holley, "Negro in the New Deal," 184.

p. 40   "musical color line": Karl Hagstrom Miller, *Segregating Sound* (Durham, NC: Duke University Press, 2010), 2–4.

p. 40   "exotic, domestic 'other'": Sonnet Retman, *Real Folks* (Durham, NC: Duke University Press, 2011), 14.

p. 40   This view of Appalachian: Filene, *Romancing the Folk*, 24.

p. 40   Eleanor Roosevelt was known: Conkin, *Tomorrow*, 255.

p. 41   "She wanted it to have": Lash, *Eleanor and Franklin*, 398.

p. 41   Collins built a folk music program: Sam F. Stack Jr., *Elsie Ripley Clapp* (New York: Peter Lang, 2004), 197–98.

p. 41   "the morale of the people": Mary LaFollette Sucher to John Carter, July 20, 1935, LOC-LFC.

p. 41   "more interest in music": Kellock, "Tygart Valley, W. Va.," [fragment, n.d.], LOC-KKP.

p. 41   Attendance at his scheduled: Dornbush to Falke, March 20, 1936, NARA-CP.

p. 42   "Mr. van Rhyn is rather inflexible": Seeger to Dornbush, March 19, 1936, LOC-CSFSA.

p. 42   "Most of them arrived": Van Rhyn in Dornbush to Falke, March 3, 1936, NARA-CP.

p. 43   "like a dream come true": Francis M. Stephenson, "Government Setting Example in Rural Settlement Field," *Chattanooga News*, December 3, 1935.

p. 43   "the farm and the city": Conkin, *Tomorrow*, 139.

p. 43   "has made a real hit": Seeger to Dornbush (confidential), March 28, 1936, LOC-CSFSA.

p. 43   "I don't think it will harm us": Falke to Tugwell, June 3, 1934, Trip Reports.

p. 44   "more extensive use of American material": Seeger to Dornbush, April 15, 1936, LOC-CSFSA.

p. 44   "I'm tired of colonies": Tick, *Ruth Crawford Seeger*, 238.

p. 45   built on six hundred acres: Conkin, *Tomorrow*, 136; "Town History," Town of Eleanor, West Virginia, https://eleanorwv.com/town-history; "Red House," The Historical Marker Database, https://www.hmdb.org/m.asp?m=85683.

p. 45   "They gave me a little bungalow": Herbert Heufrecht, interview by David Dunaway, April 14 and 19, 1976, AFC-2000/019.

p. 45   Charlie urged Haufrecht: Seeger to Dornbush (confidential), April 16, 1936, LOC-CSFSA.

p. 46   "He had to go by foot": Heufrecht interview, AFC-2000/019.

p. 46   "The split among": Seeger to Dornbush, April 16, 1936.

p. 46   "simply one more": Haufrecht interview.

p. 46   "I want to put": Seeger to Dornbush (confidential), March 28, 1936, LOC-CSFSA.

p. 47   "Miss Valiant's activities": Seeger to Dornbush, April 1, 1936, LOC-CSFSA.

Chapter 4: Cooperation Is Our Aim

p. 48   "I have marked": Seeger to Robert Van Hyning, April 11, 1936, LOC-CSFSA.

p. 48   "Congressmen just loved": Tugwell interview.

p. 48   "a cultural uplift": "Tugwell Plans Cultural Uplift of Backwoods," *New York Herald Tribune*, October 3, 1935.

p. 49   "Many persons will": "State Within a State," *Buffalo News*, October 11, 1935.

p. 49   even Dornbush's bimonthly: Dornbush, "Special Skills Division Letter No. 1" (confidential), February 20, 1936, MSU-MV.

p. 49   "The music and dramatic": Dornbush to Agnes King Inglis, November 23, 1936, quoted in Warren-Findley, "Passports to Change: The Resettlement Administration's Folk Song Sheet Program, 1936–1937," *Prospects* 10 (1985): 207.

p. 49   "Communist in its conception": "Subsistence Homesteads Fail," *Pittsburgh Post-Gazette*, November 6, 1935.

p. 49   "modeled on the collective": "GOP Says Resettlement Plan of New Deal is Communistic," AP, *Denver Post*, March 30, 1936.

p. 49   "semi-Socialistic": "To Have a Soviet Farm," *San Jose Mercury Herald*, November 29, 1935.

p. 49   "Business will logically": Bernard Sternsher, *Rexford Tugwell and the New Deal* (New Brunswick, NJ: Rutgers University Press, 1964), 99.

p. 49   "controlled to whatever": "National Affairs: Hard, Soft & Red," *Time*, January 8, 1934.

p. 49   "planned capitalism": Sternsher, *Rexford Tugwell*, 229.

p. 50   "regimentation of opinion": Ibid., 9.

p. 50   "disdainful, contemptuous": Ibid., 230.

p. 50   "discredit the bill": Ibid., 234.

p. 50   "I made the mistake": Michael Namorato, *Rexford G. Tugwell: A Biography* (New York: Praeger, 1988), 95.

p. 50   "The Director wishes": Seeger, "Music Memorandum no. 1," January 17, 1936, MSU-MV.

p. 51   "subversive harmonies": Tick, *Ruth Crawford Seeger*, 235, 242.

p. 51   "vigorous, disciplined": Pescatello, *Charles Seeger*, 133–34, 166.

p. 51   represented the two schools: Filene, *Romancing the Folk*, 24, 26.

p. 51   "Frankly," Lomax admitted: Ibid., 31.

p. 51   "To keep this widespread": Seeger to Dornbush, "Integration of Work" (draft), LOC-SRC.

p. 52   one thousand copies: Purchase Order Request, January 23, 1936, LOC-CSFSA.

p. 52   some folk songs were included: Marx and Anne Oberndorfer, eds., *The New American Song Book* (Chicago: Hall & McCreary, 1933).

p. 52   "songbook of the American": Dornbush to Mastin G. White, February 16, 1937, LOC-CSFSA.

p. 52   "build renewed respect": Dornbush in Warren-Findley, "Passports," 207–208.

p. 52   "distinctly the wrong type": Seeger to Judith Tobey, March 30, 1936, LOC-CSFSA.

p. 53   "She would like to use me": Hampton to James Dombrowski, February 22, 1936, WHS-HREC, 3.

p. 53   Hampton had been among: John Glen, *Highlander* (Knoxville: University Press of Kentucky, 1988), 29–33. Highlander would later become a critical training ground for civil rights activists, beginning in the 1950s.

p. 53   He taught piano: Hampton to Charles Peck, March 3, 1936, NARA-STL-Hampton.

p. 53   "Highlander Folk School of Communism": "Myles Horton Denies Communism Charge," *Chattanooga Daily Times*, May 7, 1936.

p. 54   "probably a first": Peck, Interview Report, [n.d.], NARA-STL-Hampton.

p. 54   "He has many friends": Myles Horton to Fred Parker, June 29, 1936, NARA-STL-Hampton.

p. 54   "special assignment": Seeger to Van Hyning, May 22, 1936, LOC-CSFSA.

p. 54   several union leaders: Fran Ansley and Brenda Bell, "Davidson-Wilder 1932," *Southern Exposure* 1, no. 3-4 (1974): 130; Charles Tollett, *The Cumberland Homesteads* (special publication of the *Crossville Chronicle*), [n.d.], 8, 11–12.

p. 55   "These homesteaders know": Seeger to Van Hyning, May 22, 1936.

p. 55   "to build up a body": Seeger to Hampton, May 28, 1936, NARA-STL-Hampton.

p. 55   "No collection of": Seeger to Van Hyning, May 22, 1936.

p. 56   "do similar work": Seeger to Dornbush, May 18, 1936, LOC-CSFSA.

p. 56   "We are ready": Seeger to Dornbush, "Song-book project," May 18, 1936, LOC-CSFSA.

p. 56   "design the covers": Dornbush to White, February 16, 1937.

p. 57   a later memorandum: "Proposed List of Songs," August 22, 1936, LOC-SRC.

p. 57   The song (and the RA's explanatory text): "The Farmer," in *American Songbag*, ed. Carl Sandburg (New York: Harcourt, Brace & World, 1927), 282–83.

p. 57   "It would put them to the test": All song-sheets in LOC-SRC.

p. 58   Charlie claimed: Warren-Findley, "Passports," 212, 240n37.

p. 58   "we had at least": Ibid., 240n37.

p. 58   noted making use: Valiant, "Journal of a Field Representative."

Chapter 5: New Wine in Old Bottles

p. 59   "The boxing green": Unless otherwise noted, all quotes from Margaret's reports are from Valiant, "Journal of a Field Representative."

p. 59   former heavyweight: "Tunney Tells Yale about Shakespeare," *New York Times*, April 24, 1928.

p. 60   tell the origin story: Van Hyning to Division Representatives, April 24, 1936, MSU-MV.

p. 60   persuading regional: Valiant, Daily Work Report, February 26, 1936, MSU-MV.

p. 60   Charlie informed: Seeger, Music Memorandum no. 7: Equipment, [n.d. ~March 1936], MSU-MV.

p. 63   down on his luck: Randy Noles, *Fiddler's Curse* (Anaheim Hills, CA: Centerstream, 2007), 63–64.

p. 63   "the very word": Conkin, *Tomorrow*, 6.

p. 66   "Paradoxically, perversely": Wesley Morris, "Music," in *The 1619 Project edited by Nikole Hannah-Jones* (New York: One World, 2021), 370–71, italics in original.

p. 66   insidious nostalgia: Michael Rogin, *Blackface, White Noise* (Berkeley: University of California Press, 1998), 177.

p. 67   amateur blackface: Rhae Lynn Barnes, "Yes, Politicians Wore Blackface." *Washington Post*, February 8, 2019.

p. 68   "appreciation of Mr. Steffen": Valiant to Dornbush, July 6, 1936, NARA-STL-Valiant.

p. 68   "I do believe": Ibid.

p. 69   It had a cast: Cast list, set design credits, and all quotes from the script from Margaret Valiant, "New Wine: A Play," July 22, 1936, MSU-MV.

p. 71   real-life $550,000: Victor Bogachoff, "Col. Westbrook Opens Cherry Lake," *Madison Enterprise-Recorder*, July 22, 1936.

p. 73   from a Broadway musical: Claire Suddath, "A Brief History of Campaign Songs: Franklin D. Roosevelt," *Time*, September 26, 2008.

Chapter 6: Delight in What It Is to Be American

p. 74   "An order was": Dornbush to Falke, February 6, 1936, NARA-CP.

p. 74   "dig out": Dornbush interview.

p. 74   "belong to the people": Seeger to Dornbush, "Integration of Work with Recorder and Song Sheets" (draft), [n.d.], LOC-SRC.

p. 75   "should be no further": Dornbush to Seeger, March 23, 1936, LOC-CSFSA.

p. 75   "held up indefinitely": Seeger, "Music Memorandum no. 7: Equipment."

p. 76   "I seem to have": Robertson to Tobey, April 29, 1936, NARA-STL-Robertson.

p. 76   "Seeger, the music": Robertson to Hawkins, May 7, 1936, LOC-SRC.

p. 76   dominated by women: Rebecca Traister, *All the Single Ladies* (New York: Simon & Schuster, 2016), 57; Judith Trolander, *Settlement Houses and the Great Depression* (Detroit: Wayne State University Press, 1975), 42–43.

p. 76   "moral and material uplift of the poor": Kennedy, *Freedom from Fear*, 146.

p. 77   High-ranking New Dealers: Judith Trolander, *Professionalism and Social Change* (New York: Columbia University Press, 1987), 17.

p. 77   "middle-class missionaries": Kennedy, Freedom from Fear, 146.

p. 77   "My God": Lash, *Eleanor and Franklin*, 135.

p. 77   came to the RA: Reed Harris to Oliver Griswold, February 15, 1936, LOC-KKP.

p. 77   ease relationships: Shannon Green, "'Art for Life's Sake'" (Ph.D. diss., University of Wisconsin-Madison, 1998), 47.

p. 78   Wald was known: Elisabeth Lasch-Quinn, *Black Neighbors* (Chapel Hill: University of North Carolina Press, 1993), e-book, 10, 26.

p. 78   "great fun": Robertson to Hawkins, July 5, 1935, LOC-SRC.

p. 78   She worked with: Robertson to Hawkins, September 30, 1935, LOC-SRC

p. 78   She tracked down: SRC, untitled reminiscence ("I have been asked"), September 21, 1989, AFC-1990/039.

p. 78   "I led a negro chorus": Robertson, Personal Data Memorandum, April 15, 1936, NARA-STL-Robertson.

p. 79   "Struggling to extend": Robertson to Tobey, April 29, 1936.

p. 79   "I'd love to come west": Robertson to Hawkins, April 23, 1936, LOC-SRC.

p. 79   Sidney was born: Unless otherwise noted, all early biographical details from SRC Chronology I, AFC-1990/039.

p. 79   her activity-filled: *Stanford Daily* Archives, https://archives.stanforddaily.com.

p. 80   progressive school that had recently: Jane Knoerle, "The Peninsula Way," *The Almanac*, June 20, 2001, https://www.almanacnews.com/morgue/2001 /2001_06_20.peninsula1.html.

p. 80   "I had a revolution": SRC, "I have been asked."

p. 81   fairy-tale cottages: Kevin Starr, *The Dream Endures* (New York: Oxford University Press, 2002), 53.

p. 81   she nicknamed her "great-grandmother": Robertson to Hawkins, "I must get," [n.d.], LOC-SRC.

p. 81   "a sort of western": Robertson to Hawkins, "I got your letter" [n.d.], LOC-SRC.

p. 81   "radical mag": Robertson to Seeger, [n.d.], AFC-1940/001.

p. 81   "The impact": Robin Howe, "Which Arrives," *Pacific Weekly*, April 26, 1935, 203.

p. 82   "The Depression crept": SRC-Goldsmith interview.

p. 82   "A transcontinental trip": Robertson to Hawkins, "I've spent the evening," [n.d.], LOC-SRC.

p. 82   "high quality": Margaret Walsh, "Gender and the Automobile in the United States," Automobile in American Life and Society, 2004, http://www.autolife .umd.umich.edu/Gender/Walsh/G_Overview1.htm.

p. 82   Still, in 1909: Marina Koestler Ruben, "Alice Ramsey's Historic Cross-Country Drive," *Smithsonian*, June 4, 2009.

p. 82   "the perpetual emergencies": SRC Chronology I.

p. 83   fewer than one in five: Walsh, "Gender."

p. 83   "This is beautiful": Robertson to Hawkins, postcards, June 15–July 5, 1935, LOC-SRC.

p. 83   "sentimental ties": SRC, undated reminiscence, Henry Cowell Papers, NYPL.

Chapter 7: What Are People Singing Now?

p. 84   designed by Walter C. Garwick: Mark Davidson, "Recording the Nation" (PhD diss., UC Santa Cruz, 2015), 258–61.

p. 84   "Yesterday I got": Robertson to Hawkins, May 26, [1936], LOC-SRC.

p. 85   "After repeated requests": SRC, "Folksongs in RA, 7/11 sequence," [n.d.], AFC-1990/039.

p. 85   "Historically as well as": Eleanor G. Pierce, "Mrs. Franklin D. Roosevelt, Attending the White Top Music Festival," *Norfolk and Western* 11, no. 9 (September 1933): 313.

p. 85   "particularly fond of American folk": Eleanor Roosevelt, "Folk Music in the White House," in *Folk Music in the Roosevelt White House* (Washington, DC: Smithsonian Institution, 1982), 8.

p. 86   The Roosevelts brought: Davidson, "Recording the Nation," 164.

p. 86   Vice President John: Ibid., 149, 159.

p. 86   "rang out at": Reuss and Reuss, *American Folk Music*, 17.

p. 86   New Dealers embraced folk culture: Rachel Clare Donaldson, *"I Hear America Singing"* (Philadelphia: Temple University Press, 2014), 21–22; Sonnet Retman, *Race and Genre in the Great Depression* (Durham, NC: Duke University Press), 13; William Stott, *Documentary Expression and Thirties America* (New York: Oxford University Press, 1973), 92–118.

p. 86   "hovered over it": Robertson, "Folksongs in RA, 7/11 sequence."

p. 86   "big round bear": Nolan Porterfield, *Last Cavalier* (Urbana: University of Illinois Press, 1996), 51–52.

p. 87   "New England Connecticut": Ibid., 391.

p. 87   "each held himself": Ibid.

p. 87   he had accompanied: John Lomax to Oliver Strunk, June 1, 1936, AFC-1933/001.

p. 87   "We were hillbillies": Steven Naifeh and Gregory White Smith, *Jackson Pollock* (Aiken, SC: Woodward/White, 1989), 303.

p. 87   "Skip to My Lou": RA recordings and "Notebook on Special Skills Division Recordings" in AFC-1939/016.

p. 88   "not, strictly speaking": Charles Seeger, "Versions and Variants of the Tunes of 'Barbara Allen,'" *Selected Reports of the Institute of Ethnomusicology* 1, no. 1 (1966): 128.

p. 88   sent her to private school: Naifeh and Smith, *Jackson Pollock*, 303.

p. 88   King-Smith Studio School: Leslie Milk, "What I've Learned," *Washingtonian*, December 1, 2008.

p. 89   brief appearance in biographies: Naifeh and Smith, Jackson Pollock, 304; Henry Adams, *Tom and Jack* (New York: Bloomsbury, 2009), 42–45; Deborah Solomon, *Jackson Pollock* (New York: Simon & Schuster, 1987), 86–89.

p. 89   "comprising some fair": Seeger to Dornbush, June 29, 1936, LOC-CSFSA.

p. 89   "There were moments": Eleanor Roosevelt, "My Day," June 25, 1936, *The Eleanor Roosevelt Papers Digital Edition* (2017), accessed February 16, 2023, https://www2.gwu.edu/~erpapers/myday.

p. 89 "The delay in getting": Robertson to Hawkins, May 26, [1936], LOC-SRC.

p. 90 "I need new shoes": Robertson to Hawkins, June 10, 1936, LOC-SRC.

p. 90 "There is a swell": Robertson to Hawkins, May 26, [1936], LOC-SRC.

p. 90 "all delightful": Robertson to Hawkins, June 23, [1936], LOC-SRC.

p. 90 "Margaret and I are giving a party": Robertson to Hawkins, July 8, [1936], LOC-SRC.

p. 91 "OPPORTUNITY TWO WEEKS": Robertson to Hawkins (telegram), July 9, 1936, LOC-SRC.

p. 91 "We have authorized her travel": Seeger to Lomax, July 10, 1936, LOC-SRC.

p. 91 "The trip seemed": Robertson to Hawkins, "Just leaving for . . ." [n.d.], LOC-SRC.

p. 92 when Lomax served: Lomax to Brown, October 23, 1912, Frank Clyde Brown Recordings, Duke University Libraries, last updated September 14, 2021, https://guides.library.duke.edu/brownfrankclyde.

p. 92 both collectors used: Davidson, "Recording the Nation," 246–50.

p. 93 "reveals a flair": Seeger to Van Hyning, July 21, 1936, LOC-CSFSA.

p. 93 Lomax also appeared: SRC, "I have been asked . . ."

p. 93 "manage the gent without offense": Robertson, handwritten note on Seeger to Robertson (telegram), July 18, 1936, LOC-SRC.

p. 93 taking notes for him: SRC, "I have been asked . . ."

p. 93 "the rough-and-tumble": Robertson, "Report on Two Weeks' Trip."

p. 94 "Her singing was extremely": Robertson to "Pat," August 20 [actually July], 1936, LOC-SRC.

p. 95 "in their near purity": Erich Nunn, Sounding the Color Line (Athens: University of Georgia Press, 2015), 83.

p. 95 White resident of tiny Estatoe: Robertson, "Contacts in Western North Carolina," LOC-SRC.

p. 95 "Stripes, 39": Robertson, "Recording at the State Prison Camp at Boone," LOC-SRC.

p. 95 "the big White man": Porterfield, Last Cavalier, 391.

p. 95 "rather ostentatiously": SRC, "I have been asked . . ."

p. 95 "Sidney made special": Robertson, "Recording at State Prison," 1.

p. 96 At sixteen, she chose: SRC Chronology I.

p. 96 admissions restrictions: Sam Scott, "Why Jane Stanford Limited Women's Enrollment to 500," Stanford Magazine, August 22, 2018.

p. 96 "sometimes included in conversations": SRC, "Field Recordings," [n.d.], LOC-SRC.

p. 96 "I came to the conclusion": Robertson, "Observations on Technique of Collecting," [n.d.], LOC-SRC.

p. 96 "You goin' to": Robertson, "Contacts in Western North Carolina."

p. 97 "The collector is after": Robertson, "Observations on Technique."

Chapter 8: Look Down That Lonesome Road

p. 99 "Ideas used": Bogachoff, "Col. Westbrook Opens Cherry Lake."

p. 100 "I cannot tell you": Seeger to Valiant, June 11, 1936, MSU-MV.

p. 100   "While it is probably": Seeger to Valiant, May 29, 1936, MSU-MV.

p. 100   She was told: Tobey to Valiant, June 30, 1936, NARA-STL-Valiant.

p. 101   "It is with extreme": Paul Vander Schouw to Dornbush, July 1, 1936,
          NARA-STL-Valiant.

p. 101   "our deep appreciation": Valiant, "Journal of a Field Representative."

p. 101   "There is a Folk Festival": Seeger to Valiant, May 18, 1936, MSU-MV.

p. 102   his Asheville festival: Loyal Jones, *Minstrel of the Appalachians* (Boone, NC:
          Appalachian Consortium Press, 1984), 66.

p. 102   "Your letters don't": Tick, *Ruth Crawford Seeger*, 238.

p. 103   "Charles suggested": David King Dunaway, *How Can I Keep from Singing*
          (New York: McGraw-Hill, 1981), 48.

p. 103   "Mr. Simmons leaves": Seeger to Dornbush, June 29, 1936, LOC-CSFSA.

p. 103   composing a set of songs: Seeger to Haufrecht, June 6, 1936, Herbert
          Haufrecht Collection, NYPL.

p. 103   Haufrecht was not included: Seeger to Van Hyning, July 21, 1936,
          LOC-CSFSA.

p. 104   They were joined: Seeger, "Daily Work Report," July 29, 1936, LOC-CSFSA.

p. 104   "visiting a foreign": Tick, *Ruth Crawford Seeger*, 239.

p. 104   "The performers came": Jones, *Minstrel*, 106.

p. 104   neglecting to invite: Kevin Kehrberg and Jeffrey A. Keith, "Somebody Died,
          Babe," *Bitter Southerner*, August 4, 2020, https://bittersoutherner.com/2020
          /somebody-died-babe-a-musical-coverup-of-racism-violence-and-greed.

p. 104   "They could sing": Jones, *Minstrel*, 106.

p. 104   A handbill for: *Along About Sundown . . . 1928–2002* (Asheville: North
          Carolina Humanities Council, 2002), 8.

p. 105   "a very good showman": Pete Seeger, interviewed by Fiona Ritchie and Doug
          Orr, *Wayfaring Strangers* (Chapel Hill: University of North Carolina Press,
          2014), 201.

p. 105   "I discovered there": Dunaway, *How Can I Keep*, 49.

p. 105   "very amiably taught": All quotes from Sidney's Asheville report in Robertson,
          Development report, July 29, 1936, LOC-SRC.

p. 106   That evening showcased: "Mountain Dance Festival Draws Large Audience,"
          Asheville Citizen Times, July 24, 1936.

p. 107   "Thursday I went": Hampton to Seeger, June 27, 1936, NPS-JWF.

p. 108   "I had heard": Hampton to Seeger, July 2, 1936, NARA-STL-Hampton.

p. 109   Cooley had come: "Cooley Learns Federal Work in Washington," *Kokomo*
          (Indiana) *Tribune*, November 14, 1935.

p. 109   "Cooley is a grand": Hampton to "Mommie" (Highlander Folk School),
          August 26, 1936, WHS-HREC, 4.

p. 109   "Mr. Cooley says": Seeger to Dornbush, "Conference with Mr. Cooley,"
          August 6, 1936, LOC-CSFSA.

p. 109   "My collection of songs": Hampton to "Mommie," August 26, 1936.

p. 110   "Do you know the classic": Robertson to Grete Franke, September 8, 1937,
          LOC-SRC.

p. 111   "with the assistance": Seeger to Dornbush, August 24, 1936, LOC-CSFSA.

p. 111   she thought Margaret: SRC, "Folksongs in RA, 7/11 sequence."

p. 111   "Having no car": Robertson to Franke, September 8, 1937.

p. 112   She held a presentation: Robertson, Development report, September 23, 1936, LOC-SRC.

p. 112   "office routine": Robertson to Hawkins, August 12, 1936, LOC-SRC.

p. 112   her activity: Weekly development reports, August 12, September 9, 16, and 23, 1936, LOC-SRC.

Chapter 9: Government Song Woman

p. 114   "We never could figure": SRC, "First Solo Field Recordings," [n.d.], LOC-SRC.

p. 114   "I bought a car": Robertson to Hawkins, September 15, 1936, LOC-SRC.

p. 115   "The Garwick Electrograph": Seeger to Dornbush, August 24, 1936, LOC-CSFSA.

p. 115   "We cannot spare": Seeger to Dornbush, September 17, 1936, AFC-1939/016.

p. 115   "all of them vital": Robertson to "Belteshazzar," [n.d.], LOC-SRC.

p. 116   "The evening guard": Robertson, Development report, August 26, 1936, LOC-SRC.

p. 116   "28 people came": Robertson to Hawkins, September 15, 1936, LOC-SRC, emphasis original.

p. 116   "sorting out all": Robertson, Development report, October 7 and 23, 1936, LOC-SRC.

p. 116   "I would like to suggest": Seeger to Dornbush, October 5, 1936, LOC-CSFSA.

p. 116   "There are a number": Seeger to Dornbush, October 22, 1936, LOC-CSFSA.

p. 117   "I'm really crazy about": Robertson to Hawkins, October 29, 1936, LOC-SRC.

p. 117   First, she met: Robertson to Seeger, October 27, 1936, LOC-SRC.

p. 117   "The day before": SRC, "Folksongs in RA, 7/11 sequence."

p. 117   "You know, it took": SRC-Goldsmith interview.

p. 118   "disregard Charlie's": Robertson, SRC Chronology II.

p. 118   "I was not to return": Robertson, "Folksongs in RA, 7/11 sequence."

p. 118   "Record EVERYthing!": Pescatello, *Charles Seeger*, 141.

p. 119   "When I set up": Robertson, November 12, 1936, LOC-SRC.

p. 120   "fine dancey": SRC, "First Solo Field Recordings, November 10, 1936," [n.d.], LOC-SRC.

p. 120   "A little before eleven": Robertson to Dornbush, November 7, 8, and 9, 1936, LOC-SRC.

p. 121   "I went on to Elkins": Robertson to Dornbush, November 12, 1936.

p. 121   "wide berth": SRC, "First Solo Field Recordings."

p. 121   "My system took": Robertson to Dornbush, November 12, 1936.

p. 122   "When is a ground": Robertson to Dornbush, November 11-12-13-14, 1936, LOC-SRC.

p. 122   "One just goes": Robertson to Seeger, "I just sent off . . ." [n.d.], LOC-SRC.

p. 122   "Because it shows": Robertson to Dornbush, November 15–16–17, 1936, LOC-SRC.

p. 123   "followed indoors": SRC, "First Solo Field Recordings."

p. 123   "I wish I could": Robertson to Dornbush, November 15–16–17, 1936.

p. 123   "We came through": Robertson to Hawkins, November 25, 1936, LOC-SRC.

p. 123   "Once at Mrs. Current's": Robertson to Dornbush, November 15–16–17, 1936.

p. 124   "government song woman": "Folk Music Program," [n.d.], AFC-1990/039.

p. 124   "Marion is after all": Robertson to Dornbush, November 12, 1936.

p. 125   "To dig in": Robertson to Dornbush, November 15–16–17, 1936.

p. 125   "pretty dang": Bob Fulcher, interview by author, September 16, 2022, Crossville, Tennessee.

p. 125   "My 4x4x4 home": Robertson to Van Hyning, November 20, 1936, LOC-SRC.

p. 125   This session would follow: Robertson to Dornbush, November 20–21, 1936, LOC-SRC.

p. 125   "retreated to the 17th century": Robertson to Joe Jones, [n.d.], LOC-SRC.

p. 125   "Don't feel I'm going antiquarian": Robertson to Seeger, "I think my two . . ." [n.d.], LOC-SRC.

p. 126   "attractive and sweet": Robertson to Dornbush, November 21, 1936, LOC-SRC.

p. 126   "Of course the thing I am most anxious": Robertson to Hampton, "Just wired you . . ." [n.d.], LOC-SRC.

p. 126   Her first exposure: Robertson to Tobey, May 29, 1936.

p. 126   "the strongest expression of government support": Ahmed White, *The Last Great Strike* (Oakland: University of California Press, 2016), 74, 75.

p. 126   "When he had recovered from the unfortunate": Robertson to Seeger (confidential), November 4, 1936, LOC-SRC.

p. 127   "Could I possibly manage": Robertson to Hampton, "Just wired you . . ."

p. 127   "The Tarwaters owned the mines": "Union Leaders Depart Today for Rockwood," *Chattanooga Daily Times*, May 7, 1936.

p. 127   "As to Rockwood": Hampton to Robertson, November 7, 1936, LOC-SRC.

p. 127   "I went out to Lockwood": Robertson to Dornbush, November 20, 1936, LOC-SRC.

p. 128   Phillips had written: See Highlander Songbooks 1935, 1936, and 1937, Tennessee Virtual Archive, accessed May 25, 2023, https://teva.contentdm .oclc.org/customizations/global/pages/collections/highlander/highlander. html.

p. 128   The Phillips family: "Original Homesteaders," *Cumberland Homestead Families 1933–2007*, Cumberland Homestead Tower Museum, Crossville, TN.

p. 128   Phillips seemed: Robertson to Dornbush, "Recording of Hershel Phillips' Strike Songs (confidential)," [n.d.], LOC-SRC.

p. 128   Sidney's official: Robertson to Dornbush, November 22, 1936, LOC-SRC.

p. 129   "I never did": Robertson to Dornbush, "Recording of Hershel Phillips."

p. 129   "The management has": "Crossville Union Calls for Probe," *Chattanooga Daily Times*, November 21, 1936.

p. 129   "non-interference": "Homesteaders Given Right to Organize Union,"
          Chattanooga News, November 21, 1936.
p. 129   "old miner": Robertson to Dornbush, "Recording of Hershel Phillips."
p. 130   "I won't again": Ibid.

Chapter 10: We Ain't Down Yet

p. 131   "There's a hitch": Seeger to Robertson, "Your delightful memorandum . . ."
          [n.d.], LOC-SRC.
p. 131   "There is some talk": Robertson to "Belteshazzar," November 26, 1936, LOC-SRC.
p. 131   "Handsome Tugwell": *Knoxville News-Sentinel,* November 18, 1936.
p. 132   "Resettlement Rex": "Landon Volunteers Ask Roosevelt about Tugwell,"
          Brooklyn *Times Union,* October 13, 1936.
p. 132   conservative coalition: James T. Patterson, "A Conservative Coalition Forms
          in Congress, 1933–1939," *Journal of American History* 52, no. 4 (1966): 757–72.
p. 132   "I am afraid": Tugwell interview.
p. 132   "Things like that": Robertson to Seeger, "I just sent off . . ."
p. 133   "the outstanding cultural interest": Kellock to Dornbush, October 28, 1935,
          LOC-KKP. Among the residents at Dyess County was a young Johnny Cash,
          who later expressed his gratitude for the homestead, confessing, "I don't know
          what we would have done otherwise." Christopher S. Wren, "The Restless
          Ballad of Johnny Cash," Look, April 29, 1969.
p. 133   "It's a long time": Powell to Robertson, November 7, 1936, LOC-SRC.
p. 133   "It seems that Mrs. Dusenbury": Robertson to Seeger, November 29, 1936,
          LOC-SRC.
p. 133   that week's incessant rain: Robertson to Van Hyning, December 5, 1936,
          LOC-SRC.
p. 134   "Other Great Migration": Story Matkin-Rawn, "'The Great Negro State of
          the Country,'" *Arkansas Historical Quarterly* 72, no 1 (2013): 3–4.
p. 134   "We were engaged": Robertson to Dornbush, November 30, 1936, LOC-SRC.
p. 134   "continually making": "Mister Roosevelt," song lyrics, SRC Box 25; also see
          "Notebook on Special Skills Division Recording," AFC-1939/016.
p. 135   Wright begins: "Mister Roosevelt," song lyrics; recording in "Resettlement
          Administration, Special Skills Division Songs," SRD 74-12, FDRL-RGT.
p. 135   "This seemed a particularly": Robertson to Dornbush, November 30 and
          December 1–2, 1936.
p. 135   hoped to hire a Black choral conductor: Seeger to Dornbush, "Music
          Program, using present personnel."
p. 135   "Too hot": Seeger to Dornbush, September 4, 1936, LOC-CSFSA.
p. 135   "not to risk running afoul": SRC, "First Solo Field Recordings."
p. 135   Sidney's idea of including: Robertson to Joe Jones, October 28, 1936, LOC-SRC.
p. 136   "new form": "40 Jobless Spend Night Encamped in the City Hall," *St. Louis
          Post-Dispatch,* April 29, 1936.
p. 136   "Most often repeated": "40 Jobless Persons Camp at City Hall in Hunger
          Protest," *St. Louis Globe-Democrat,* April 29, 1936.

p. 136   "that there was an active group": Unless otherwise noted, all quotes related
          to this session from Robertson to Dornbush, December 11, 1936, SRC
          correspondence file, AFC (hereafter AFC-CF).

p. 136   "I don't know *what* to say": Robertson to Seeger, December 22, 1936,
          LOC-SRC, emphasis original.

p. 136   "I've written Adrian": Robertson to Tobey, [n.d.], LOC-SRC.

p. 139   The cover for "We Ain't Down Yet": All song-sheets in LOC-SRC.

p. 139   "Turkey in the Straw" existed: Natalie Escobar, "An Ice Cream Truck Jingle's
          Racist History Has Caught Up To It," Code Switch podcast, NPR, August
          14,
          2020, https://www.npr.org/sections/codeswitch/2020/08/14/902664184
          /an-ice-cream-truck-jingles-racist-history-has-caught-up-to-it.

p. 140   those lyrics were created: John Greenway, *American Folksongs of Protest* (New
          York: Octagon, 1970), 225; Alan Lomax, Woody Guthrie, and Pete Seeger,
          Hard Hitting Songs for Hard-Hit People (New York: Oak Publications, 1967),
          284.

p. 140   "hidden transcript": James C. Scott, *Domination and the Arts of Resistance*
          (New Haven, CT: Yale University Press, 1990).

p. 141   McCord had missed: Robertson to Dornbush, November 15–16–17, 1936.

p. 141   "very much alive": Robertson to Seeger, "I just finished," [n.d.], LOC-SRC.

p. 141   "What Mr. Lunsford": SRC, "Field Recordings," [n.d.], LOC-SRC.

p. 141   With the headline: "Old Ballads Resettled," *Springfield News-Leader*,
          December 16, 1936.

p. 141   "I was of course alarmed": SRC, "Field Recordings."

p. 142   thirteen local folk musicians: Wayne Glenn, "Transcribed Music of the 1930
          Ozarks," *Ozarks Mountaineer* 23, no. 11, (December 1975): 18–19.

p. 142   she received a telegram: Robertson to Tobey, "Judy, my love," [n.d.], emphasis
          original.

p. 143   "Attack of flu": Robertson to Van Hyning, telegram, December 21, 1936,
          NARA-STL-Robertson.

p. 143   "sickly, frail": Robertson, "Mrs. Dusenbury," [n.d.], LOC-SRC.

p. 143   "sung in a leaky-roofed": Robert Cochran, "All the Songs in the World":
          The Story of Emma Dusenbury," Arkansas Historical Quarterly 44, no. 1
          (1985): 3.

p. 143   "the serene face": Ibid., 3, 4.

p. 143   "The only time I ever paid": SRC, "Narrative on Mrs. Dusenberry," [n.d.],
          LOC-SRC.

p. 144   "There is no way for Resettlement": Robertson, "Mrs. Dusenbury."

p. 144   She calculated: Robertson to Van Hyning, January 5, 1937, LOC-SRC.

p. 144   Instead of expressing: Robertson to Tobey, [n.d., ~December 1936].

p. 145   "You are needed": Seeger to Robertson, December 28, 1936, LOC-SRC.

p. 145   There was talk: Conkin, *Tomorrow*, 180.

p. 145   "We expect to": Seeger to Robertson, December 22, 1936, LOC-SRC.

Chapter 11: Wayfaring Stranger

p. 146   "with houses and barracks": Unless otherwise noted, all Margaret's Skyline-related quotes in this chapter from Valiant, "Skyline Farms," [n.d.], LOC-CSFSA.

p. 146   Families were large: Flynt, *Poor But Proud*, 307.

p. 146   "cultural pattern of fierce": Ibid., 308.

p. 147   Kirk reported that people: Ibid., 310, 420n73.

p. 147   Flynt argues that the condescension: Ibid., 310.

p. 148   augmented by animal masks: Seeger to Robertson, December 17, 1936, LOC-SRC.

p. 148   "new barn": All quotes from play in Valiant, *A Christmas Masque* script, MSU-MV.

p. 149   "Having Lunsford": Seeger to Robertson, December 22, 1936, LOC-SRC.

p. 149   "We must have more than": Seeger to Dornbush, "Drama as KL activity," October 19, 1936, LOC-CSFSA.

p. 150   "He would go to the place": Bernard Eisenschitz, *Nicholas Ray* (Minneapolis: University of Minnesota Press, 2011), 41. Ray would go on to become a Hollywood film director, best known for *Rebel Without a Cause* in 1955.

p. 150   "Look, here we have": Ibid. Slightly different lyrics appear in the recordings in AFC-1939/016.

p. 150   scrapbook assembled by the Special Skills Division: Handwritten note [n.d.], LOC-LFC.

p. 150   Sidney made a compilation: "Resettlement Administration, Special Skills Division Songs," SRD 74-12, FDRL-RGT.

p. 151   "surprising and ludicrous": SRC, "Wayfaring Stranger," [n.d.], LOC-SRC.

p. 151   "The manuscript of this song": Dornbush to Tugwell, "Wayfaring Stranger," November 4, 1936, NARA-CP.

p. 152   "very controversial": Oral history interview with Will Winton Alexander, 1952, Columbia Center for Oral History.

p. 152   "found it particularly difficult": Baldwin, *Poverty*, 109.

p. 152   terse memo: Seeger to Dornbush, January 4, 1937, LOC-CSFSA.

p. 152   "most important job": Seeger to Dornbush, January 29, 1937, LOC-CSFSA.

p. 152   nine of the fifty-two songs: "Proposed List of Songs," August 22, 1936, Folder 20, LOC-SRC.

p. 152   with two more waiting: Dornbush to Francis Bosworth, March 18, 1937, LOC-CSFSA.

p. 152   cooperative-friendly lyrics: Seeger to Robertson, December 17, 1936, LOC-SRC.

p. 152   "The songs were very well received": Hampton to Van Hyning, November 6, 1936, NARA-STL-Hampton.

p. 152   "luxurious" symbol: "Tugwell Report on R.A. Baffles Even His Aids," *New York Herald Tribune*, December 25, 1936.

p. 153   "We have been informed": Dornbush to White, February 16, 1937.

p. 153   "distributed at the request": Falke to Will Alexander, March 17, 1937, NARA-FHA.

p. 154   the Music Unit's trouble began: Seeger, *Reminiscences of an American Musicologist*, UCLA Oral History Program, 1972, 255–56.

p. 154   "magnificent dodger himself": Stephen Winnick, "Election Week Special," *Folklife Today* blog, American Folklife Center, November 3, 2016, https ://blogs.loc.gov/folklife/2016/09/the-candidates-a-dodger-an-electoral -folksong-from-oral-tradition-to-aaron-copland.

p. 155   "to the Skyline situation": Franke to Valiant, March 11, 1937, NARA-STL-Valiant.

p. 155   "I was so incensed": Robertson to Valiant, March 11, 1937, LOC-SRC.

p. 155   "It will be such as I experienced": Flynt, *Poor But Proud*, 311.

p. 155   In March 1937, a delegation: Michael K. Honey, *Sharecropper's Troubadour* (New York: Palgrave Macmillan, 2013), 1, 5, 52.

p. 155   "The man who had brought them": SRC-Goldsmith interview.

p. 156   "poet laureate of the STFU": Honey, *Sharecropper's Troubadour*, 97.

p. 156   "much more conservative": Seeger to Robertson, May 7, 1937, AFC-CF.

p. 156   "Drastic cuts": Robertson to Hawkins, March 10, 1937, AFC-CF.

p. 156   "great shame": Robertson to Lunsford, March 10, 1937, LOC-SRC.

p. 156   constant stream of criticism: Conkin, *Tomorrow*, 182.

p. 157   "He considers that his best bet": Robertson to Hawkins, March 10, 1937.

p. 157   "with some impatience": SRC, "First Solo Field Recordings."

Chapter 12: Let the People Themselves Make the Music They Need

p. 158   "Tonight I was sitting": Robertson to Hawkins, "It is awfully . . ." [n.d.], AFC-CF.

p. 159   "My goodness but it was": Robertson to Seeger, April 4, 1937, AFC-CF.

p. 159   At first, she worked: Robertson to Franke, April 6, 1937, AFC-CF.

p. 159   "I found I had to": Robertson to Dornbush, April 18, 1937, AFC-CF.

p. 159   "I do like it here": Robertson to Seeger, May 7, 1937, AFC-CF.

p. 159   nearly all Austin Acres': Conkin, *Tomorrow*, 112, 193.

p. 159   with a garden club: Robertson to Dornbush, May 11, 1937 and June 26, 1937, AFC-CF; Robertson to Harold Stewart, June 28, 1937, LOC-SRC.

p. 159   unleashed an exasperated tirade: Robertson to Dornbush, June 19, 1937, LOC-SRC.

p. 160   Compared to the narrow focus: Donaldson, *"I Hear America Singing,"* 25–26.

p. 160   She found songs and instruments: Robertson to Seeger, June 14, 1937, AFC-CF; AFC-1939/016.

p. 160   "occasionally trying": Nicholas Ray to Robertson, May 24, 1937, LOC-SRC Box 6.

p. 161   "The piano was surrounded": Valiant, "Penderlea," [n.d.], LOC-CSFSA.

p. 161   The pageant opened: Penderlea Pageant program, NARA-ATL.

p. 161   "The chorus was": Valiant, "Penderlea."

p. 162   Collins noted: Ann M. Campbell, "Reports from Weedpatch, California," *Agricultural History* 48, no. 3 (1974), 402.

p. 162   region's information chief: Seeger to Robertson, May 19, 1937, AFC-CF.

p. 162   sung by a men's: Martha Smith to George S. Mitchell, "Penderlea Pageant manuscript," July 1, 1937, NARA-ATL.

p. 162   "We'll raise our": Penderlea Pageant program.

p. 163   "The eyes of the nation": Carl Thompson, "First Lady Brings Message of Cooperation to Wallace," clipping [n.d., June 1937], MSU-MV.

p. 163   with glowing newspaper stories: Ibid.; "Mrs. Roosevelt Dances and Smiles During Visit," *Raleigh News and Observer,* June 12, 1937.

p. 163   "subsequent conversation": Valiant, "Penderlea."

p. 163   "the remarkable performance": Mitchell to Alexander, June 14, 1937, NARA-ATL.

p. 164   "There were no hitches": Seeger to Robertson, June 18, 1937, AFC-CF.

p. 164   Penderlea's community manager: J. O. Walker to Mitchell, June 17, 1937, NARA-STL-Valiant.

p. 164   "We are gradually": Seeger to Robertson, June 18, 1937.

p. 164   Attending all-night: Eisenschitz, *Nicholas Ray,* 42.

p. 164   The couple married: Wedding announcement, WHS-HREC.

p. 164   Although Lunsford was: Caroll Van West, "Skyline Farms," Center for Historic Preservation, Middle Tennessee State University, January 2012, https://digital.mtsu.edu/digital/collection/p15838coll4/id/565/rec/21.

p. 164   "I have really unearthed": Robertson to Seeger, "Someplace in Minnesota," [n.d., before July 15, 1937], LOC-SRC.

p. 165   "Things here have": Dornbush to Robertson, July 15, 1937, AFC-CF.

p. 165   but Sidney's mail held: John O. Walker to Robertson, July 15, 1937, LOC-SRC.

p. 165   "We have fought": Franke to Robertson, July 17, 1937, LOC-SRC.

p. 165   "Suffice to say": Seeger to Robertson, July 23, 1937, AFC-CF.

p. 165   She ignored increasingly insistent: Seeger to Robertson, July 19, August 4, and September 4, 1937, Dornbush to Robertson, July 27, 1937, AFC-CF.

p. 166   thirty-six discs: Recordings and track notes in AFC-1939/016. For details, see James P. Leary, *Folksongs of Another America* (Madison: University of Wisconsin Press, 2018), 21–72.

p. 166   she was among the first collectors: Joseph C. Hickerson, *Ethnic Recordings in America* (Washington, DC: American Folklife Center, 1982), 73.

p. 166   "I've been seeing the world": S. Robertson to Kenneth Robertson, August 24, 1937, LOC-SRC.

p. 167   "The main question should be not": Seeger, foreword, "Journal of a Field Representative."

p. 167   He worked on the manual: Seeger to Dornbush, January 29, 1937, LOC-CSFSA.

p. 167   "guiding principles for group-work": "Music Manual," [n.d.], LOC-CSFSA.

p. 168   In his final months, Charlie oversaw: Tick, *Ruth Crawford Seeger,* 240.

p. 168   After the intermission: Ibid.; AFC-1938/011.

p. 168   community singing by the audience: Seeger to Robertson, "Seems like a . . ." [n.d.], AFC-CF.

p. 168   "keep the song-sheets": Seeger to Robertson, September 4, 1934, AFC-CF.

Chapter 13: New Ground

p. 170   "Has Tugwell's Daughter": *Chattanooga News*, August 23, 1938.

p. 170   "resembles Don Ameche": "Sevier Watley Won't Give Up Miss Tugwell," *Knoxville News-Sentinel*, August 25, 1938.

p. 170   "husky mountaineer": "Homesteader's Son Jilted By Miss Tugwell," *Urbana* (IL) *Daily Citizen*, August 24, 1938.

p. 170   Sevier's father, Lon Watley: "Homesteader Says 'Son, Girl' Tore Up License," *Nashville Tennessean*, August 24, 1938.

p. 171   "Tugwell Loses Wife": *Knoxville News-Sentinel*, August 26, 1938.

p. 171   "You'd love the drive": Valiant to R. Tugwell, July 16, 1938, FDRL-RGT, emphasis mine.

p. 171   "promptly fell": Leta Smith Colditz, "Cumberland Homesteads," *Crossville Chronicle*, December 27, 1977.

p. 171   Tugwell had asked FSA administrator: Tannis Tugwell to C. B. Baldwin, [n.d., August 14, 1937]; R. Tugwell to C. B. Baldwin, August 23, 1938, UI-CBBC.

p. 171   Tugwell "thought Margaret would": Robertson to "Risto," November 21, 1938, AFC-1940/0001.

p. 171   "I can't imagine what": Valiant to Baldwin, August 27, 1937, UI-CBBC.

p. 171   "a little second-hand car": Valiant-Rinzler interview.

p. 172   "a brilliant girl": Colditz, "Cumberland Homesteads."

p. 172   "dramatic effectiveness": Sande Jaffray to Hallie Flanagan, October 11, 1938, MSU-MV.

p. 173   "trace the struggle": Valiant to Walker, May 7, 1938, NARA-ATL.

p. 173   "for the most part": Jaffray to Flanagan, October 11, 1938.

p. 173   But on July 28, 1938: "5,000 Spectators Cheer Pageant Put on at Cumberland Homesteads," *Chattanooga Times*, July 29, 1938.

p. 173   The first scene: All cast information from Program, Cumberland Homesteads' Day, July 28, 1938, MSU-MV.

p. 173   including Congressman J. Ridley Mitchell: "Mitchell Gets Pageant Role," *Nashville Tennessean*, July 29, 1938.

p. 174   Longtime residents: Oren Metzger, "New Ground of Yesterday and Today," *Crossville Chronicle*, July 28, 1938.

p. 174   a "Homesteader" arriving: Stuart Patterson, "A Brave New Deal World," in *Rural Life and Culture in the Upper Cumberland*, edited by Michael E. Birdwell and W. Calvin Dickinson (Lexington: University of Kentucky Press, 2009), 205.

p. 174   there were calls to make it: "Make Pageant Annual Event," *Knoxville News-Sentinel*, July 29, 1938.

p. 174   "Leaving today for Washington": Valiant to Walker (telegram), August 4, 1938, NARA-STL-Valiant.

p. 174   "Margaret disliked the job": Robertson to "Risto."

p. 174   "I have heard of her work": "Cross Reference: Walker from Garst," August 5, 1938, NARA-SF.

p. 175   "from hill and valley": Valiant to Walker, October 10, 1938, FDRL-RGT.

p. 175   German-Russian immigrants: Brian Q. Cannon, *Remaking the Agrarian Dream* (Albuquerque: University of New Mexico Press, 1996), 2, 20–21.

p. 175   "dancing fools": Ibid., 108.

p. 175   "I can't send": Valiant to Tugwell, October 15, 1938, FDRL-RGT.

p. 175   "with whole-hearted cooperation": Valiant to Walker, October 10, 1938.

p. 176   "still as much": Dornbush to Robertson, December 25, 1937, AFC-CF.

p. 176   "sent to the migrant": Valiant-AFC interview.

p. 176   "fine chap": Dornbush to Robertson, December 25, 1937.

p. 176   "quite something": Oral history interview with Roy Emerson Stryker, 1963–1965, SI-AA.

p. 176   "didn't like women": Valiant-AFC interview.

p. 176   "that the only jobs open": Robertson to Dornbush, February 21, 1938, AFC-1940/0001.

p. 177   "I think Miss Valiant": Garst to Tugwell, 22 November 1938, FDRL-RGT.

p. 177   "I can truthfully say": Falke to Tugwell, "Southern California," Trip Reports 1934-35.

p. 177   "the empathetic value": James Noble Gregory, *American Exodus* (New York: Oxford University Press, 1991), 81.

p. 177   After spending Thanksgiving: Valiant-AFC interview.

p. 178   "in accord with the President's plan": Giulana Muscio, *Hollywood's New Deal* (Philadelphia: Temple University Press, 2010), 39.

p. 178   "a most delightful and entertaining": Tugwell to King Vidor, November 22, 1938, FDRL-RGT.

p. 178   "keep her away from Hollywood": Tugwell to Garst (wire), November 22, 1938, FDRL-RGT.

p. 178   "set a record for brevity": "Tugwell Is Married at City Hall," *New York Times*, November 24, 1938.

p. 178   "would like to marry Margaret": Robertson to Risto, November 22, 1938.

p. 178   "Bless you. I saw Vidor": Valiant to Tugwell, November 29, 1938, FDRL-RGT

p. 178   "one-third of the nation ill clothed": "Christmas Party for 1/3 of the Nation," press release, December 10, 1938, NARA-SF.

p. 179   seven thousand toys: "Information Bulletin No. 2," [n.d.], and Charles E. Barry to Garst, December 15, 1938, NARA-SF.

p. 179   Cars began to arrive: "8000 Kern People Join in Migrant Party," *Bakersfield Californian*, December 26, 1938.

p. 179   "home talent": "Film Luminaries Stage Party at Migrant Camp," *Fresno Bee*, December 25, 1938.

p. 179   "so popular that there was": Brian Q. Cannon, "'Keep On A-Goin'," *Agricultural History* 70, no. 1 (1996): 10.

p. 179   "combed the migrant camps": Valiant, untitled manuscript, "Several years ago . . . ," [n.d.], FDRL-RGT.

p. 179   "As we traveled": "The Migrant" poem in Ibid.

p. 180   "song of the 'Okies'": Valiant, "Migrant Camp Recordings," [n.d.], Phillip S. Brown Papers, FDRL.

p. 180   "Ladies and gentlemen": All quotes from broadcast from "Christmas
          in a Migrant Camp," December 24, 1938, NBC broadcast recording,
          LOC-RSRC.
p. 181   Gahagan later wrote: Sally Denton, *The Pink Lady* (New York: Bloomsbury,
          2009), 2. Gahagan went on to launch a political career, serving three terms in
          the US House of Representatives before being defeated by a young Richard
          Nixon in a nasty 1950 Senate race at the height of the Red Scare.
p. 182   "If several thousand": Harold James to Fred Soule, December 29, 1938,
          NARA-SF.
p. 182   "toys, sandwiches, oranges": Garst to Tugwell, [n.d.], FDRL-RGT.
p. 182   She helped create a youth group: Valiant to Walker, "Report of Activities
          from January 13 to February 23, 1939," NARA-SF.
p. 183   "The FSA has sent me": Valiant to Alan Lomax, February 6, 1939,
          AFC-1939/017.
p. 183   "the Indian School": Valiant to Walker, "Report of Activities."
p. 183   her recordings include boys and girls: All available recordings from this
          period in AFC-1939/017 and AFC-1940/008.
p. 183   "I was the first person": Valiant-Gaume interview.
p. 183   "Recordings from other parts": Valiant to Walker, "Report of Activities."
p. 183   "to say, look friends": Valiant-Gaume interview.
p. 184   "I began to learn the trick": Valiant-Rinzler interview.
p. 184   "Four members of the Franklin family": "Old Blue," AFS-3564-B1,
          AFC-1940/008.
p. 185   "So long as our least-privileged": "Farm Workers' Songs Lauded," *Los Angeles
          Evening Citizen-News*, March 2, 1939.
p. 186   "The value of documentary": Valiant, manuscript ("These recordings . . ."),
          March 1938, MSU-MV.
p. 186   "Miss Margaret Valiant, who has": Eleanor Roosevelt, "My Day," April 26,
          1939.
p. 186   "I have tried to interest": Valiant to Eleanor Roosevelt, July 25, 1939,
          MSU-MV.
p. 187   "My Dear Mr. Secretary": Franklin D. Roosevelt to Henry Wallace,
          September 15, 1939, MSU-MV.
p. 187   "Here are the voices": Valiant, "Migrant Camp Recordings."

Epilogue
p. 189   "Grace had charge": Tugwell interview.
p. 190   on a humid June morning: Dornbush interview.
p. 190   "applied arts": Ibid.
p. 190   In May of 1938, they arranged: Eleanor Roosevelt to Dornbush, May 13,
          1938, 90-192, Office of Social Entertainments papers, FDRL; Flynt, *Poor but
          Proud*, 314.
p. 190   "insisted that a program": Eleanor Roosevelt, "Folk Music in the White
          House," 8.

p. 190 Performers included: *Folk Music in the Roosevelt White House*, 23–27.

p. 190 managing a small handicraft business: Seeger to Valiant, 2 November 1976, MSU-AEC.

p. 191 an anti-gay crusade: David K. Johnson, *The Lavender Scare* (Chicago: University of Chicago Press, 2003).

p. 191 "What we did do": Dornbush interview.

p. 191 show up in printed folk music: B. A. Botkin, *Treasury of American Folklore* (New York: Crown, 1944), 874–80, 902. Ruth Crawford Seeger, American Folk Songs for Children (Garden City, NY: Doubleday, 1948), 5–6; Lomax, Guthrie, and Seeger, *Hard Hitting Songs*, 32, 38, 188, 208, 258, 260–67, 278, 298.

p. 191 "Without realizing it": Bill C. Malone, *Music from the True Vine* (Chapel Hill: University of North Carolina Press, 2014), 23.

p. 191 "It never occurred": SRC, "Wayfaring Stranger," [n.d.], LOC-SRC.

p. 191 she created and directed: Catherine Hiebert Kerst, "Sidney Robertson Cowell in Northern California," Library of Congress Digital Collections, accessed June 26, 2023, https://www.loc.gov/collections/sidney-robertson-cowell -northern-california-folk-music/articles-and-essays. Also see Catherine Hiebert Kerst, *California Gold* (Berkeley/Washington, DC: University of California Press/Library of Congress, forthcoming).

p. 192 "it was probably more through": Peter Stone, "Sidney and Henry Cowell," Association for Cultural Equity, accessed June 25, 2023, http://www .culturalequity.org/alan-lomax/friends/cowell.

p. 192 Cowell had recently: Michael Hicks, *Henry Cowell, Bohemian* (Urbana: University of Illinois Press, 2002), 134–43.

p. 192 in the 1950s: *Songs from Cape Breton Island* (1955); *Wolf River Songs* (1956); and *Songs of Aran* (1957), all from Folkway Records. Also see Deirdre Ní Chonghaile, "In Search of America," *Journal of American Folklore*, 126/500 (2013): 174–200.

p. 192 she had stopped collecting: SRC to Vance Randolph, February 25, 1964, AFC-1941/001.

p. 192 "Have you seen any": Seeger to Valiant, April 7, 1973, MSU-MV.

p. 192 "perfect balance": Pescatello, *Charles Seeger*, 263.

p. 193 "I have always": Valiant, notebook of writings [n.d., c. 1976], MSU-MV.

p. 193 Margaret collaborated with the conductor: Valiant to Leopold Stokowski, January 14, 1941, MSU-MV.

p. 193 recording African American youth: Recordings in AFC-1939/025.

p. 193 she tried to launch: Valiant, Application for Federal Employment, April 15, 1951, MSU-MV.

p. 193 accepting Sidney's offer to sublet: Valiant to SRC, June 10, 1946, LOC-SRC.

p. 194 started over in Memphis: Thomas BeVier, "A Glass of Sherry with Margaret Valiant," *Commercial Appeal Mid-South Magazine*, April 30, 1972.

p. 194 She lived at: "Lauderdale Courts, Memphis, TN," The Living New Deal, accessed June 25, 2023, https://livingnewdeal.org/projects/lauderdale -courts-memphis-tn/.

p. 194 She scraped by: H. L. Mitchell to Anita S. Williams, May 24, 1972, MSU-AEC.

p. 194 "Miss Margaret Valient [*sic*]": Eleanor Roosevelt, "My Day," January 10, 1955.

p. 194 "Abraham Lincoln's ghost": Helen Hosmer and Randall Jarrell, "Helen Hosmer: A Radical Critic of California Agribusiness in the 1930s," Regional History Project Oral Histories, UC Santa Cruz.

p. 195 "I have no doubt": Fred Soule to John Fischer, April 12, 1939, NARA-SF.

p. 195 set of master discs created: Walker to Garst, May 1, 1939, NARA-SF; Fischer to Soule, September 14, 1939, NARA-SF.

p. 195 Interest in using the recordings from Hollywood and elsewhere: see Fischer to Nancy Naumburg, June 9, 1939, and Frank Ross to Valiant, June 20, 1939, NARA-CP.

p. 195 "May I call your particular attention": Valiant to Fischer, October 11, 1939, NARA-CP.

p. 195 reporting his "discoveries": Charles Todd to Alan Lomax, January 23, 1940; Lomax to Todd, February 7, 1940, AFC-1985/001.

p. 196 "an amateur folklorist": Gregory, *American Exodus*, 265n55.

p. 196 this was the King family: Fischer to Valiant, October 23, 1939, NARA-CP.

p. 196 guitar quartet: "Los Carlistas," May 16, 2018, Strachwitz Frontera Collection of Mexican and Mexican American Recordings, https://frontera.library.ucla .edu/tag/los-carlistas.

p. 196 ace fiddler: "Chubby Wise," Bluegrass Music Hall of Fame, accessed June 25, 2023, https://www.bluegrasshall.org/inductees/chubby-wise.

p. 196 exemplifying all the reasons: Conkin, *Tomorrow*, 140; Spear, *Cherry Lake*, 199–200; Nick Wynne and Joe Knetsch, *Utopian Communities of Florida* (Charleston, SC: History Press, 2016), 155–56.

p. 196 In 1943, the co-op store: Spear, *Cherry Lake*, 197.

p. 196 "a small number of the families": Ibid., 201.

p. 197 "little more than an esoteric": Leighninger, *Long-Range Public Investment*, 139.

p. 197 "fascinating adventure in idealism": Conkin, *Tomorrow*, 6.

p. 197 "I suppose you always hold dear": Spear, *Cherry Lake*, 200–201.

p. 197 "For sixty years,": Cook, *Eleanor Roosevelt, vol. 2*, 151–52.

p. 197 66 percent of whom: Kelly and Power, "Norvelt," 335.

Acknowledgments

p. 199 This book is a book because: adapted from A. A. Milne, *Winnie-the Pooh* (New York: Dutton, 1988 [orig. 1926]), 155.

INDEX

A

Alexander, Will, 132, 152–153, 163
Allen, Chester, 149
Amateur Night events, 31, 64, 100
amateur programs, 31, 42, 64, 67, 100, 149, 168
American Ballads and Folk Songs, 51
American Conservatory, 6
American Folklore Society, 92
American Friends Service Committee (AFSC), 38
American Songbag, The, 8, 57
American Workers' Union, 136
Archive of American Folk Song, 86, 92, 116–117, 183
Archives of American Art, 189
art colonies, xvii, xx–xxii
art programs, xvi, xx–xxi, 12
art projects, xvi, 91, 135–136
Arthurdale, West Virginia, 38–42, 45–46, 77, 85, 89, 108–109, 116, 121, 164, 197
Arvin camp (California), 162, 178, 184
Asheville Folk Festival, 102–106, 108, 141, 160, 164
Associated Farmers, 177, 195
Association for Cultural Equity, 192
Astaire, Fred, 66
Atchley, Whitney, 90
Austin Acres, Minnesota, 159–160

B

Babes in Arms, 67
Bach, Johann Sebastian, 34
Baldwin, C. B., 171
Baldwin, Sidney, 152
ballads
    Child ballads, 40–41, 88, 95, 123–125
    cowboy ballads, 57, 80, 89–90
    English ballads, 40–41, 51, 125, 144
    folk ballads, 8, 51, 56–57, 80, 88–96, 125–133, 140–144, 149, 152, 160, 165–166
    prison ballads, 129–130, 140
    See also folk music
"Baptist, Baptist Is My Name," 124
"Barbara Allen," 87–88, 123, 127
"Barbourville Jail," 140
Barnes, Rhae Lynn, 67
Baur, Bertha, 3
Baxter, Jere, 173
Beethoven, Ludwig van, 34
Benton, Rita, 9
Benton, Thomas, 9, 13, 15, 35, 56, 86, 88–89, 169
Berle, Adolf, 77
"Billy Boy," 58
Binns, Archie, 80
"Birmingham Jail," 140
Blitzstein, Marc, 7
Blue Grass Boys, 196

bluegrass music, 9, 196
Bluegrass Music Hall of Fame, 196
blues, 45, 95, 135, 156, 184
"Bonnie Annie Laurie," 87
Boswell Sisters, 138
"Bought Me a Cat," 144
Brahan, Margaret Valiant, 1–4. *See also*
  Valiant, Margaret
Brain Trust, xix, 8, 77, 176
Brawley camp (California), 178, 184
Brico, Antonia, 90–91
Brookwood Labor College, 107, 150
"Brother Are You Ready?," 95
Brown, Frank C., 92–98, 106
Bruce, Edward, xvi
Bruce, Virginia, 181
Buchanan, Annabel, 121
Buck, Pearl S., 194
Buffalo News, 49
Bumgarner, Aunt Samantha, 105
Burkett, Mrs., 96

C
Calapatria camp (California), 184
California Folk Music Project, 191
Calloway, Cab, 176
Cannon, Brian Q., 175
"Careless Love," 168
Carr, Freda, 69
Carr, Pierson W. (Bill), 27, 64, 69,
  111–112
Carter, Joe, 182
Casa Grande Farms, Arizona, 182–183
Chattanooga News, 170
Cherry Lake Community Players, 64–71,
  101
Cherry Lake Farms, Florida, 1, 12,
  14–32, 43, 47, 57–59, 63–73, 90,
  99–104, 110–112, 115–120, 146–155,
  166, 184, 192–193, 196–197
Cherry Lake Orchestra, 27, 63–64
Cherry Lake Self-Governing Club, 20–21
"Chicken Reel," 64
Child, Francis, 40

Child ballads, 40–41, 88, 95, 123–125.
  See also ballads
"Chiseler's Sorrow, The," 129
Christmas carols, 148–149, 178–179, 181
"Christmas for One-Third of the Nation,"
  178–179
Christmas Masque, A, 148–149
Cincinnati Conservatory of Music, 2–3,
  43
"Cindy," 9, 168–169, 172
Civil War, 134, 143
Civilian Conservation Corps (CCC),
  173–174
Clam-Bake Cats, 179
Cleveland Institute of Music, 44
Coffey, O. L., 94, 97
Cold War, 191
Collier, John, 90
Collier, Nina, 90–91
Collins, Fletcher, 41
Collins, Tom, 162, 179
Columbia University, 10–11, 102, 105
Columbia University Library, 105
Commonwealth College, 133
Community Players, 64–65, 67–69, 71, 101
Composers' Collective, 7–9, 34, 44, 53,
  88, 150
Conkin, Paul, xxii, 19, 63, 197
Cook, Blanche Wiesen, 197
Cooley, J. C., 36, 52, 108–109
Coon Creek Boys, 105
Coon Creek Girls, 190
Co-op Players, 150, 164
"Co-operation Is Our Aim," 57, 109
Cooperative Education Unit, 53, 108–109
Copeland, Aaron, 7
Corcoran, Tommy, 86
"Cotton-Eyed Joe," 172
Council of the Unemployed, 126
cowboy songs, 57, 80, 89–90
Cowboy Songs and Other Ballads, 80, 89–90
Cowell, Henry, 7, 76, 192
Cowell, Sidney Robertson, 192. *See also*
  Robertson, Sidney

Cradle Will Rock, The, 7
Crawford, Ruth, 6–7. *See also* Seeger, Ruth Crawford
Crossville Band, 174
Cumberland Homesteads, Tennessee, 12, 43–46, 54, 104–109, 125, 129–132, 146, 171–174, 197
Current, Mrs., 123–124

D
Daily Worker, 7–8
dance tunes, 74, 111, 149
D'Arle, Yvonne, 4
Davis, Elmer, xiv, xvii, xix
Day, David, 36–37, 39
Denny-Watrous Gallery, 81
Denoon, Jim, 142
Denoon, Ray R., 142
Denoon, Roy, 142
Department of Agriculture, xix, 10, 145, 152–153, 165, 168, 172, 187
Dett, Nathaniel, 95
Dickmann, Barney, 136
"Dickmann Song," 136, 138
discrimination, 18–19, 39–40, 78, 87, 94–96, 104
Division of Subsistence Homesteads (DSH), 12, 38–45. *See also* homesteads
"Dodger, The," 153–154, 163
Doolittle, J. L., 27
Dornbush, Adrian
  Key West experiment and, xvi–xxiii
  Music Unit and, 33, 52–53, 58, 74–75, 85, 101, 112, 115–123, 127–130, 135–137, 149, 151, 153, 157–158, 165, 176, 190–191
  Puerto Rico and, 190
  recording equipment and, 115, 117–119, 121–123, 127–130
  Resettlement Folk Singers and, 168
  Special Skills Division and, 10–11, 13–14, 48–49, 68, 104
Dorton String Band, 174
Doud, Richard, 189–191

Douglas, Melvyn, 178, 180–181
"Down in the Valley," 140
"Down Under," 120
Duke University, 92
Duluth Homesteads, Minnesota, 159, 165–166
Dunne, Irene, 67
Dusenbury, Emma, 133, 142–144, 154
Dusenbury, Ora, 143–144
Dust Bowl, 116, 177, 196
Dyess Colony, Arkansas, 12, 133

E
Easter: Its Origins and Celebration in Many Lands, 155
Easter pageant, 59–61, 69, 148, 154–155, 161
Ediphone, 92
Electrograph, 74–75, 84–88, 105, 115–119, 122, 183
Elizabeth, Queen, 190
Elks Club, 67, 119
English Folk Songs from the Southern Appalachians, 51
Exhibition of Rural Arts, 168

F
Fairfield Bench Farms, Montana, 175
Falke, Grace, 10–11, 43, 74, 152–153, 177–178, 189, 193
Farm Security Administration (FSA), 166, 171–179, 182–196. *See also* Resettlement Administration
"Farmer Comes to Town, The," 56–57, 139
Farmers' Union Cooperative Education Service, 139
Federal Art Project, 91
Federal Emergency Relief Administration (FERA), xiv–xx, 11–12, 17–22, 37–39, 43–45, 60, 116, 146
Federal Music Project, 78, 91
Federal Theatre Project, 78, 150, 172
FERA. *See* Federal Emergency Relief Administration

Fischer, John, 194–195
Fletcher, John Gould, 143
Flynt, Wayne, 18, 146–147
folk music
  archives of, 86, 92, 116–117, 183
  ballads, 8, 40–41, 51, 56–57, 80, 88–96,
    123–133, 140–144, 149, 152, 160,
    165–166
  bluegrass, 9, 196
  blues, 45, 95, 135, 156, 184
  collecting, 9, 52–58, 87–93, 96–130,
    133–145, 152–157, 164–167, 172–187,
    191–196
  cowboy songs, 57, 80, 89–90
  hymns, 8, 30, 45, 51–52, 60, 111–112,
    123–125, 149–151, 155, 184
  power of, 5–9, 52–55, 80, 138–140,
    155–156
  prison songs, 129–130, 140
  propaganda songs, 7, 52–53, 71–73,
    136, 139
  protest songs, 7–9, 53–56, 107, 126–
    130, 135–140, 156, 166
  roots of, 40, 104
  selecting, 50–58, 74–76
  spirituals, 4, 51, 79, 95, 108, 134–136,
    156, 190
  work songs, 7–9, 34, 56, 95, 126, 128–
    130, 156, 165
Franke, Grete, 110–111, 158, 165, 168
Franklin family, 184–185, 187
Fresno Bee, 179
From Settlement to Resettlement, 161
FSA. See Farm Security Administration
fundraisers, 63, 65, 159

G
Gahagan, Helen, 178, 181
Garland, Judy, xiii, 67
Garment Workers Union, 126
Garner, John, 86
Garrett, Carl, 128–130
Garrett, Henry, 128–130
Garrett, Ida, 128–130

Garst, Jonathan, 174, 176–178, 182
Garwick, Walter C., 84, 105
Garwick Electrograph, 74–75, 84–88,
  105, 115–119, 122, 183
Gaspar, Jose, 30
"Gasparilla," 30–31, 61, 67, 69
Gee's Bend, Alabama, 147, 197
Gellert, Lawrence, 9, 56, 135
George VI, King, 190
Gilbert and Sullivan, xvi
"Gilderoy," 144
"Goin' Down the Road Feeling Bad,"
  180, 184
Gold, Mike, 8
Grapes of Wrath, 162, 196
Great Depression, xiii–xiv, xviii–xxii,
  11–12, 37–38, 44, 66, 80–82, 162, 174,
  177, 194
"Great Open Spaces," 57
Great War, 79–80, 103, 134
Greensburg Tribune, 37
Gregory, James, 177
Guerrero, Lalo, 196
Guggenheim Fellowship, 6

H
Hall, Helen, 82
Hampton, Rupert
  Music Unit and, 53–57, 74–75, 104,
    107–110, 120–121, 125–128, 139, 147,
    152, 164
  recordings and, 107–110, 125–128
  reports by, 107–110, 152
  Special Skills Division and, 53–57, 104
Handcox, John, 156
Handel, George Friedrich, 60
"Happy Days Are Here Again," 71, 73,
  174
Harmonica Rascals, 9, 13, 86–87
Harper's magazine, xiv, xix
Harvard University, xv, 34, 87, 103
Haufrecht, Herbert, 44–46, 103
Healey, Don, 46
Heifetz, Jascha, 79

Held, Fred, 127
Hemingway, Ernest, xvii
Henderson, Leon, 90
Hendrick, Frank, 142
Henry Street Settlement House, 76–78, 82, 126
Henry Street Workers Education Center, 126
"He's a Jolly Good Fellow," 58
Hickok, Lorena, 11, 37–38, 43, 177
Hidden Figures, 197
Highlander Folk School, 53–54, 107–109, 128, 133, 139
"Hill-Billy Heartbeats," 141
"Hills of Roane County, The," 129
Historical Unit, 11
Hitler, Adolf, 7
"Home on the Range," 80
Homestead Informer, 36
homesteads
 Arthurdale, 38–42, 45–46, 77, 85, 89, 109–109, 116, 121, 164, 197
 Austin Acres, 159–160
 Cherry Lake Farms, 1, 12, 14–32, 43, 57–59, 63–73, 90, 99–104, 110–112, 115–120, 146–155, 166, 184, 192–193, 196–197
 Cumberland Homesteads, 12, 43–46, 54, 104–109, 125, 129–132, 146, 171–174, 197
 Duluth Homesteads, 159, 165–166
 Dyess Colony, 12, 133
 explanation of, xix–xxiii, 10–16
 Gee's Bend, 147, 197
 Key West experiment, xiii–xxiii, 17
 Penderlea Homesteads, 160–164, 173, 186, 191, 197
 Pine Mountain Valley Farms, 12, 42–43, 46
 Prairie Farms, 147
 Red House Farms, 12, 45–46, 103, 109, 197
 segregation of, 18–20, 39–40, 65–67, 78, 94–96, 104, 116, 135, 147, 197

Skyline Farms, 146–155, 161–164, 190
subsistence homesteads, 12, 38–45, 178
Tygart Valley Homesteads, 12, 41–42, 45, 101–103, 109, 121, 152
Westmoreland Homesteads, 12, 33–39, 44, 52–53, 103, 109, 118–119, 164, 197
Hope, Bob, 181
Hopkins, Harry, xviii, 11, 22, 37, 77
Horton, Myles, 54
"House Carpenter, The," 123
Howard, J. T., 51
Howe, Robin, 81–82
Hughes, Langston, 81
Hughes family, 107–108, 120, 125–128
Hull, Cordell, 173
Hunter, Nell, 135, 190
hymns, 8, 30, 45, 51–52, 60, 111–112, 123–125, 149–151, 155, 184
"Hymns to Apollo," 60

I
"I Am a Union Woman," 8
Ickes, Harold, 39, 86
"Ida Red," 9
"I'm Just Here To Get My Baby Out of Jail," 172
Indiana Cooperative Association, 109
Indio camp (California), 178, 184–185
Inglis, Agnes King, 53–54, 75
Institute for Ethnomusicology, 192
Institute of Musical Art, 6
International Ladies' Garment Workers Union, 126

J
Jackson, Aunt Molly, 8, 35, 88
Jackson, George Pullen, 51, 95
Jaffray, Sande, 172–173
Jeffers, Robinson, 81
Jefferson, Thomas, 72
Jim Crow segregation, 18–20, 39–40, 65–67, 78, 94–96, 104, 147, 197. *See also* segregation

Jim Crow South, 18–19, 39, 65, 67, 78, 94–96, 104, 139–140, 159
John Steinbeck Committee to Aid Agricultural Organization, 178
Johnson, Avery, xvi
Johnston, June Frazier, 196–197
Jones, Joe, 135–137
"Journal of a Field Representative," 167, 193
Juilliard School, 6, 8, 14, 34, 44
Jung, Carl, 80

K
Kellock, Katharine, 13–14, 21–23, 35–37, 41, 77
Kennedy, David, 77
Kerr, Florence, 90–91
Key West, Florida, xiii–xxiii, 17
Key West Players, xvi
Key West Volunteer Corps, xv
King Family string band, 184, 186–187, 196
King-Smith Studio School, 88
Kirk, Leonard, 44, 103–106, 128–129, 142, 145, 147, 156
Knoxville News-Sentinel, 171
Kromer, Tom, 81

L
labor unions, 8, 53–55, 107, 126–130, 136–139, 155–156, 184, 194–195
Ladies' Garment Workers Union, 126
"Lady McDuff," 59
LaGuardia, Mayor, 178
"Landlord, What in the Heaven Is the Matter With You?," 156
Lash, Joseph, 38, 41
Le Sacre du Printemps, 79
Lee, Ruth, 90
legacies, 189–198
Lenin, Vladimir, 7
Lewis, Mrs. Sinclair, 112
Library of Congress, 75, 86–87, 92, 112, 115–116, 165, 167, 195

Library of Congress Music Division, 75, 116, 167
Limestone Dance Team, 106
Lincoln, Abraham, 72, 194
"Little Silver Cup," 124
Littlest Rebel, The, 66
Lomax, Alan, 85–86, 183, 192, 195
Lomax, John, 51–52, 80, 84–98, 103, 106, 112, 133, 143–144, 154
"Look Down That Lonesome Road," 111
Loomis, C. B., 22–23, 25, 28, 61–63, 67, 71
Lorentz, Pare, 178
Los Carlistas, 196
Lunsford, Bascom Lamar, 101–106, 122–125, 141, 145, 149, 156, 160, 164, 190
Lunsford, Nelle, 104–105

M
Marlor, Mrs. Nate, 123
Marlor, Nate, 122–124
Mattox, H. R., 21
McCord, May Kennedy, 141–142
McCrea, Zanadia, 184
McDowell, L. L., 108, 120, 125, 151
McLean, Evalyn Walsh, xxi
McNeeley, Estelle, 134–135
McNeeley, Hazel, 134–135
Memphis Academy of Art, 194
Messiah, 60
Mick, John, 17
"Migrant, The," 179–180
migrant camps, 116, 162, 174–185, 194–196
Miller, Karl Hagstrom, 40
Mims, Edwin Jr., 4–5
Mims, Edwin Sr., 5
minstrel shows, 65–67, 69, 139–140, 147–149, 159, 184
"Mister Roosevelt," 135, 157
Mitchell, George S., 163
Mitchell, H. L., 194
Mitchell, J. Ridley, 173
Monroe, Bill, 196

Morales, Antonio Pena, xvii
Morgenthau, Henry Jr., 77, 86
Morris, Wesley, 66
Mountain Dance Contest and Mountain Music Festival, 104
Mountain Folk Festival, 102–106
"Mourn, Jerusalem, Mourn," 124
Music Division of the Library of Congress, 75, 116, 167
"Music for Everyone" program, 25, 27–28
"Music Manual," 167
Music Unit
    Adrian Dornbush and, 33, 52–53, 58, 74–75, 85, 101, 112, 115–123, 127–130, 135–137, 149, 151, 153, 157–158, 165, 176, 190–191
    assistant at, 53, 76, 78, 90, 104, 110, 136, 142, 156
    attacks on, 141–142
    birthplace of, 9
    Charlie Seeger and, 25–27, 31–38, 40–60, 65, 74–75, 86–89, 100–107, 112, 115–118, 127, 135–136, 139, 145–159, 163–169, 191–193
    director of, 33–35, 50, 65
    first recording sessions, 86–89, 127
    first songs for, 56–57
    legacy of, 189–198
    Margaret Valiant and, 15–16, 23–32, 59–73, 90, 99–112, 146–155, 160–187, 189–196
    music selections and, 50–58
    new phase for, 74–79
    propaganda songs and, 7, 52–53, 71–73, 136, 139
    representative of, 54–55
    "respectable propaganda" and, 52–53, 71–73, 139
    Rupert Hampton and, 53–57, 74–75, 104, 107–110, 120–121, 125–128, 139, 147, 152, 164
    Sidney Robertson and, 75–98, 105–106, 112, 114–145, 151, 155–168, 191–192
Music Vanguard, 9

musical engineering, 33, 35–45, 103, 133, 168
musicals, 7, 43, 45, 53, 67
"My Day" column, 89, 186, 194
"My Horses Ain't Hungry," 88

N
NAACP, 78
NASA, 197
Nashville Tennessean, 170
National Archives, 117
National Folk Festival, 102, 160
National Miners Union, 8
National Recovery Administration (NRA), 7–8
National Youth Administration (NYA), 91, 193
NBC, 179
New American Song Book, The, 52, 58
New Deal, xiv, xvii–xxii, 1, 7–8, 11–14, 18–22, 37, 46, 49–50, 65–77, 85–91, 112, 132, 156, 193–194, 197
New Dealers, xvii–xxii, 77, 86, 89–91, 194
New Ground, 173
New Masses, 9
New School, 6, 9
New Wine, 68–72, 90, 99, 106, 149, 196
New York Herald, 4, 153
New York Times, xvii, 178
New Yorker, xvii, 81
News-Leader, 141
"Night Before Christmas," 179
Ninth Annual Mountain Dance Contest and Mountain Music Festival, 104
Nordmark, Olle, 148, 161
North Carolina Spiritual Singers, 190

O
"Okies," 177, 180
"Old Ballads Resettled," 141
"Old Blue," 184
"Old Rose Tree, The," 139
O'Neil, George, 75

opera, x, 4, 43
operetta, xvi, xviii, xxiii, 45, 53
Our American Music, 51
Our Daily Bread, 178

P
Pacific Weekly, 81–82
Packard, Walter, 112
pageants, 59–61, 69, 148–149, 154–155,
    160–164, 170–177, 186, 191–193. *See
    also* plays
Paris Conservatory, 4
Peck, Charles, 54
Penderlea Homesteads, North Carolina,
    160–164, 173, 186, 191, 197
Penderlea pageant, 160–164, 173, 186,
    191
Peninsula School of Creative Education,
    80
Penner, Joe, 181
Perkins, Frances, 77
"Personal Interlude," 144
Phillips, Hershel, 128–129
Pine Mountain Valley Farms, Georgia,
    12, 42–43, 46
"Pioneer Song: Who's That Guy?," 7–8,
    150
Pirates of Penzance, The, xvi, xviii, xx
plays, 30–31, 59–73, 90, 99, 106, 148–
    149, 154–155, 196. *See also* pageants
Plow That Broke the Plains, The, 178
Pollock, Charles, 9, 13, 56, 86, 88, 139
Pollock, Jackson, 9, 88
"Powder Mill Jail," 140
Powell, Dick, 181–182
Powell, Laurence, 56, 132–134, 154
Prairie Farms, Alabama, 147
Presto Corporation, 84, 195
Priest, Granville, 26, 30–31
Priest, Zelma, 26–27, 29–30
prison ballads, 129–130, 140
prisons, 94–96, 140, 192
propaganda songs, 7, 52–53, 71–73, 136,
    139

protest songs, 7–9, 53–56, 107, 126–130,
    135–140, 156, 166
Public Works Administration, 135, 194
Public Works of Art Project, xvi

Q
Quartet 1931, 192
"Queen of the Hillbillies," 141
Queer, Tink, 119–120, 164

R
RA. *See* Resettlement Administration
racism
    discrimination and, 18–19, 39–40, 78,
        87, 94–96, 104
    minstrel shows and, 65–67, 69, 139–
        140, 147–149, 159, 184
    segregation and, 18–20, 39–40, 65–67,
        78, 94–96, 104, 116, 135, 147, 197
Radioscriptions, 183, 195
"Raggedy, Raggedy Are We," 156
Ramsey, Alice, 82
Ray, Nicholas, 149–150, 160–165
recording equipment, 74–76, 84–96, 105,
    110–111, 114–125, 134, 142, 150, 160,
    165, 183, 195
recording studios, 68, 86, 136–137, 142,
    179
Red House Farms, West Virginia, 12,
    45–46, 103, 109, 197
Red Star, 6
Reedsville, West Virginia, 37, 39
Reeves, Curley, 184
"Rehabilitation of John Doe, The," 68–72
Religious Folksongs of the Negro, 95
Resettlement Administration (RA)
    attacks on, 131–132, 141–142
    beginning of, xxi
    Business Management Division, 48, 152
    Cooperative Education Unit, 53,
        108–109
    director of, xix, xxi–xxiii, 10–11, 34,
        38, 43, 48–50, 86, 90–91, 110, 129
    documentaries for, 178

Education Division, 22, 36, 53, 75, 108–109, 165, 187
explanation of, xix–xxiii, 1–16, 18–32, 36–46
Farm Security Administration and, 166, 171–179, 182–196
Franklin D. Roosevelt and, xxi–xxii
Information Division, 11, 185–189, 194
legacy of, 189–198
politics and, 131–132
recordings and, 105–130, 133–145, 150–154, 160–167, 183–186, 191–196
Rural Resettlement Division, 12, 40, 49, 112
Special Skills Division, 10–16, 22–23, 28–29, 34, 41, 44, 48–58, 66–68, 71, 75–77, 86–93, 103–104, 109–116, 127, 135, 141–154, 160–165, 169–182, 189–191
See also homesteads; migrant camps
Resettlement Folk Singers, 168–169, 172
"respectable propaganda," 52–53, 71–73, 139. See also propaganda songs
Retman, Sonnet, 40
Rice, Ben, 142
Rice, David, 142
"Risselty, Rosselty," 142
Rite of Spring, The, 155
River, The, 178
"Roane County (Strike at Harriman, Tennessee)," 129
Robertson, Kenneth Gregg, 80
Robertson, Sidney
    as apprentice, 90–99
    birth of, 79
    marriage to Henry Cowell, 192
    marriage to K. G. Robertson, 80
    Music Unit and, 75–98, 105–106, 112, 114–145, 151, 155–168, 191–192
    recording equipment and, 114–125, 160, 165
    recordings and, 114–130, 133–145, 164–167, 191–192
    reports by, 84–98, 105–106, 110–113, 121–130, 133–145, 171, 191–192
    termination of, 165
    trip to California, 166
    trip to Midwest, 158–168
    trip to South, 116–145
"Rock-a-bye Baby," 138
Rockefeller Foundation, 192
Roffe, Larry, 27
Rooney, Mickey, xiii, 67
Roosevelt, Eleanor
    column written by, 89, 186, 194
    folk music and, 40–41, 85–86, 89, 121, 157, 160–163, 186–187, 190, 194
    homesteads and, 37–42, 85–86, 173, 197
    poverty conditions and, 37–40
    role of, 11, 37–40
Roosevelt, Franklin D.
    administration of, 7–8, 14, 21–22, 40, 46, 50, 85, 112, 129
    campaign of, 38, 73
    folk music and, 73, 85–86, 94, 187, 190, 194
    homesteading project and, 38–40
    migrant camps and, 178
    New Deal and, xix, xxi–xxii, 7–8, 20–22, 46, 49–50, 67, 85–86, 112, 193–194
    re-election of, 132
    Resettlement Administration and, xxi–xxii
    segregation issues and, 39–40
    settlement houses and, 77
    song about, 135, 157
"Round Up," 187
Rude, Carl, 23
rural resettlement projects, 12, 40, 49, 112
Russell, Joe, 121–122
Russell, S. F., 121–122
Rutherford College, 101

S
"Sacco, Vanzetti," 7
Sacred Harp, 95

Sandburg, Carl, 8, 57
Sands, Carl, 7
Sanger, Margaret, 3–4
Scott, James C., 140
Seeger, Charles "Charlie"
  at Asheville festival, 102–106
  birth of, 34
  as director, 33–35, 50, 65
  early years of, 6–9, 13–15, 34
  first recording sessions and, 86–89, 127
  later years of, 191–193
  legacy of, 191–193
  marriage of, 6–7
  music selections and, 50–58
  Music Unit and, 25–27, 31–38, 40–60,
    65, 74–75, 86–89, 100–107, 112,
    115–118, 127, 135–136, 139, 145–159,
    163–169, 191–193
  musical engineering and, 33, 35–45,
    103, 133, 168
  recording equipment and, 115–118
  Resettlement Folk Singers and, 168
  Special Skills Division and, 13–15
Seeger, Constance, 34
Seeger, Michael, 14, 102, 191
Seeger, Peggy, 14, 102
Seeger, Pete, 6, 34, 102–106
Seeger, Ruth Crawford, 6–9, 14, 57,
  102–106, 168, 192
segregation, 18–20, 39–40, 65–67, 78,
  94–96, 104, 116, 135, 147, 197
settlement houses, 76–78, 82, 126
"Seven-Cent Cotton and Forty-Cent
  Meat," 191
Shafter camp (California), 178–184
Shakespeare, William, 59
"Sharecropper's Lament," 162
"Sharon," 120
Sharp, Cecil, 40, 51
Shirley, Anne, 181
Sholtz, David, xiv, 17, 99
Showboat, 67
Simmons, W. Jefferson, 33, 36–37, 43,
  46–47, 103

Skillet Lickers, 120
"Skip to My Lou," 87
Skirvin, Anna Mae, 26–27
Skirvin, James, 26
Skyline Farms, Alabama, 146–155,
  161–164, 190
Slee, Margaret Sanger, 3–4
Slee, Noah, 3
Smith, Ellison D. ("Cotton Ed"), xix
Smith, Leta, 172
Smithsonian Archives of American Art,
  189
Smoky Mountain String Band, 106
Soco Gap Square-Dance Team, 190
"Solidarity," 152
"Song of Welcome," 161
Songs of the Old Camp Ground, 125
Soule, Fred, 194
Sound Preservation Division of the
  National Archives, 117
Southern Tenant Farmers Union (STFU),
  155–156, 194
Special Skillets, 106, 115, 190
spirituals, 4, 51, 79, 95, 108, 134–136,
  156, 190
Spivacke, Harold, 112
square dancing, 40–41, 45–46, 68, 85–86,
  111, 116, 120, 142, 149, 160–164, 190
Stalin, Joseph, 7
Stanford Daily, 79
Stanford University, 79–80, 82, 96
Starr, Mark, 126
Steffen, Bernard, 9, 68–69, 86, 88, 103–
  104, 111–112, 114
Steffens, Lincoln, 81
Stein, Gertrude, 81
Steinbeck, Carol, 81
Steinbeck, John, 80–81, 162, 178
Steuart, Matilda, 3–4
Stevens, Clarence H. "Red," 23–27, 63,
  65, 67, 69, 111
Stevens, Mary, 69
Stokowski, Leopold, 193
Stone, Julius F. Jr., xiv–xviii, xx, 17–18, 99

Stone City Art Colony, xx
Stravinsky, Igor, 79, 155
Strawberry Festival, 160
Stryker, Roy, 11, 176, 189
subsistence homesteads, 12, 38–45, 178
"Sweet Betsy from Pike," 152
Swingtime, 66–67

T
Tarwater, Penelope "Nippy," 87–88,
   127–128
Tarwater, Rebecca "Becky," 87–88,
   127–128
Taussig, Charles, 176
Temple, Shirley, 66
Tennessee Folklore Society, 125
"There Is a Tavern in the Town," 57
"There Is Mean Things Happening in
   This Land," 156
Thompson, Dorothy, 112
Three Musketeers, The, 4–5
To Have and Have Not, xvii
Tobey, Judith, 53, 76, 78, 90, 104, 110,
   136, 142, 156
Todd/Sonkin Collection, 195–196
Tolegian, Manuel, 9
"Tomorrow's My Birthday," 181
Trump, Donald, 197
Tsiang, H. T., 7
Tugwell, Florence, 171
Tugwell, Grace, 178, 189, 193. *See also*
   Falke, Grace
Tugwell, Rexford G.
   as director of RA, xix, xxi–xxiii, 10–11,
      34, 38, 43, 48–50, 86, 90–91, 110, 129
   interview with, 189–190
   Key West experiment and, xix–xxiii
   marriage of, 178
   Puerto Rico and, 190
   resignation of, 131–132, 145–146,
      150–152
   Special Skills Division and, 10–11,
      145–146, 150–152, 170–178, 182,
      189–190

Tugwell, Tannis, 170–174
Tunney, Gene, 59
"Turkey in the Straw," 139
"Twenty-One Years," 129–130
Tygart Valley Homesteads, West
   Virginia, 12, 41–42, 45, 101–103, 109,
   121, 152

U
UCLA, 192
Union Theological Seminary, 53
University of Arkansas, 133
University of California, Berkeley, 34

V
Valiant, Margaret
   amateur programs and, 31, 64, 67, 100,
      149, 168
   in Arizona, 182–186, 196
   birth of, 2
   in California, 174–184, 196
   at Cherry Lake, 1–2, 15–16, 23–32,
      59–73, 90, 99–101, 146–151, 166–167,
      192–193, 196
   at Cumberland Homesteads, 171–174
   early years of, 1–9, 14–16
   Easter pageant and, 59–61, 69, 148,
      154–155, 161
   in Europe, 3–6
   as field instructor, 1–2, 15–16, 23–32
   later years of, 189–196
   legacy of, 189–196
   migrant camps and, 174–184
   minstrel shows and, 65–67, 69
   in Montana, 175
   Music Unit and, 15–16, 23–32, 59–73,
      90, 99–112, 146–155, 160–187,
      189–196
   musical talent of, 2–7, 14–16, 28
   pageants and, 59–61, 69, 148–149,
      154–155, 160–164, 170–177, 186,
      191–193
   at Penderlea Homesteads, 160–164,
      173, 186, 191

Penderlea pageant and, 160–164, 173, 186, 191
plays and, 30–31, 59–73, 90, 99, 106, 148–149, 154–155, 196
reassignment of, 100–101, 110–112, 174–176
recording equipment and, 183, 195
recordings and, 110–112, 115, 183, 186, 191, 194–196
reports by, 58, 65–67, 70–71, 146–148, 174–187, 193–194
Resettlement Folk Singers and, 168
at Skyline Farms, 146–155, 161–162
Vallee, Rudy, 57
Van Hyning, Robert, 55
Van Rhyn, Rene, 41–42, 103
Vander Schouw, Paul, 22–25, 61, 68, 100–101
Vidor, King, 178
Visalia camp (California), 184

W
Wagner Act, 126
Waiting for Nothing, 81
Wald, Lillian, 77–78
Walker, Major John O., 173–175, 195
Walker, Winkie, 125
Wallace, George, 86
Wallace, Henry, 187
Wallace, Robert, 43, 46–47, 52, 103
Ware, Susan, 11
Warm Springs, Georgia, 43, 85, 101, 103
Washington, George, 45
Watkins, Margaret, 20
Watley, Lon, 170–171
Watley, Sevier, 170–171, 173–174
"Wayfaring Stranger," 108, 151
"We Ain't Down Yet," 139
Westbrook, Lawrence, 99–100, 110, 112

Westmoreland Homesteaders Cooperative Association, 36
Westmoreland Homesteads, Pennsylvania, 12, 33–39, 44, 52–53, 103, 109, 118–119, 164, 197
Wheeler, Lorenzo, 181
White, Ahmed, 126
White, Chauncey, 39
White, Helen, 39
White, Martin G., 153
White Spirituals of the Southern Uplands, 51
White Top Folk Festival, 85, 121, 160
Williams, Aubrey, 91, 112, 193–194
Wilson, Mrs. Leander, 94
Wilson, Slim, 142
Wilson, Sticky, 80
Winnick, Stephen, 154
Winter, Ella, 81
Wise, Russell "Chubby," 63–64, 111, 120, 196
Wood, Grant, xx
work songs, 7–9, 34, 56, 95, 126, 128–130, 156, 165
Works Progress Administration (WPA), 21–23, 67, 77–78, 91, 99–100, 112, 164, 172, 190–191
World War I, 79–80, 103, 134
WPA. *See* Works Progress Administration
Wright, Will, 134–135, 157

Y
Yale University, 5, 41
Yale University Press, 5
"Yankee Doodle," 58
Young Communist League, 138

Z
Ziegfeld, Florenz, 4
"Zip Coon," 139–140

ABOUT THE AUTHOR

Sheryl Kaskowitz is the author of *God Bless America: The Surprising History of an Iconic Song*, which won an ASCAP Deems Taylor/Virgil Thomson Book Award for music writing. Her writing has appeared in the *New York Times*, *Slate*, *Humanities* magazine, *Bloomberg News*, and other outlets, and her audio storytelling has appeared on KALW Public Media. She is the recipient of a Public Scholars Fellowship from the National Endowment for the Humanities, a Kluge Fellowship from the Library of Congress, and the Anne Firor Scott Mid-Career Fellowship from the Southern Association for Women Historians. She has also received research awards from the American Musicological Society, Franklin & Eleanor Roosevelt Institute, Music Library Association, and Society for American Music. Kaskowitz earned her PhD in music with an ethnomusicology focus from Harvard University and her BA in music from Oberlin College, and she has served as a lecturer at Brandeis University and Brown University. She lives with her family in Berkeley, California.